Ultimate Fashion Doll Makeovers

Tips
From the
Experts

by Jim Faraone

Published by Hobby House Press, Inc.
Grantsville, Maryland
www.hobbyhouse.com

Hobby House Press

Dedication

To all the artists on my Yahoogroups™ list, especially to those contributing artists who helped make this book possible.

Plus: William Stewart Jones, Dorothy Fannin, Fran Czosnek, Debbie Lima, Loanne Hizo Ostlie, Scott Shore, Pamela Bachmayer, J'Amy Pecheco, Carolyn Marnon, Amy Nardone and Kerry Anne Faraone for helping with the how-to photos.

In Memory Of

Barb Rausch

Acknowledgements

Thank you to my father and mother Albert and Florence Faraone for their support; Charles Faraone for his computer expertise; Kerry Anne Faraone for doing the majority of the How-To photos; David W. Simpson for his belief in me when I first started out, and my gang at FashionDollMakeovers@yahoogroups.com for sharing their tips, techniques and adventures for this unique look into the Fashion Doll Makeover world.

Front Cover: Kristina Ammons
Title Page: Faraone Originals
Back Cover: (left to right) Donna Felton, Deborah Cates, Kathy J. McLeod

Additional copies of this book may be purchased at $24.95 (plus postage and handling) from
Hobby House Press, Inc.
1 Corporate Drive, Grantsville, MD 21536
1-800-554-1447
www.hobbyhouse.com
or from your favorite bookstore or dealer.

©2002 by Jim Faraone

Printed in the United States of America

ISBN: 0-87588-625-6

Table of Contents

Introduction

In 1999, I began my own Onelist™ on the Internet where Fashion Doll Makeover artists and enthusiasts could gather together, as a whole, to share techniques, experiences and friendships. In 1999, Onelist™ and eGroups™, Inc. merged and in 2000 Yahoo!™ Inc., a global Internet communication commerce and media company acquired eGroups™, Inc. which is now Yahoogroups™.

Yahoogroups™ is a wonderful community of on-line groups getting together to share common interests. These groups are formed by individuals and are composed of any topic that you can imagine and then some. Yahoogroups™ is a free email group service that allows you to create and join email groups. Individual messages, daily digest and no mail/web only are available to suit your needs and email handling.

Back in 1999, I found that there was a need for a Yahoogroups™ list run by a professional artist on the Internet. There was a lot of misinformation being handed out and many artists were finding that the techniques they were learning were ruining their dolls over time. Some of the "accidental information" was quite humorous and we've all messed up at times. But if one wants to teach, one needs to know and understand their craft well. Getting someone to listen is a whole other ballgame, but with time and patience, everyone can learn.

At the moment, my Yahoogroups™ list consists of over 400 artists from around the world, from teens to great grandmothers, males and females, newbies and the professionals, domestic goddesses, lawyers and doctors. I try to moderate my list well. As many on the Internet know, lists, chat pages and bulletin boards can get quite nasty at times. I like keeping my list fun for all subscribers. At times, we get into "semi-heated" discussions about techniques and such, but I like to consider this brainstorming because all ideas are helpful in learning. We "discuss" whether to glue or not to glue knowing that I don't approve of over-gluing one's dolls. But I've learned that each individual has to find out things for him or herself. There is always more than one correct way to do things. But those "semi-heated" discussions are stopped before they get out of hand. Another thing that is not allowed on my list is the petty bickering about other artists and their creations and spreading gossip or falsehoods. My group knows to take care of their own work and not go looking at what others are doing or what they think they are doing. They know to use that time on their own creations rather than wasting their talented energy worrying about what others

are doing. I say to read everything on the Internet and believe a quarter of it.

I decided to create this book with the help of my Yahoogroups™ to show how all artists, from the first timers to the professionals, can work together well and help one another with expert tips. The Fashion Doll Makeovers world does not have to be a competitive force, but a working group that can grow as a group and as individuals.

I feel this book will become the Encyclopedia for the Fashion Doll Makeover world. This book will begin to teach you just about EVERYTHING, the good, the bad and yes, unfortunately the sometimes ugly side of the fashion doll makeover world, but it will help you grow in this creative world. I decided to give this book an Internet feel, so all the tips, techniques and

experiences of each chapter are done as if you're lurking on a chat site. For those not familiar with the Internet, here are a few descriptions of some of the cyber-symbols you'll find throughout the book:
LOL = Laughing Out Loud; BRB = Be Right Back, :-) = Smile, ;-) = Wink, :-(= Sad, ROTFLMBO = Rolling On The Floor Laughing My Butt Off and OOAK = One-of-a-Kind.

Though this book features all artists from newbies to the professionals, I can honestly say that their shared tips are definitely Expert Tips that will help all. There is certainly more ways than one to achieve that special effect or get yourself organized and prepared.

Now put your feet up and begin to lurk at a special group of artists who are dear to my heart.

Starting Out

Everyone has to start somewhere and starting at the beginning can be a scary experience. Not everyone wakes up one day as an artist. Yes, some are born with inner talents, yet everyone still has to work and work hard at it. Like a baby, one has to start out crawling and taking baby steps before one can learn to run. But, before you know it, you'll be running with the best of them.

The scary part of creating is really just the thought of trying something new. We all experience that with other aspects in life, but we've all learned that as we progress, the fears begin to fade. The fears fade, and your confidence grows and you're taking off in your own artistic direction.

As the Broadway song goes, "It's not where you start, but where you finish........and you're gonna finish on top!"

Jim Faraone: As for myself, my mind is constantly buzzing, so ideas come pretty easily. Sometimes just working on one doll will give me ideas for future dolls. For instance, I was working on my "insect" line of dolls and decided to try creating a "reptile" doll. I began making my "Queen of the Cobras" and was working on my own pattern for the cobra hood. When I placed the buckram hood on the doll, it reminded me of an Easter Lily. (Light bulb goes off!) That sparked the idea of creating another line of dolls representing different flowers. Keeping your creative mind one step ahead is a way to go, but I know there are various ways people like to create.

Laura Fern Fanelli: Jim, I keep a pad and pencil by my bed. Inspiration may strike during the night or on waking up and you want to be ready to jot down all new ideas. You can place your doll where you can see her when you go to sleep so that she is the last thing you see when you close your eyes and the first thing you see when you wake up. Ask yourself, who is she?

Jean Birk: I agree with you Laura and creating ideas often come to me when I am lying down or trying to go to sleep. I also keep a pencil and pad next to my bed so it's easy to write them down the minute I think of them. If you don't write them down, most likely you will lose the idea. But thinking of ideas can be very spontaneous and hit you at any time of the day, so always write them down immediately. Jot your ideas down even if they seem too far-fetched or impossible to do. You can always make changes to the idea. Or, if your talents are currently not up to tackling an idea, maybe you will be able to create the doll or find tips later that will help you get the job done.

Laura George: Not just during the night, but carrying a small, pocket-sized notebook with you all the time to jot down ideas is good. Creative ideas come from everywhere including fashion magazines, television, history books, costume stores and even real people. When you see something that puts an idea in your head, you can quickly jot it down so you will not forget

Jim Faraone: Sketching out ideas that pop into your mind is great. I do that at times and don't think that you have to do elaborate, full color works of art. When ideas hit me I'll sometimes do a quick sketch with notes and ideas for the outfits that appear in my mind. I'll jot down notes like hair color for doll, whether it will have real hair or molded hair, color schemes or design patterns. What types of beads or sequins I will use and what

Vonda Silliman: I started a notebook with dividers for creating. Whenever I run across a helpful tip on the Internet, I print it out and insert it in the appropriate category. Magazine articles, instructions on making anything, lists, ideas for new dolls, doll show information, etc. all goes in there. Before or while I am working on a certain area of the doll, I browse through that category in the book to see if I want to try anything new. This has become one of my favorite books.

Jennifer L. Brown: When starting out, do not expect to perfect everything at once. Keep it simple until a technique is perfected or to your liking. Practice will lead to improvement. Never be afraid to ask questions of other doll artists.

William Stewart Jones: For ideas for color schemes just save big pictures of flowers in magazines. Nature combines colors in beautiful ways. You can see color combinations of greens and shades you might never think to use together.

Charlie Dale: I get many of my ideas from my years of being involved with the theater and with female impersonators. Many of my ideas also come from fashion I may see or especially fashion I wish to see. I took two years of Fashion Design in college. Here lately, a lot of my ideas are coming from actual people who are either now alive or once were. I love to research an idea and do research extensively.

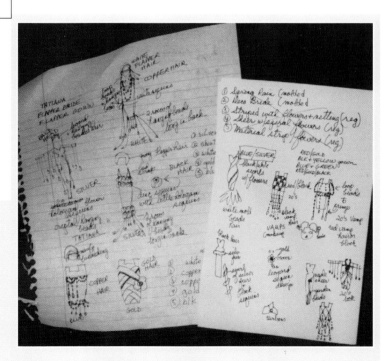

accessories will work with the doll. Just little notes and sketches will help you in the long run.

Jean Birk: No one starts out being an expert. It takes practice, practice, practice! And more practice! A "newbie" needs to learn what works and doesn't work for them. The best way to learn what works for you is to play with the tools and different techniques. Do not expect a masterpiece the first time. Just experiment and have fun. Start with a simple project. Otherwise you will become frustrated and the fun is no longer there. The object is to set a reachable goal and feel good about the outcome.

Jim Faraone: Well put Jean, and even for the experts, practice and experimenting are still important. We all need to practice and learn because when the day comes that you think you know it all, you're ready for a downhill spiral!

Jennifer Urbaniak: If you have Internet access, USE IT. Join doll lists. Members are always willing to help and answer a question. You can also learn a lot of tips from other artists. Make a visit to your local bookstore and check out the Fashion Doll Makeovers series. These are a must for any beginner. Not only will you learn the basics, you will also see a variety of artists' wonderful work. Most of all, have fun and enjoy. This is really a great hobby and for some, a livelihood.

Aurora Mathews: The best way to start out is to try to keep your mouth closed unless you can help someone. The 3 L's—LOOK, LISTEN and LEARN—are very important when starting out. LOL!

Jim Faraone: That was short and sweet Aurora! LOL!

Rachel Steinberger: A lot of us are scared to do a first makeover. But think about it - what do we really have to be afraid of? The Barbie® doll costs $5, another $3 will get you fabric and thread and then another $8 if you want jewelry or beads or new hair. For less than the price of two movie tickets, you can make a doll, which I guarantee will give you more than 4 hours of enjoyment. Before you say, "I can't," just try it. You'll probably find out you can. (Disclaimer: This does not apply to jumping off buildings and trying to fly. The latter is reserved for birds and the former has permanent side effects.) One way I like to work on my doll skills is to look at other artists' dolls and mentally dissect them. I figure out how I would do what they did, which is almost like creating a virtual custom. It's always a good way to keep your mind occupied during boring meetings. Like others have said, practice makes perfect. Your first doll is probably not going to look like a professional's latest creation. However, if you were given the chance to compare your first doll to that professional's first doll, odds are it would be a fair comparison. So don't think of professional artists as being unreachable elite (though some are), think of them as people with a BIG headstart.

Jim Faraone: Good points Rachel! I'm sure many of you are doing much better than I when I first started out. Like you said, never say "I can't" and don't ever let others tell you you can't! When I wanted to write my first book, I had a family member tell me I couldn't do it. They told me I would never get a publisher, how the publishers would laugh at me and on and on. Well, I can be a bit stubborn when anyone tells me "I can't" and if you truly believe in something (which is an <u>original</u> idea and not trying to play off of someone else's accomplishments) in your heart then go for it. I also like your comment that the "unreachable elite" artists should be thought of as people with a BIG head start. You're right about that and it's true that if everyone saw the top artists' first creations, yours would be a fair comparison or even better than their first creations. Mine were wonderful

Kert Hoogstraat: Create dolls you would most want in your private collection. Never compare your work to the work of others. Remember that inspiration comes from everywhere. One of my favorite designs ever was based on an outfit I saw worn by a vivacious 85-year-old grandmother. Also remember that everyone will have an opinion of your work. Just keep in perspective that an opinion is not the gospel truth. Develop relationships with really good customers. Some of the people who have bought my dolls have been instrumental in my growth as an artist by offering ideas and criticism and letting me know about what they would love to see.

Jim Faraone: In starting out, just jump in there with both feet. There are plenty of artists out there willing to help you along the way if you get stuck on anything. If you're unsure, get a cheap doll and experiment with that one. Before you know it, your family will be screaming for you to spend more time with them and to stop popping in TV dinners for supper. LOL! I know you can all do it!

with 3 foot, over-frizzed Afros from over boiling! LOL! Talk about frightening!!! Okay Rachel, I'll bite and here's a shot of some of my first dolls. As you can see, many of you are starting out better than I did!

The Basics of Face Painting

Looking at a doll's face as a blank canvas can be exhilarating, studying the overall dimensions of hills and valleys. Your mind will race with excitement and your hands will be anxious to reach for those brushes. You prepare your paints, you dip that brush into the paints and PLOP! OOPS! What went wrong?

My first book showed you the basics of painting your doll's face, but there are numerous techniques to create the image that you want. Each individual artist has to discover the way that works best for them. A technique that works well for one artist does not necessarily mean it will work well for the next artist.

Painting a doll's face is quite the challenge, but it can be done with some patience, experience and practice.

Brad Jensen: I find that cotton swabs (like Q-Tips®) work best when completely removing the face paint, **(see step 1)** especially if you conserve them by wrapping the cotton around the ends of a toothpick, making a miniature swab. **(see step 2)** I find it's better to work in small areas when paint removal is necessary. I find it is best not to use the same cotton swab over again as it absorbs the paint and can deposit it again once you soak it in the non-acetone nail polish remover. Try not to rub an area, rather soak it and twist the cotton swab in that small area and remove. Good brushes are also important in painting faces. I use (10/0, 12/0 and

18/0) brushes by Loew-Cornell®. I have also thinned out an old 10/0 brush to 5 bristles or so to outline the iris and do the eyeliner. I only use acrylic paints and use a toothpick to mix my colors. The best secret I've learned while painting faces is to use water with the paints. If you let the water smooth out the paint, you get fewer brush strokes and more even color. Once I have finished painting, I like to add a little shine. I've been using a satin varnish that is made for acrylic paints and cleans up the same as acrylics. I also use this varnish to protect the doll's fingernails and they seem to last longer.

Susan Yslas: I also keep a package of Q-tips® around, along with water and a paper towel when working with any acrylic paint on anything. If you make a mistake you can immediately dip a Q-tip® into the water and remove the paint or boo-boo, wipe it off and start all over again.

Jim Faraone: Also if you finished painting your doll (even if you finished it months ago) and you just hate the face painting you did, you can still remove all the paint with non-acetone nail polish.

William Stewart Jones: I've been experimenting! Acrylic paints are soluable in alcohol. While you are repainting the face, you can erase mistakes or clean up your work by using alcohol and a Q-tip®. Acrylic varnish doesn't seem to be soluble in alcohol. You need acetone for that. So when you paint something you like, you can varnish it to protect it. Then continue working with acrylic paint that can continue to be erased with alcohol, leaving the part you protected by the varnish.

Jim Faraone: Great Bill, but for newbies, just be careful with that acetone. Only experienced crafts people should use that because it could damage your dolls. If you choose to use acetone, as soon as you remove what you wanted, really scrub that doll to get all the acetone off so it will not seep into the vinyl. It does do nasty things to dolls.

Jennifer Hughey: To remove all the makeup, I use non-acetone nail polish remover also but applied with an item called a "micro-brush." These are plastic sticks with fuzzy bristles on the tip. They work really well because the slight fuzziness is enough to remove

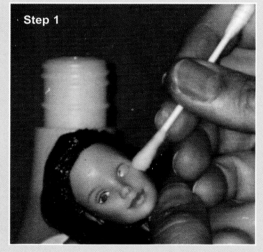

Step 1

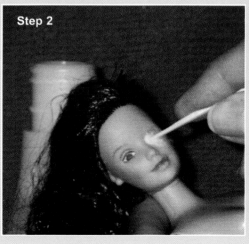

Step 2

the paint easily without smearing. You just dip it in the nail polish remover and gently rub the paint to loosen it. Wipe on a napkin, then dip again in the remover and repeat until the paint is gone.

Kim Burie: A problem I ran into with removing the face paint from a doll with non-acetone nail polish remover is smearing. Also, the chemicals gave me a headache, and made me nauseous. I would get to the point of tears whenever I had to remove the face paint. As a last ditch effort, I tried something I had heard about using erasers to remove the face paint. It didn't sound to me like it would work, but it did! Any type of eraser that can be used to remove ink will work, but I have been using the non-abrasive Magic Rub® artist erasers from Sanford®. You just rub and erase like you would any ink. At first it will seem like nothing is happening, but then you will see the eyeshadow fade, then the eyelashes. Once it gets going, the paint comes off quickly. You can squeeze the head in order to reach all the little cracks and crevices, and for stubborn paint usually a toothpick will loosen up the last of it. I have used this method on Mattel™ dolls, the Candi® doll and the Charice® doll. I have not yet tried it on larger fashion dolls. If anyone had any of the frustrations I had with removing face paint, give this a try. No fumes, no mess, no worrying about what chemicals might do to the vinyl over time and I found it is actually faster than the other methods. The biggest ordeal is vacuuming up eraser crumbs afterward. :-)

Jim Faraone: I'll have to check that out Kim because it sounds like a great idea especially for those with weak immune systems, allergies or for those who are pregnant. It could be a good way to even just lighten up enough of the paint on the doll's face so you have some sort of "stencil" to work with when repainting especially the doll's eyes. For those that still use the non-acetone nail polish, the brand I use is the Sally Hansen® For Artificial and Sensitive Nails, Acetone Free. It doesn't seem to smear things at all. I'm sure all brands work differently.

William Stewart Jones: Powdered or cake eye shadow can be mixed with clear acrylic medium and used as paint. The pearlescent shades are especially beautiful. Flesh tone (non-oil) cake makeup can also be mixed with medium for skin tones.

Vonda Silliman: After I take the doll's head off for repainting, I use a baby bottle dryer (a plastic rectangular base that has 8 tall and 8 short plastic rods that are inserted vertically into the base) for holding the heads upright while the paint on the face dries. Just insert one of the tall rods into the neck hole and then put it into the base. The fit is perfect. It can also be handy to hold onto the rod while painting the face.

Laura George: Good one Vonda, and here's what I do. When I paint or style a doll's head, I remove the head and put it on the end of a wooden spoon. It helps me to maintain control while painting and is great for hanging onto while dipping her in hot water to set her curls.

Jim Faraone: The wooden spoon is a great idea Laura, especially if you need to whack someone who's annoying you while working on your dolls. LOL! You can also use a craft glue bottle to put the heads on so you can hold them better when painting or letting them sit to dry. When I do my molded-hair dolls, I put the heads on the top of Sharpie® Ultra Fine Point Permanent Markers and then stick the pens into Styrofoam till each layer dries.

Steph Gazell: I wrap the doll's hair with paper towels, tucked under, and taped in place, nun-like in appearance. This is very useful for keeping pesky hairs out of the paint while painting the face.

LaDonna Moore: I find it's always better to apply thin layers of pain. Then you can add as many coats as needed. I also coat with an acrylic varnish to give a nice finishing shine.

Jim Faraone: You're absolutely right about painting in thin coats. It's better to use 5 thin coats of acrylic paint to get the color you want than to apply one harsh coat. The thinner coats will blend better and give you a less streaky and more natural look to your doll's face paint. That is one of the big secrets to painting faces....guess, that secret's out of the bag now. LOL!

Michelle Candace: One of my favorite tools to paint with is a double ended stylus, especially for lips and eyeball painting. With the stylus, the paint can be moved around on the doll easily and evenly without leaving brush strokes.

Vonda Silliman: I like using a small angular brush (I use Loew-Cornell® 10/0 7400 angular), which is useful when applying eyeshadow and blush. I've even used it turned sideways (long side towards me) to paint eyelashes. It is stiff and tends to paint a more precise line.

Joelle Cerfoglia: To make my doll's eyes brighter I put a veil of acrylic varnish on them, but do not put a lot on. Otherwise it will make your doll look like she's crying.

William Stewart Jones: I wasn't happy with using acrylic paint for the fine lines like eyeliner and lashes or eyebrows. I experimented and settled on permanent colored inks. Higgins® and Windsor & Newton® inks are waterproof. Dr. Martins® comes in great colors but smears when it is given a coat of water base varnish.

Sheryl Majercin: I have a few ideas to share! WARNING—do not attempt to repaint your gal after having more than one cup of coffee! ;-) Seriously, like Brad mentioned, trimming down a paint brush can give you the fine tip you need for detailed repaints. Also, a drop or two of acrylic medium added to your paint will give a nicer finish. Three thin layers looks smoother than one thick layer. Also, acrylic blending gel works wonderfully on the eyeshadow and shading. Just follow the directions on the bottle.

Jenny Sutherland: I remove all the original paint first, so I have a clean slate with which to work. I've experienced that when you keep the original paint on the face, you tend to follow those same lines instead of creating a face from your imagination. A MUST for me is a blending medium. This slows down drying time on acrylics. This will help you "play" with the paint on the eyes and shadow of the eyes. As you practice working with the medium and a touch of water on the brush you can obtain "soft edges". The blending medium will help you achieve really nice results for the eyeshadow! I recommend a soft look with soft colors. If you want definition, use the same color, but in a little darker tone around the crease of the lid which gives a dramatic look without appearing "gaudy." I

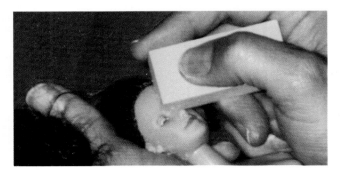

also use acrylic matte, gloss and Satin sealers. I use matte for the eyelids, gloss for the eye itself, and sometimes the lips, and satin for the lips. The best tip I can give you is practice, combined with the love of the art! Study faces and compare to them the work you have done. I'm always criticizing my own work, trying to see how I can do better on the next face.

Jim Faraone: I like your last few lines Jenny. Too many out there are more into studying and criticizing what others are doing and if more would concentrate on their own work, they'd see a big change in their own creations. Being critical of one's own work is very good. Just don't get to the point of being too critical of your own work that it stifles your creativity.

Laura Fern Fanelli: I paint my doll's face near a window since the natural lighting is the truest. I also purchased at my local store/pharmacy those magnifying reading glasses to assist in seeing those tiny features. Also, hold your breath when painting the tiny eyes. It seems to take a steady hand to do eyebrows and eyeliner. Nix the 16 cups of coffee just before you paint! LOL!

Juan Albuerne: Unless you're making a fantasy item, look at all the faces around you before starting. Different shapes of facial features, lips, eyes, eyebrows, eyelashes, noses, cheekbones; different colors of skin, shades, lights; different hairstyles and hair colors—all are there in front of you for reference. All you have to do is watch. First of all, make your choice. You'll have to know what you want to do, and then do it. If you're looking for a likeness with a particular character, in my case a movie star, put some photos of her around you. Let that woman look at you and you look at her. Then try make the doll that you have in your hands reflect those characteristics. That woman becomes your doll, or your doll becomes that

woman. If you don't get it on the first try, don't be impatient. Try again. Perhaps you might start with the easier characteristics and stronger features. NEVER get desperate. We all felt the same at some time. Remember, what you don't get today, you can get tomorrow.

Jim Faraone: Good point, Juan. Many seem to want to run before they learn how to walk and it does take time to master a technique. It does take patience (and some cursing at times) to achieve what you want. But do go slow and the time does go fast and before you know it you're there! But I hope no one ever achieves that goal of being "there," because we all should be striving with each doll to do even better.

Natalie Tetzlaff: To practice my painting I buy the cheapie dolls from the dollar store. Since they are the same size as the 11½ in (29cm) you can try new things, like side glancing eyes, light eyeshadow and blush without ruining a good doll. These are great practice "canvases." I also use wax paper as my palette for painting. It covers my workspace, cleans up easily and provides me lots of space for mixing colors. Also, with painting, replace your brushes frequently. Frayed bristles can lead to unwanted stray marks. I keep a soft cloth handy when painting to wipe my brush on after rinsing.

Jim Faraone: I use aluminum foil for my palette and that works just as well as the wax paper. Also, though sounding yucky, after washing your thin brushes, use your mouth to form your paintbrush to a point before putting it away. This will keep your brushes nice with sharp points for those fine lines.

Tricia Hill: For painting, I like to use the following acrylic paint products and brushes. Folkart® Acrylic Paint and Delta® Creamcoat Acrylic Paint. I also use Delta® Creamcoat Color Float (Color Blending Medium & Water Conditioner) and Delta®

Creamcoat Gloss Varnish (for sealing eyes and lips). For mixing colors, I like to mix 2-3 different colors to get my own unique color. I use a small saucer (coffee cup saucer) and place just a drop of each color. Then I start with my wet brush, dipping into the 3 colors until I have the tone that I want. I also use a drop of water to get the right consistency and/or drop of paint medium to prevent the acrylics from drying out too soon. For correcting errors, I use a small shot glass with a tiny bit of rubbing alcohol so I can dip either a cotton swab or toothpick with cotton around just the end to wipe away any mistakes. Sometimes I just use the toothpick dipped in alcohol depending on how fine the area is.

Rachel Steinberger: To add some extra sparkle to a paint job, I like to use the glitter colors of fabric paint. After you squeeze a small dab onto your palette, you dip your paintbrush in and the glitter acts just like paint.

Lori Strawn: You will find that half of the doll's face seems harder to paint than the other simply because you hold the brush in your dominant hand and you have to position the hand awkwardly at some point. You will find it easier to paint the difficult side of the face if you turn the doll upside down.

Pamela Bachmayer: Keep one or two beat up Malibu era Barbie® doll bodies on hand to use as substitute bodies while creating dolls. Put the head of the doll you are working with onto the old body. This allows you to work on the outfit of your design while you're waiting for paint, hair or sealant to dry. The Malibu body has a small neck knob that allows you to pop the new head off and on easily without having to reheat the neck each time. It also gives you a body for additional support as you work on the head or something to hold onto if you need it. You won't mind getting paint, etc. on the Malibu body of this doll, which is

beyond repair anyway. You will have the freedom to change your mind about hairstyles and other details, as a last minute perm won't mess up an outfit. It also helps if you find that the head doesn't go with the outfit. You can start a new head with no hassles, keeping the finished head for another doll.

Aurora Mathews: I like to use Graumbacher® Transparentizer for thinning paint and a little water. It's so much smoother than water thinning alone. Also, when using a sealant, use it like you are painting and don't let it run over the edges of the area you are sealing. You can also mix your own paints to get a special color and save it in an airtight jar. I do this especially with "transparentized" glazes. If your painting hand wants to shake, put your other hand or arm under it and create a balance to steady your paintbrush.

Jim Faraone: Great Aurora! Now we coffee drinkers don't have to give up our 42 cups of coffee a day! LOL!

Anke Scharfenberg: For beginners, it is a little bit difficult doing make-up on a doll and getting the eyes and everything straight. So maybe they can try this. Don't remove the old make-up of the doll but paint over it. This is easy when you want to change the color of the eyes, or the eyeshadow. It sure is a lot easier and you get a feeling for the proportions.

Jim Faraone: Painting right over the original paint sure is an easy and helpful way for beginners. There is nothing wrong with that, and at times, it can save you from creating those "alien-eyed dolls," the "deer caught in the headlights eyes" or that look just before you say, "The dog did it!" Just enhancing the doll's original make-up still completely changes the look of a doll. But like we mentioned before, visuals and practice makes perfect!

The Specifics of Painting

Sometimes instead of looking at a whole project, it's best to break it down into small sections. At times it's easier to concentrate on a small piece of the puzzle instead of the whole puzzle. Let's concentrate on certain areas of the doll's face like the eyes, nose, eyebrows, cheeks, lips and anything else pertaining to painting your doll's face. Taking things one step at a time teaches you to become more focused so you can perfect one area before moving on. We're going to break down the doll's face with this chapter and see if we can all help you become more relaxed at face painting.

EYEBROWS

Becky Kelly: I like to free-hand the eyebrows, so in order to place them correctly, I carefully remove all of the eyebrow paint except for a tiny dot on either side of the nose so that I have a starting point for the new eyebrow.

Luci North: I sort of use dots as well, Becky. When I repaint anything, first I take a pale shade of paint and put dots where I am going to paint the eyebrows, eyes, etc. That way I can make sure they're even before I actually start painting. It's sort of like connect the dots. I also like to use a monochromatic pallet. I think it makes the doll look pulled together.

Barbara Fowler: For realistic eyebrows or "feathery" eyebrows, I use 3 or 4 colors within the same family but in various shades. You will also need a skin tone color. Start with the darkest color and paint in the eyebrow arched in "feathers." **(see step 1)** On top, paint a lighter color, then a lighter color on top of that, **(see step 2)** ending with the skin tone. It will appear that the eyelashes have actual hairs with skin showing beneath.

Aurora Mathews: I like to lightly draw the eyebrows on with a lead pencil in the shape I want them. That way I can inspect them to see that they are the same on both sides and are placed in the same area. It acts as a guide for applying paint. I also use a fine lead pencil to draw lips, eye shape and brow shape before I start painting on a portrait repaint. This way I know if I can see a likeness of the subject first. Also, look at your doll upside down, Look at shapes, not facial features. You will see if the face is symmetrical this way.

Lori Strawn: If you have difficulty painting eyebrows and don't want to simply paint over the existing paint, try a stencil. You needn't make one. The hobby store has tons of small 3in (8cm) square stencils with patterns that include shapes that are small and curvey and shaped like eyebrows.

Barb Wood: For painting eyebrows for fairies and butterflies, I usually remove only the outer half of the eyebrow with the non-acetone nail polish remover (to about the pupil of the eye) and then use this guideline for a "fairy" eyebrow painting upward on the ends of the eyebrow.

Laura Fern Fanelli: Eyebrows sure can be tricky! A couple of ideas that helped me are investing in a small fine point brush and hold your breath when you take a brush stroke on the brow. This will help you from shaking. As long as you start the brow in the same place (inner corner of eye) even if one eyebrow is slightly higher, it can sometimes look fine— remember Vivian Leigh in *Gone With The Wind*? A lot depends on the expression you want to convey.

Jaun Albuerne: For the eyebrows, you'll only have to be careful with the symmetry of the arch. You can paint them also in many shapes. Look at real people and how their eyebrows differ. Don't paint them in black. Try it with dark or medium brown. You can also paint over them with some fine lines of a darker color to accent them.

Aurora Mathews: Look at your doll's painted face in a mirror reflection. This helps to see if eyebrows, etc. are even.

Jean MaDan: To get nice eyebrows, try drawing the weak side first. If you're left handed, your weak side would be on the right, and if you're right handed, the weak side would be on the left. If you're ambidextrous, then you can come over and do the eyebrows on MY dolls! LOL! Another option on the eyebrows is to draw your weak side upside down then turn the doll right side up to do the strong side.

Jim Faraone: Good one Jean. And to make it simpler, if you're right handed, paint the left side of the doll's face (doll facing you) first and if you're left handed, paint the left side of the doll's face first. This way, when you move to the other side of the doll's face, your arm will not be blocking the side you painted and you can use the painted side as a guide.

Joyce Marie La Fave: I like to use white, gray or ivory paint to lightly outline the eyebrows and lips before the actual color, especially on the Gene® doll's vinyl. Also I do this holding the Gene® doll upside down for better balance of eyebrows.

Step 1

Step 2

EYES

Jim Faraone: Years ago the talented Ken Bartram sent me a set of doll heads showing how he works on the doll's eyes. **(see step 1)** First Ken removed all the original makeup from the doll's face. **(see step 2)** He then paints in the whites of the eyes. **(see step 3)** Ken then applies the color of the eyes. **(see step 4)** Next he outlines the eyes and paints in the pupils. **(see step 5)** Ken finishes up with rooting in the eyelashes **(see step 6)**, which are now ready to be trimmed. **(see step 7)** As you can see, Ken Bartram has come a long way from his beginning days of creating.

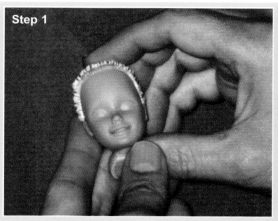

Step 1

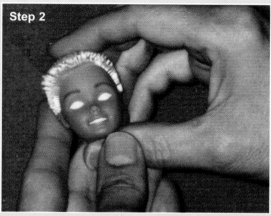

Step 2

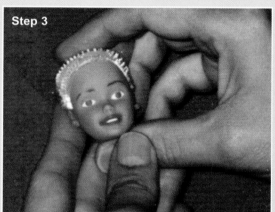

Step 3

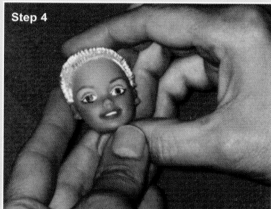

Step 4

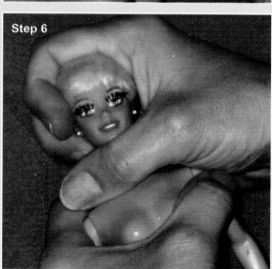

Step 5

Step 6

Step 7

Jenny Sutherland: Study eyes from fashion magazines, showing make-up and different eyes/eye colors, etc. You will notice a lot that you probably never noticed before. I use many colors in the eye itself. No one's eyes have just one solid color. There are various colors in each of our eyes, and doing this, will help you to achieve some realism.

Juan Albuerne: If you want the eyes to seem more stretched than the originals, use a dark color to line the eye BELOW the molded line. The wider the line, the more stretched. For irises, you'll obtain a better result if you do them smaller than they seem originally, painting it as rounded as possible and reserving a tiny space below (this way they won't reach the lower line of the eye and you'll see a white line below them). You can also try to place them in a different area of the eye— not just the center. Be careful with the symmetry. With a side-glance you will get a more mysterious look, but try different ways of setting the irises, and you will be amazed at the results. You must paint at least 3 different graduations of color in the irises: The first one will be the darkest (for all the iris); the second one will be lighter (in the low side of the iris to the middle of it, more or less); and finally, the third one will be the lightest (only a half-moon line in the low side of the iris). About the colors, be natural. Don't paint the apples (irises) too big and do put a spot of white light on one side of the apples, but don't cover them. In the upper side, a little bit displaced to right or left will look fine.

Tricia Hill: When painting eyes, I start with the whites first. I mix white paint with a very minute amount of black to make a slightly grayish white tint. I do this so the whites have a more natural look than if I were to paint them pure white. After letting the paint dry for approximately 15-20 minutes, I start painting the iris

of the eyes using the color of the eye that I have chosen ie. green, blue, brown, etc. For a narrow eye, I paint a smaller circle or oval. For a more rounded look, I paint a larger circle that is more round. Placement depends on the final look also. You can set the eyes in the center or to either side. After this dries, I paint the pupil of the eye in either black or a dark blue depending what would correspond with the iris color. I make my dot somewhere inside the eye color, again depending on what look I want. I let that paint dry again and do my final sparkle to the eye. I like to use pure white and do a very small dot in each eye for that "twinkle" look. This can be a dot or starburst or even a few lines coming out of the pupil. (These lines can also be done with a lighter shade of color that was used for the iris). I like to use a needle or the end of a toothpick dipped in the paint to do this. While that dries, I begin my lash lines. If I've rerooted the lashes, I use a dark color and finally dot the paint in between the lash holes for the top, and then a fine line either along the top or below the lashes. I like to use a straight pin for painting the fine line below the eye. Again, experiment with the length— either half way across the lower part of the eye or for a longer slimmer eye or all the way across. Also, turning the sides the eyes up or down will give it an entirely different shape.

Rachel Steinberger: I have two ways to make eyes look more mystical. The first is to make the outer edge of the eye slant far up on the face and have very long lashes. The other is to use either a sparkle paint or a metallic paint (especially gold) to paint the gleam and light-spots in the eye. To make the eyes look just a little creepy at the same time, leave the centers very, very light to create the illusion that you can see through the doll's head.

Pamela Bachmayer: I use toothpicks as a substitute for a paintbrush when trying to shape

the iris of the eye. Just use the very tip to dab paint where you want it slowly shaping the iris. You can also use it to add tiny details to the iris. Do be careful using toothpicks to avoid the tiny paint "volcanoes."

Vonda Silliman: I use a small metal stylus for painting the highlight in the eye.

William Stewart Jones: I have a tip for getting the eyes (iris and pupil) the same size—I stamp them!!! I use small tubes as a rubber stamp. (Flexible clear plastic aquarium tubing, soda straws, broken ballpoint pens, etc.) Lightly paint the end of the tube with the appropriate color acrylic, and press it onto the white eyeball. This gives me two circles exactly the same

with which to work. After the color is done, I stamp a black dot in the center. I then free hand highlights or anything else I want. I paint the upper and lower lines after that, so I can cut off part of the top and bottom of the eye as needed.

Jim Faraone: Great idea Bill! I've been experimenting as usual, and I find for the larger dolls like the Gene® doll you can use a 3mm or 2mm sequin as a stencil to trace around for the eye. You can place the tiny sequin on a round toothpick **(see step 1)** and hold the sequin in place on the doll's eye. **(see step 2)** Then just trace around the small sequin with a lead pencil to get your eye outline. **(see step 3)**

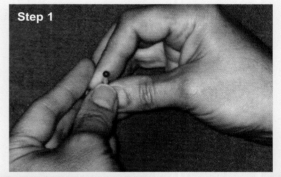

Step 1

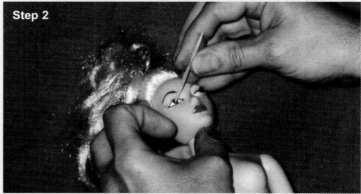

Step 2

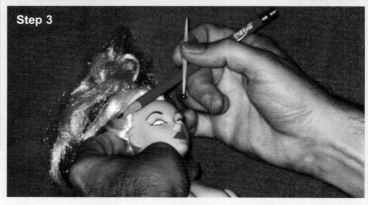

Step 3

LIPS

Juan Albuerne: To remake lips, noses or other facial features, I use a modeling paste such as Duro (Kdneattite) or Milliput.

Jim Faraone: Be careful in outlining your doll's lips. If you really want to outline your doll's lips, use the paint a half shade darker than the color you choose for the lips. If you do the liner too dark, your doll will come across looking like a platypus.

Juan Albuerne: (see step 1) When painting the mouth, you can try painting on the same molded line. You'll get better results if you don't choose a color that is too harsh. When you have filled the lips with the chosen color, **(see step 2)** add a touch of the same color mixed with a bit of white in the middle side of the lower lip, and smooth it from side to side for a bit of a pouty look. **(see step 3)** Then paint the line between the two lips a darker color. I always varnish the mouth except when I add metallic paint to the lips.

Lori Strawn: Remember that you don't have to paint within the lines. You can change the shape of the doll's lips and eyes by painting inside or outside the face mold contours.

Step 1

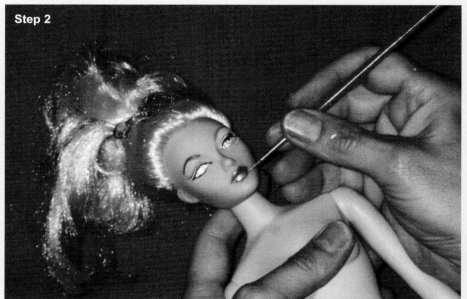

Step 2

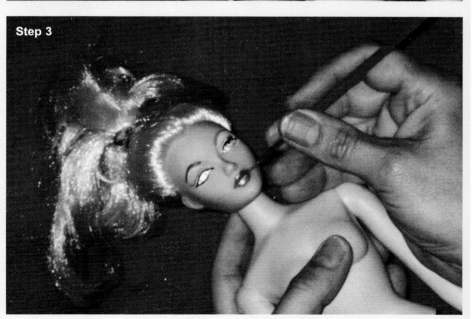

Step 3

BLUSH

Natalie Tetzlaff: I use the same color or a similar color as the one I used for the lips to apply as blush to my dolls. Take your small paintbrush, and dot 3 or 4 spots on the "apple" of the cheek for a natural look, and slightly below the "apple" for a more dramatic look. With a CLEAN finger, gently blend in an "upsweeping" motion. If it looks too heavy, wipe off excess with a wet paper towel. As always, best to practice this first on a cheap doll.

Juan Albuerne: You can reserve and maintain the original blush for the cheeks, but if you want to change it, it's a simple job. Mix a light pink color (I use a color named Old Rose) with the blending gel, and paint a line across the cheek. Then smooth that line with a dry, plain paintbrush till it mixes with the color of the face. You can also do other things with the cheeks such as simulate the cheekbone shadows, but it's difficult and you can ruin the face. Anyway, if you want to try this, I use a mixture of brown and dark red colors with the blending gel. I use this mixture to draw the line of the cheekbone; then I smooth the line till the shadow looks almost invisible on the face.

Susan Yslas: (see step 1) For blush, I use a Q-tip® and lightly dip one end into the acrylic paint. **(see step 2)** Then I blot it on a paper towel until I can barely see the faint color. **(see step 3)** I then blot it onto the cheek area and **(see step 4)** when I have blended it enough with the Q-tip®, I seal it with acrylic matte sealer. I do the same for eyeshadow.

Tricia Hill: I use a dry brush or the end of my finger tip (could even use a dry cotton swab for this too.) After lightly dabbing into the wet paint, I pat it onto a paper towel to remove the excess. Finally, I lightly apply it to the cheeks.

William Stewart Jones: When I was faced with the Barbie® doll's cheeks, I bought the smallest doe foot stippler brush. I made a soft cheek color in acrylic and didn't dilute it. In fact, I spread it out thin on a plate and let it thicken slightly but didn't allow it to dry out completely. Then I took an acrylic medium gel, dabbed a tiny-tiny amount on my finger and then onto the Barbie® doll's cheek. I spread it in a circle till the cheek was barely shiny and damp. Then I stippled a small circle of color onto the apple of the cheek. I pounced the rest of the paint off the brush onto a rag, and use the dry empty brush to blend the cheek color to the shade I want.

Jim Faraone: I once watched how my friend David Simpson added blush to his dolls. He took red carbon paper, dabbed his finger onto the carbon paper and rubbed it onto the doll's cheek area, which worked.

NOSE

Juan Albuerne: Paint the nostrils with a reddish brown color that is very watered down. If you do that, you'll get a look of bigger nostrils. If you want the nose to look wider, you can draw a thin line with that reddish brown color at both sides of the edges of the nose.

Aurora Mathews: Carefully inspect your entire nude doll after you finish a repaint. You may find that paint accidentally got into the doll's most unusual places.

Jim Faraone: While you're at it, you should check yourself also. Many times I've gone out with blotches of paint on me in the most usual places. LOL!

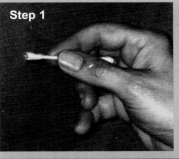

Step 1

Step 2

Step 3

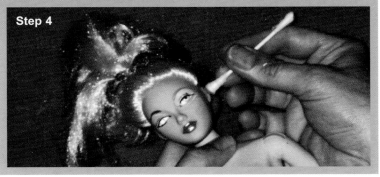

Step 4

Eyelashes

Adding eyelashes to your doll is like adding accessories to your outfits. They're that little added feature that can make your doll stand out from the rest. Although I have taught many of the basic techniques in my series of books, once again, there's always more than one way to do things. Flirty, sultry, sleeping or bright eyes, eyelashes make the difference.

Melissa A. Klein: I like to use thread to root the lashes on the dolls that I have done. I use quilting thread, which has a heavier consistency than regular sewing thread. It doesn't tend to go limp as lighter thread will. Depending on the doll's coloring, I use either a dark brown or black thread.

Aurora Mathews: There is a ridge along the Gene® doll's upper eyelid which is a great guide to apply false eyelashes.

Shirley Amador: The ridge is a great guideline Aurora. I found when applying eyelashes to the Gene® dolls, I use one of those tiny little screwdrivers that are for eyeglasses. I push the eyelashes into the little groove on the doll's eye with the screwdriver and the screwdriver fits perfectly for pushing them into place. Also, I put a tiny bit of white glue on the screwdriver and go over it. Super glue seems to get all over. Let it dry and then you can bend the eyelashes up or do whatever you want with them.

Sharon Marquiss-Morris: To curl rerooted eyelashes, I use toothpicks while applying the hairdryer.

Debbie Jane Cates: I use a homemade punching tool to root eyelashes for the Barbie® doll. I use very small quilting needles, and cut the eye of the needle in half with wire cutters used for jewelry or small electronics. I then use pliers to set the needle (point end first) into the end of a pencil eraser. The pencil is then used as the punch. I place the rooting material into the half-eye of the needle and "punch" it into the Barbie® doll's eyelid. When I'm done I seal the lashes with the sealant I used to seal the repaint. This really holds the eyelashes in place.

Susan Yslas: I do just about the same thing Debbie! **(see step 1)** I take a large-eyed sewing needle and cut the eye in half, leaving a set of prongs like a pitchfork. For the eyelashes, I like to use brown or black quilting thread. I cut about twelve 3in (8cm) pieces of thread per eye. **(see step 2)** I then take one piece of thread and lay equally across the middle of the set of prongs. **(see step 3)** I hold onto both sides of the thread and insert the prongs into the top of the eyelash line starting at the left side or inside of the eye. I continue this process until I cover the eyelash line to my satisfaction. I then crop or cut the eyelashes to the length I want. I then curl them with a human eyelash curler, and paint the lash line with a light line of acrylic paint to complete the eyeliner. I apply an acrylic sealer or non-yellowing clear nail polish to the lashes to give them a gentle push up to where I want them to be. I then let them dry and wah-lah a new set of eyelashes. If only it were that easy for us! LOL!

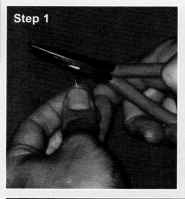

Step 1

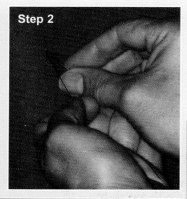

Step 2

Step 3

Jim Faraone: When trimming your eyelashes on the doll, keep them VERY short at the inner eye and longer at the outer eye like natural eyelashes. Having eyelashes too long gives the doll a "camel" look flapping in the Sahara desert!

Joan Champagne: I'm very picky about getting a natural look with my eyelashes so, after I root them with the smallest (in diameter) needle that I can use, I take the tweezers and pull on several at a time to get a blended look. Be careful that you don't pull too hard with the tweezers or you can break the lashes.

Barbara Fowler: Polyester rope is a great substance. I buy it by the foot or yard from the local home improvement store. I use black for the eyelashes and I am very pleased with the look. I unbraid it and iron it between pressing clothes to straighten it for the lashes. The number of strands used depends on "the look" desired. It gets a great "flirty" look.

Jen Hughey: When rooting eyelashes, start from the front of the doll. You can put the lashes exactly where you want them that way. I seal the inside end with a lighter burning them a tad. Smells icky, but it works. :-) No need to make a teeny knot.

Juan Albuerne: Women have bigger eyelashes than men. If you paint them in black, the eyes will seem deeper. I prefer the painted lashes over the rooted ones, but that's my own opinion. I varnish the eyelashes with gloss one by one.

Jenny Sutherland: I use the original lashes for the Gene® doll mostly, but I do sometimes use human lashes as well. When using human lashes, take care in the "length" of the lashes. If you are trying to achieve a "real" effect, make sure you trim them to a realistic length. A tip for trimming real lashes, trim the tips at various lengths so they appear to have a "choppy-straight across" look.

Gael Singer Bailey: I try and save the Gene® doll's original eyelashes, but if I can't, I use human false eyelashes for the lower lids. They are not as full as the upper lashes and you can get them at beauty supply shops. Also, they make individual false eyelashes for lower lids. I glue these on with her original lashes or with the line of false eyelashes. The extra length really looks good.

Vonda Silliman: When rooting eyelashes, make sure you are careful about the angle in which you insert the needle into the vinyl. If you want the lashes to show more of the eye, angle the needle into the vinyl (downward from the top) at the eyeliner. If you want a sleepier look, insert the needle into the vinyl at less of an angle, maybe even horizontally. These two methods give you different looks to the doll.

Angel Mitchell: Trimming rooted lashes with hot scissors will put a slight curl in them.

Joan Champagne: I use other fashion doll hair, or hair from Sally's Beauty Supply® or Lynn Smith®. Furthermore, Halloween is a great time to pick up those packs of synthetic hair.

Jean MaDan: I also use doll hair at times, Joan. I like using the hair from one of the Kira® dolls. Their hair is a great color and texture for lashes.

Brad Jensen: I do the Halloween hunt as well, Joan. I use hair from black Halloween wigs. It tends to be a little coarser and is more rigid than thread. I usually put about 9 - 11 strands per hole and about 7 - 9 holes per eye. I do not double the plugs. I curl the lashes with a spoon, or if I am

doing a boil perm I will curl the long, uncut eyelashes with a bobby pin and cut off the excess after the boil perm.

Sandy Cunningham: I do not remove heads to reroot lashes. **(see step 1)** I use swatches of long synthetic hair and cut a long piece to thread my needle. Do not tie a knot and do this before you style your doll's hair. **(see step 2)** Start at the outside corner of the eye. Go in the front of the doll's eyelid with your needle and out the back of the doll's head in the hair area. Pull the needle and hair all the way through the doll's head and out the back, slowly leaving a long piece about 1in (3cm) hanging out of the eyelid. **(see step 3)** On the back of the doll's head where you came out, clip the eyelash hair very close to the scalp. **(see step 4)** Then from the front of the doll's head pull gently just a tiny bit till the hair at the back of the head disappears into the doll's head and trim. You then continue across the doll's eyelid.

Jean Majercin: If rooting lashes bores you to tears, get a favorite video, sit down in front of the TV and root the lashes of several dolls at once. Then you will have a supply ready to go.

Jim Faraone: When rooting eyelashes on my dolls, I also do several dolls at once. Believe it or not, it only takes about 15 minutes to root lashes onto a doll.

William Stewart Jones: For Gene® dolls, I don't reroot because I think they're too heavy. I use bits of human false eyelashes and occasionally the fake plastic clown lashes for special effects. Lashes are available in colors like blue and purple, metallics, as well as black and brown. I glue them onto the doll on top of the eyeliner with glue and trim them for length after they are on the doll. It helps to first trim them so they are wide at the outside corner of the eye and

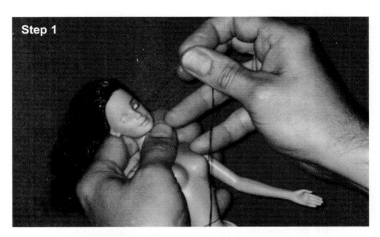

Step 1

Step 2

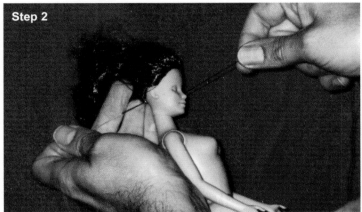

Step 3

Step 4

narrower at the inside corner. Then I snip into the lashes to give them a saw tooth shape. Sometimes I glue on just half a lash from the middle of the eye to the outer corner and trim quite short. Lashes can be bought in a long strip from doll suppliers and from theatrical stores and can be cut to the desirable length.

Doris Griswold: Use a quilter's needle threader to pull hair through your needle when rooting eyelashes or rerooting hair. They are strong and do not bend as the little metal ones do. You can find these in fabric stores.

Leslie Hampton: When using a package of curly hair for eyelashes, I straighten the hair first to make it easier to work with. Thread a large doll needle with about 1yd (.91m) length of hair. Holding the hair by the ends dip the needle into boiling water. The weight of the needle straightens the hair as it cools. Watch your fingers! I do two or three needles at one time. This is usually good enough to complete a project.

Tricia Hill: I've used synthetic hair, rope and even decorative (metallic) sewing threads for rooting lashes.

Jim Faraone: Don't forget that you can also paint your doll's eyes closed or give them a seductive wink. **(see step 1)** Just paint the doll's eye with a mixture of burnt sienna and white (which gives you a nice flesh color to match the doll's coloring) and **(see step 2)** highlight the center on the "closed" lid with a lighter flesh tone. **(see step 3)** Paint your eyeliner at the bottom ridge of the eye instead of the top. **(see step 4)** Then just root the eyelashes (as explained in my first book) on the bottom line of the doll's eye instead of the top line. Just something a little more unique to make your dolls stand out.

Loanne Hizo Ostlie: I've found that a toothpick used to spread black fabric paint onto the eyelashes acts as a miniature mascara.

Scott Shore: Regarding human hair for eyelashes, I use about 5 to 10 hairs per "lash". It is harder to thread the human hair, so I use more hairs than needed, because all the hairs don't make it through the needle's eye. I buy human hair by the bulk, probably used by people who make wigs. The hair is a little thicker and comes in different lengths, all in one bundle. I pay about $4.50 for a good amount of hair. I pull the longest hairs and cut it at the base. Then I dip the end I want to use into setting gel and clip off the excess of the short end on a slight angle (the end I put through the eye of the needle). That makes it easier to thread. When I pull the hair down through the neck of the doll, there is enough to tie off if that is what you want to do. I trim off all the loose ends inside the doll's head and trim the lashes to the length I want. Sometimes I leave them longer than usual depending on the look I want. Women who wear false eyelashes usually have shorter day lashes and longer evening lashes.

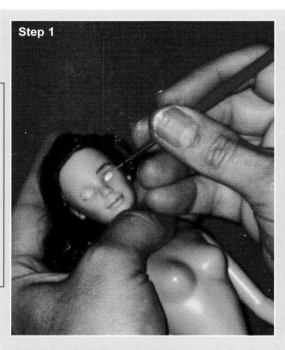

Step 1

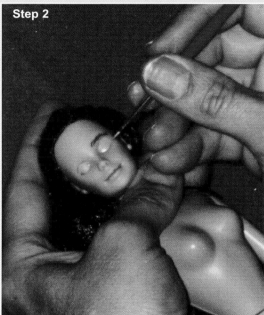

Step 2

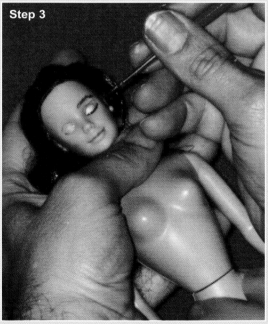

Step 3

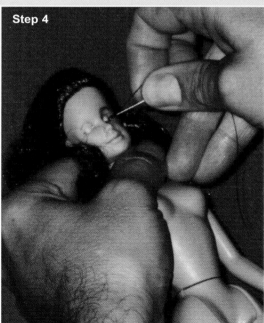

Step 4

Hair, Hair and More Hair

Most everyone loves to play beautician and create fabulous hairstyles on their dolls. It can be a challenge at times, but the end results are worth it. Creating different hairstyles seems to have an unending wealth of creativity for you. From long flowing hair, beehives, bouffants, pink hair, straight hair, curly hair to even molded hair, it will keep your imagination overflowing with ideas.

Kim Burie: A soft sculpture needle works great for rerooting doll hair or adding streaks to existing heads of hair. It is about 6in (15cm) long so it is impossible to lose inside the doll's head. The eye of the needle is also large enough that I usually do not need a needle threader. Sometimes I find it hard to find suitable rerooting fibre, but hair scavenged off of other dolls will work, and synthetic Kanekalon hair extensions made for people work well also. Sometimes this has a wave to it that can be relaxed or straightened with either a quick trip into a pot of hot water or a light ironing on the cool setting between 2 sheets of paper towels. Curly craft hair can also be straightened with an iron.

Deborah Fagan: I use a LoRain® needle threader for threading the needle while rerooting. Also, those real long needles which are about 5in (13cm) long makes for fast rooting on the top and crown of the head. I then switch to a shorter needle for the nape, above the ears and hair line. Also, different textured, rope type yarn is great to use for the look of dreadlocks.

Barb Wood: For curly, curly hair I usually wrap the hair with either coffee stirrers or small straws using tiny strips of cellophane on the tips of the hair as to catch any stray hairs. After dipping the hair in boiling water for about 30 seconds, let the doll sit for a while to let it dry a little. While the hair is still wet, carefully remove the rollers and cellophane and lightly spray with hair spray. I find this helps cut down on frizz.

Sarah Worley: Barb, I unset the hair while it's still damp also and find it gives it a looser curl. Once dried, I then use Aussie® Freeze Spray, but have found that you really have to shake it well to make sure it doesn't end up looking like "dandruff" on the doll.

Lynn K. Johnson: I use large-headed straight pins to hold hair adornments in place. Stick the pin through the confection and into the doll's head.

Laurie Samford: I had fun experimenting with rerooting an inexpensive doll with 4-ply yarn, but because I couldn't find a needle with a large enough hole to accommodate the yarn, which was small enough to go through the hair plug hole, I used beading wire. Basically bending a large piece in half and pinching the fold over the yarn. Then I poked the two cut ends of the beading wire through the hole. When I got enough wire through the neck opening, I wrapped the wire around something so that I would have something besides wire to tug on to pull the yarn through. If the wire gets twisted up inside the head, it can be retrieved with a crochet hook. The wire held up well and it only took me about three Star Trek® episodes to reroot the whole head. LOL! I untwisted the 4-ply yarn into kinky one-ply strands.

Tricia Hill: When I reroot, I use small plastic little girl barrettes to keep the hair that has already been rerooted out of the way and to keep from getting tangled as I continue to work. They come in fun colors and are very inexpensive.

Leslie Hampton: To make a perfect stand to hold the doll's head while you style the hair, you can drill a hole in the center of a large base. A fairly heavy wooden base will do. (I used the marble base from an old trophy because the hole was already in it.) Glue about a 1ft (31cm) length of a ½in (1cm) dowel into the hole and voila!

Tess Barton: Many people have trouble with short hairstyles, and therefore resort to up-dos and long curly styles. The most frequent factor is too much hair. Most fashion dolls are rooted too thickly for achieving a nice compact short hairstyle. To thin the hair, separate the plugs along the hairline all the way around, and in the part. If you want a 60's bouffant type hairstyle, also separate hair out at the crown. You can use bobby pins or clips to hold the hair away from the rest of the hair. Then using small scissors trim away the other plugs as close to the scalp as possible. You may want to start along one row of plugs and trim away only every other row first, so you don't thin too much. Once you have trimmed the hair you can, cut it and style it as is. If you plan to curl it, I find it is better to cut each section as you separate it out to place in the curler. Once you have finished curling the hair and have boiled it, take it out of the curlers while still wet (after cooled completely). Trim away any frizz and further trim the edges to get the shape you want. Brush or style as you had

planned. Then spray with a generous helping of hairspray, glue water or finger hair gel throughout. Wrap the hair (not too tight) in a stocking or wide ribbon until dry. When you unwrap it, you will have the shape you wanted and the hair will not be too poofy.

Joan Champagne: My latest discovery is using "invisible thread" to sew hair into the hairstyles I'm creating.

Carolyn Marnon: I have bought micro braids at a beauty supply store. I use them to wrap around the base of a ponytail. I did this with a Madonna look-a-like doll I did. Micro braids also come in some children's dress up toy sets. I have found it in lavender, pink, lime green and a few other assorted colors.

Jen Hughey: I found the perfect "rollers" for the Gene® doll sized curls. My dad actually suggested it, and told me I could share his tip with the group. Use the clear plastic tubing they have in hardware stores. It is flexible and cuts easily. I cut some small rollers, wet the hair, applied some gel, rolled up the roller, secured with a bobby pin near the head and VOILA! The perfect medium because they sell the tubing in several sizes, and it's CHEAP! :-)

Aurora Mathews: I always wash, condition and then comb the hair in the direction I plan to style it. I look for bald spots before I finalize my plans for each doll's hairdo. Do NOT use dry heat on the Tyler Wentworth® doll's hair because it will melt. Sometimes I blow the Gene® doll's hair with a blow dryer/comb combination. This way I can dry her hair with heat in the direction I plan on styling it. It makes styling so much easier and less bald spots occur.

Joan Champagne: I discovered that my electric dog clippers could be used to shape the hair when doing short hairdos. You could also use human hair electric clippers that are sold in drugstores. Invisible thread works well for sewing hair in place when creating hairdos. Do this while the head is removed and use a long needle. I always reroot the head hair before rooting eyelashes otherwise there is a possibility that you will ruin the eyelashes by getting head hair tangle in them.

Tricia Hill: I use the synthetic "Jumbo Braid" or hair from donor dolls for rerooting, but my ultimate preference is soft nylon rope that can be purchased by the foot at any hardware store and comes on a spool.

Stefanie Baumler: When doing micro-braiding or corn rows, use orthodontic rubber bands to secure the ends. If you want to add beads to the braids, complete your braiding and then one at a time, remove the rubber band and dip the end of the braid in some water or apply a small amount of hair gel to keep the ends together. Slide a bead on (the small pony beads look nice for this and fit just right) and all the way up the braid. Take a small piece of aluminum foil and wrap it around the end of the braid leaving a bit of a "tail" showing, then slide the bead back down and over the foil. This will keep the bead from falling off. The bead should fit very snugly over the foil. If it doesn't, add a little more foil.

William Stewart Jones: Watered down white glue is wonderful for setting hair. I used this for over 20 years on human size synthetic wigs. It can be used slightly watered

down, as a hair gel, or very thin as a hairspray. It will stick to rollers or straws, so I wrap a bit of wax paper around the straw, or coat the straw with melted wax. If you steam set or boil perm the hair, then arrange it and you can mist the hair with the watered down white glue. This is quite stiff and permanent, so don't use glue if you want to restyle the hair, but it's wonderful for fantasy hairdos.

Brad Jensen: I've learned that to get a firm hold on a French Twist it is best to set the twist with a boil perm. My secret to a firm set that won't fall or take 10 pins is to do the boil perm as usual and after the hair is set and dried completely, saturate the hair with hairspray and work with it wet. You will need a wet cloth because your fingers will get sticky. You can work with the hair for quite a while before it is not manageable. I use one or two stickpins to help hold the style.

Natalie Tetzlaff: Cans of compressed air or "dust remover spray" available at electronics stores are WONDERFUL! They are great for removing the little pieces of trimmed hair from your dolls after a haircut as well as for dusting them. It runs about $10 a can and will last for a while if used in short bursts.

Kevin Kilmer: If you have trouble getting braids or a twisted updo to stay in place, try monofilament fishing line. You get the 21lb strength line that is completely colorless and is finer than a strand of hair. Take a needle you would normally use for sewing and thread the fishing line through the needle as you would normally do with thread. Then just tack the thread through the end of the braid or twist of hair and sew it right through the head of the doll and then go back through the head again to secure the fishing line. Works like a charm to fix those

troublesome hairstyles that sprays and other fixatives will not hold in place and you don't have hair going all over the place.

Natalie Tetzlaff: I have a perming technique for wild, wavy locks. Divide the doll's hair into sections. If you want a wilder look, make them of varied thickness. Holding onto the end, twist the hair until it curls up upon itself. Secure the end with a rubber band and then pin to the scalp. Once all the hair is twisted and secured, dip into boiling water for 15-30 seconds and then immediately dip into ice-cold water. Now is a good time to trim the ends of the hair. Once dry, remove the pins, then the rubber bands and untwist the hair. Gently separate with a fine pick or your fingers and mist with hairspray.

Carol Jones: I use spray gloss varnish as a final finish rather than hair spray. It should be sprayed in a fine mist. I cover the doll's face with a piece of curved plastic (cut from a water bottle). This technique works especially well with sleek up-dos and springy ringlets. For sleek up-dos, use a flat paintbrush (preferably sable) and strong-hold gel. Paint it on in the direction of the hair. Finish (when dry) with a spritz of gloss lacquer. Be careful not to use too much gel or else you will get flakes.

Anita Healy: I have a quick and easy technique for up-do rolls on fashion dolls. First, saturate the doll's hair with an extra hold hairspray. Next, tie the hair up with rubber bands. Comb the ponytail straight up and respray with the hairspray and let dry. As the hair is drying plug in a small rod curling iron and set it to medium/low heat. When the ponytail dries, smooth a small amount of gel onto it and divide into sections to roll. After each roll is curled with the iron, thread a needle with the same color thread as is the hair and wrap it around the

tip of the roll. Then sew a stitch directly into the base of the skull of the doll's head. Repeat as necessary. When completed, respray with the same hairspray you started out with.

Pamela Bachmayer: Some dolls come with "wild" hair and there's just too much of it or it appears dull. This type of hair can be difficult to work with. One way to tame this hair and give it a shinier appearance is to place the doll in a sitting position in a sink and pour about 1 cup of boiling water over her head. This is a great method to change a doll's part as well. You can still boil perm or use a curling iron on her hair after this treatment.

Linda Lynch Holman: To make embroidery floss hair ponytails I cut embroidery floss into 12in (31cm) lengths and then separate the strings into 2 sections of 3-4 strands. Using a tapestry needle, thread it, knot one end and use the same procedure for regular rerooting but only do 2 or 3 rows around the face. Pull the floss up on top of the head and secure it using a retainer size rubber band or another piece of embroidery floss. If using the embroidery floss, wrap it twice around the ponytail then tie it tightly into a knot. You'll have a unique ponytail and you can trim it to any desired length.

Shirley Amador: The way I make long spiral curls is to first I shampoo and condition the doll's hair. This makes the hair easier to work with. Then I use end papers used for regular perms and medium perm rods. I comb the hair out, and starting around the face, I take a small section and comb it smooth and then twist it. Twist the hair toward her face. After it is twisted, I put an end paper around the end of the section of hair and then start curling it onto the rod. Curling it under toward her face, I roll it very tightly and then secure the rod. If the rod is one of those with the elastic, I wrap the elastic around the rod for a tight fit. I usually do half the hair in one direction and then the other half in the other direction always going toward the face. After the hair is all rolled on the perm rods, I pour approximately 2 cups of boiling water over it. Holding the doll over the sink. I use a teakettle to pour boiling water directly on the curls being careful not to pour it on my hands and making sure that every curl is covered with the boiling water. Then I pour cold water over that. I dry the excess water off with a towel and then take the rods out very carefully keeping the curls intact. I then set her up somewhere and let the hair dry naturally. If the rods are left in the hair it takes a very long time to dry. After the hair is completely dry, I play with the curls to make them the way I want them.

William Stewart Jones: I use a hand held steamer. I set the hair wet, with papers, on straws and coffee stirrers and occasionally use tiny perm rods. I spray the hair with VERY strong spray, the kind they use for punk hairdos. I save hairstyle pictures from magazines because I'm not a hairdresser!!! I save website pictures of great hairstyles on other dolls because it shows me what is possible. I like to use a ½in (1cm) pin made by Clover™. It's called an Applique pin. Art. no, 231 which has a white glass head. They are very handy because they don't tend to snag the other hair as you work. They are just long enough to go through the curler into the doll's head. However, they are VERY small, and you have to keep track of them, or you'll end up sitting on one.

Imelda Sanchez: When fashion dolls have too much hair, I always remove the hair from underneath the top layer of hair. I cut it close to the scalp and then remove the head and pluck out the hair like you do for a reroot. Do not remove any hair from anywhere along the hairline! You can remove as little or as much as you want. This is especially good when doing upsweep hairdos.

Joyce Marie La Fave: I like to use diluted Downey® fabric softener on the frizzy ends of a doll's hair or dolls that are over sprayed and well traveled.

Dorothy Fannin: I've taken my molded hair tips in Jim's book 3 a step further. After the second coat of modeling paste dries, I build up with another thicker coat and before it thoroughly dries, I take a sculpting tool to create wavy hair. Also, for the molded bobbed hairstyle, I shave the ears to just above the earring hole to give the molded hair a smoother look.

Barb Alexander: When doing hair, I have found some judicial use of super glue at certain areas is beneficial. Use carefully. This is very useful in period style hairdos.

Scott Shore: I keep the hair that I cut from dolls that I give short haircuts to and use that to reroot other dolls.

Laura Fern Fanelli: If you can't get orthodontist rubber bands, I discovered a clear thin rubber band (non-tangle) at my local Longs® drug store. They are called no damage play bands and can be used for ponytails and braids.

Jim Faraone: Good one Laura and I found the Goody® brand Mini Ouchless clear rubber bands at Wal-Mart®. Saves faking having braces when you check with an orthodontist!

Jenny Sutherland: Sculpting gel works amazingly well to keep the desired hairstyle you want to achieve. Small bobby pins work nicely to hold the hair in place.

Sheryl Majercin: I found that cosmetology books are great for those of us who know close to nothing about hair setting. If you find one with pictures, even better!

Sarah Worley: An effective way to achieve a softly curled bob or page-boy style is to remove the drinking straw curlers while the hair is still wet, style and let it dry. Clips and spray or setting foam or gel can be used to hold the style in place while it dries.

Doris Griswold: When cutting hair off a doll to get the head super clean use an electric razor or clippers to get it done fast. It makes it easier to get the stubble through the scalp if it is micro short.

William Stewart Jones: For fantasy hair, try using non-hair materials: wire, feathers, fake fur, embroidery floss, rayon fringe, etc. Wire can be strung with beads, or flocked, or glued and glittered. Marabou and feathers can be sprayed with hairspray and shaped which changes the look entirely. Embroidery floss can be braided, twisted and left loose and sprayed. Rayon fringe makes wonderful long straight hair. Fake fur can be sprayed and combed into wonderful shapes and streaked with felt pens. When it is combed while still wet with spray, it forms into strands and looks very much like hair.

Gael Singer Bailey: I discovered small curlers covered with Velcro that are much easier to work with. They are about the same size in diameter as straws and I cut the length in half. They are about 2in (5cm) long and available in beauty supply stores.

Andrea Densley: When I am using a doll with bangs, and need the hair all brushed back off the face to go under a hat or headpiece, I do a "mini-boil" hair set. Wet all the hair, and brush the bangs either back off the face, or part in the middle and back off the face. Then tear off a strip of very clingy plastic wrap about 1-½in (4cm) wide. Hold the bangs in position and tightly stretch the center of the length of wrap over the doll's forehead and hairline. Pull the plastic wrap ends behind the doll's head, cross them and bring them to the front, or twist together in the back. The object is to have the wrap tight around the bangs. Turn the doll upside down and dip the top of head in boiling water for about 15 seconds. Then dip the head in a small dish of ice water and let the doll sit for a few minutes. Finally peel off the plastic wrap.

William Stewart Jones: You can dye synthetic hair by boiling in Rit® dye. Be sure to wrap the hair around rollers before dying it, otherwise the hair will be set in odd shapes. The hot dye will color the hair and set the curl at the same time. You can reroot with already curled hair. If you don't want much curl, wrap the hair around a small tin can; then dye it.

Michelle Candace: To get a microbraid look without using braided hair or braiding it yourself, try rerooting using fringe that can be bought by the yard at your local fabric store. Black fringe makes great African-American microbraids and you can use other colors for different effects.

Jillian Manning: I have a different method I use for setting my doll's hair. First, I wash, condition and set the hair as usual. Then I wrap my doll's head in a plastic bag. I put an elastic band around her neck to keep it in place. How my dolls suffer for my art! LOL! I then boil some water and pour it into a heatproof bowl. I dunk the doll's head into it and leave it there until the water cools. Then I un-bag her and allow the hair to dry naturally. I find this gives a nice firm but natural result.

Sandy Cunningham: I like to take some hair to match the doll's hair or even a different shade for contrast to make tendrils. Using **(see step 1)** a big eyed needle, I thread the hair through it and **(see step 2)** put the needle at the sideburns area of the doll's head. Insert it through the doll's head and **(see step 3)** out the other end. Pull through. **(see step 4)** Then you can set the hair on soda straws to make great curly tendrils.

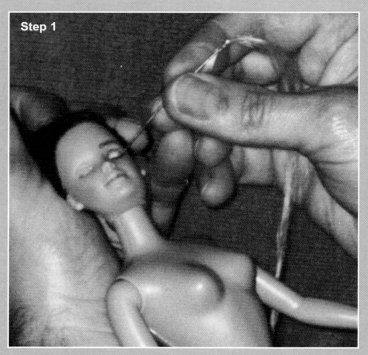

Step 1

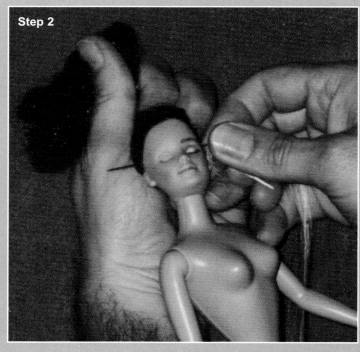

Step 2

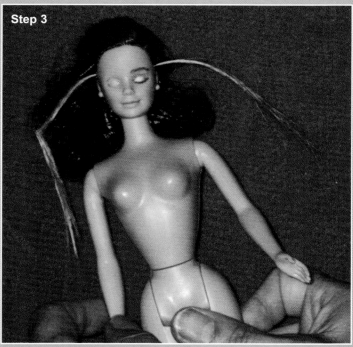

Step 3

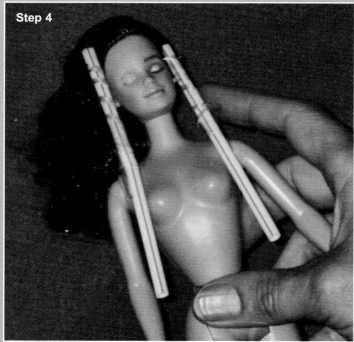

Step 4

Scott Shore: Jim, would it be okay if I post my directions for doing Architectural/Pyramid Hairdo?

Jim Faraone: Sure Scott, we're all here to learn and are always appreciative of those willing to share their tips with everyone.

Scott Shore: Cool! **(see step 1)** Well, you will need plastic straws and pipe cleaners to make the rollers and a good super hold setting gel and end papers. **(see step 2)** Make a ponytail in the center of the doll's head and put the setting gel throughout. This helps keep the rest of the hair standing straight up and out of the way. If you want spiral curls at the face or in the back of the head, leave them out of the ponytail. **(see step 3)** Take a doll brush and at the bottom of the ponytail just above the rubber band, take 2 equal sections of hair (front to back), one on the left and one on the right and let them flop down on each side of the doll's head, making sure that you keep the hair parallel to the ground. **(see step 4)** Put another rubber band around the ponytail and right up against the 2 sections of hair you just separated. **(see step 5)** Cut the end papers in half lengthwise and put more setting gel on one of the lengths of hair. Cut the straws to about 1in (3cm) to 1-½in (4cm). Place the end papers on the piece of hair, making sure that it is flat and as even as possible. Then take your roller and pipe cleaner and start rolling towards the base of the pony tail. Roll and curl under, not up. It is very important to keep the curl as tight and even as you can. (The hair can be a little narrower at the starting end), but keep the rest of the curl even. When you get to the base of the ponytail, secure the straw with 2 pins (one in front of the hair and one in back of the hair). Repeat on the other side of the head.

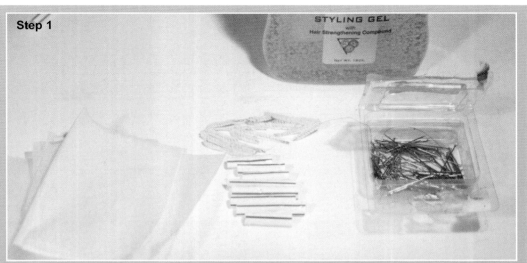

Step 1

Step 2

Step 3

Step 4

Step 5

(see step 6) Now, start all over again for the next set of curls. (Most dolls you can get 3 sets of curls and 1 on the top. Don't forget to use a rubber band between each set of curls. (see step 7) KEEP EACH CURL ON TOP OF THE ONE BELOW!!! The fact that you are using the hair from a thinner ponytail each time is what makes the final hairdo wider at the bottom, and narrower at the tops. Check to see that all curls are in a straight row, directly on top of the one below, then boil for 15-18 seconds; then give it an ice bath. Blot up the excess water and let dry. Remove the pins first, then the rollers and pipe cleaners along with the end papers. Start at the top. After you are satisfied with the results, and there is little room to move the curls if they stray a little, spray with super hold hairspray or freeze and shine. Let it dry and spray again. TIPS: Make sure you use setting gel on each curl even though you saturate the ponytail at the beginning. Always use 2 pins for each curl—1 pin in the center will hold the curl, but you will have a pin hole in the finished hair-do. (see step 8) Keep the curls directly on top of one another and if necessary, cut the ends off to make them even prior to rolling. Let everything dry thoroughly. I set the doll in front of a fan on low overnight. (see step 9) When all the curls are where you want them, trim off any loose or stray hairs, then with a small paint brush, paint setting gel on each curl following the direction the curl is going. (see step 10) You can then embellish your new hairstyle in any way you desire and (see step 11) have an exotic beauty you can be proud of.

Step 6

Step 7

Step 8

Step 9

Step 10

Step 11

Jim Faraone: Great one Scott!

Scott Shore: Jim, I'm on a roll here and I have another technique I'd like to share with everyone.

Jim Faraone: Let it rip Scott!

Scott Shore: This is my technique for doing spiral curls. I always start at the face if I want curls in front of the ears. I let some space in between the

hair as I roll it up on the straw and pipe cleaner "roller" (like in your book 3) for these, so I can have a cork screw effect. **(see step 1)** I pull all the left over hair up into a lose ponytail and **(see step 2)** coat the hair with setting gel. Next, I separate it into sections. **(see step 3)** Starting at the right side, I do a spiral. **(see step 4)** I wrap the strip of hair with end papers and **(see step 5)** starting at the bottom of the hair strand, I roll

Step 1

Step 2

Step 3

Step 4

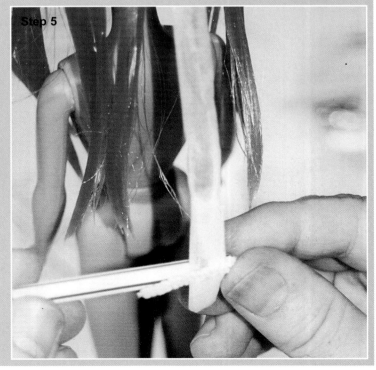

Step 5

25

Step 6

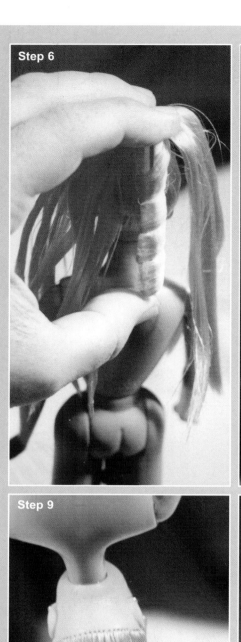

Step 7

Step 8

Step 9

Step 10

Step 11

it up and **(see step 6)** then angle the straw so it is parallel to the head. I then move to the other side and do 1 spiral. It takes about 2-½ end papers to wrap each curl (on long haired dolls, such as the Cool Clips Barbie® doll). **(see step 7)** I work my way to the center of the doll's back, **(see step 8)** curling the spirals on the right in the same direction as the one at the face and the spirals on the other side likewise. I pull a small amount of hair from the ponytail for each curl and I do about 2 or 3 rows of curls. On the Cool Clips Barbie® doll, I also pulled back a second ponytail using the top portion of hair to create it. I sectioned it off and rolled them up in the same fashion. I got 4 or 5 from that section of hair. A BIG TIP is to use lots of super firm setting gel on each spiral. Apply the gel to all the hair. USE END PAPERS from the base of the scalp to just past the ends of the hair. This will insure that you will catch all the hair. Keep the portion of hair you want to spiral as flat and as even as you can. As you roll, keep the hair that has been rolled close to the next section of hair you are rolling—sort of like a barber shop pole, but close together. Cut off the tops of the straws so they don't get in the way. Put 1 or 2 pins into the head to secure the "rollers" from moving because they seem to have a mind of their own at times. Then it's off to the boiling pot for about 18 seconds and then a dunk in icy cold water. I then absorb most of the water with a towel and set the head next to a fan for a few hours or until almost completely dry. Once it is nearly dry, I remove all the pins. Then starting on the curls close to the neck, I remove the curler and pipe cleaners. The last thing I do before spraying it, is removing the end papers. Once again I start at the bottom (near the neck) and actually pull the papers from

the end of the spirals. If the curl gets a kink in it, I just twist it back into the direction it should be in, sort of like a phone cord. The last curls I take out are the corkscrews in front of the ears. **(see step 9)** I cover the doll's face and then spray. Turn the head upside down and spray some more. **(see step 10)** Now with a little imagination, you can cover the rubber band with beads or trim and **(see step 11)** your new spiral haired beauty is ready for a night on the dance floor.

Jim Faraone: Super Scott and you sure are on a roll today. I bet you $5 you have a coffee machine next to your computer! LOL!

Carolyn Marnon: I have used ribbon to wrap around the base of a ponytail and then wound the ribbon up (or is that down?) the ponytail to create a higher looking ponytail. The effect is quite dramatic.

Aurora Mathews: Do NOT cut bangs on a doll unless you know they will lay flat or the way you want them to. Doll hair has a mind of its own and when cut, it sometimes will NOT lay flat.

Jim Faraone: I agree, Aurora, that doll hair can have a mind of its own. If the bangs won't lay flat, you can always use a piece of rolled paper toweling and wrap it around the doll's forehead (like she has a headache) and secure it. Then pour boiling water over the paper toweling in the bangs area and let it dry. When you remove the paper towel, the bangs should lay flat.

Joyce Marie La Fave: I like to use sponge rollers in the smallest size. I remove the plastic clip from the foam part and cut the foam in half or thirds. Then I attach the foam pieces to the hair with a pipe cleaner through the center to hold them in place.

Sandy Cunningham: I take a doll and cut away all her hair with no need to remove the head. When I have it all cut off, I shave it even closer with a disposable razor (be careful here and go slowly as you can slice a big hole in the doll's head.) Once you get her fairly bald (it's okay if a few hair bristles remain because they won't show) you are ready to apply a neat new kind of hair. Just trim a piece of feather boa in your choice of color to wrap around the doll's head. Leave it longer than you will need because you can trim it later. Position the boa along the original hairline and apply it to the doll's head with several straight pins being careful not to stick them through her face. If the boa is too fluffy for your taste, you can give it a haircut just like hair. But when cutting, go slow and just cut a little at a time, as the feathers are delicate and you will not want to have gaps.

Tricia Hill: I curl my doll's hair by using a small, ¼in (.65cm) diameter curling iron. I've played around with the settings for different types of hair. Some doll's hair I can use it with the hair damp and the setting on high and some I have found it works best with the hair dry and the curling iron set on low. LOW is the safest way to go, but even with that, TEST a small unnoticeable strand of hair first. It could very possibly melt the hair. The curling iron is also great for kinky hair to straighten and for looser "wispier" curls.

Leslie Hamptom: I pick out the right size medicine bottle and drop the head face down into the bottle up to the hairline. This makes a perfect shield for the face while you are spraying the hair.

Working with Patterns

Working with patterns can be a fun experience or a terrifying endeavor for those not use to patterns. All the pattern pieces can look like a giant jigsaw puzzle. Patterns are really easy to work with if you follow the instructions. Once you have the basics down, future patterns will be a breeze to work with. The best patterns I have found for beginners are the old 1960's Advance® patterns that you can find at times on on-line auctions or at doll events. Not only are the fits perfect with these patterns, but they were manufactured for little girls and the instructions are so easy to follow and so self explanatory that even I learned a few new things from them. Now if we can only figure out how to fold up those patterns to get them back into their envelopes neatly.

Carolyn Marnon: A quick way to make a pattern is to use paper towels. I have made clothing for dolls just by placing the doll on the paper towel and tracing around the doll to get the shape I wanted. When I had the pattern pieces cut out, I could play around with them on the doll to get a rough idea of what I wanted. The paper towel doesn't hold up well like a regular pattern would, but if you are just looking for a rough "sketch," the paper towel is inexpensive, plentiful and drapes well enough for starters.

Rachel Steinberger: When creating new patterns, I use dryer sheets or plastic bags. Not only do these materials fold and drape more like fabric, they're also easy ways to reuse trash and that's environmentally sound. One easy shortcut I use when creating a pattern, I make a paper cut-out in the exact shape and dimension I want the piece to be. I trace around this piece on my fabric with a water-soluble marker.

Then I cut out around the piece leaving about ½in (1cm) around the edge as a seam allowance. Then I just sew along the traced line.

Tricia Hill: When cutting fabric and patterns for sewing, I cut it about ¼in (.65cm) wider than the standard commercial patterns call for. This way it's easier to piece the outfit together and sew and then later go back and trim the excess along the seam line with my scissors. Then I go along the edges with Fray No More® for a more professional/quality look.

Debbie Jane Cates: I photo-copy my new doll patterns twice. One set I use to cut out my doll clothes, and the other set is used to recopy when the first set is worn out. This way you only have to unfold the original pattern once. This is also good with vintage patterns. It keeps them in good condition and you still can use the pattern. Also, I have a 3-ring notebook with page protectors in which to keep my original patterns. Then I can just flip through the book when I'm looking for a particular pattern.

Bunny Dedes: I spent the entire day using clear contact paper, the kind you use to line the bottom of your cabinets, and laminated all my favorite doll patterns. They are so much easier now for pinning and cutting. No more crease where you want to cut and they don't rip when you pin them.

Natalie Tetzlaff: I scan my patterns into my computer, so I will always have a copy if the originals get too well used. Also, I write notes next to the sewing instructions that come with the pattern. (ie: gathers must be tight here, darts need to be eased gently.) This is a tip I learned from my grandmother who was a seamstress.

Patriciann Palka: I scan my patterns also, Natalie. I VERY carefully scanned each pattern piece into my computer, saved as a bitmap, then printed out what I needed onto tear-proof paper available at your local office supplier. The benefit of this is that you create a master that you can scale up/down for other dolls, merely by toggling the points of the bitmap picture on the computer. I use a master pattern that I draft via draping on each doll to compare fit as well as measurements. It takes a bit of practice, but once you develop the skill it saves a LOT of time and gives you more flexibility with your pattern investment.

Amy Nardone: Patterns are a great way to start for the beginner. Try altering the pattern slightly to get your own look. With stretchy, clingy fabric, it is easier to lay the doll on the fabric and trace with a chalk wheel, allowing for seam allowance. A great curvy sexy fit is a sure hit with this fabric and method.

Jim Faraone: You're right, Amy, about altering patterns you have and it's actually very easy even for beginners. For instance, this collar pattern. **(see step 1)** The important part of this pattern is the section where it connects to the collar of the bodice (shown in a solid line). You know that those two sections need to remain the same to fit together perfectly while sewing them together. But, you can change the shape of the rest of the pattern. If it's a curved collar, you can trace it onto graph paper (keeping the section that is sewn to the bodice the same) and **(see step 2)** change the outside edge to a rounded collar or whatever shape you'd like. With the graph paper you can center the section that is sewn to the bodice on one of the lines, **(see step 3)** fold the graph paper in

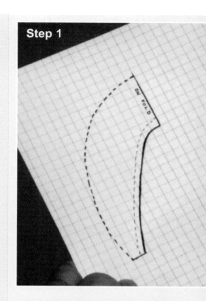

Step 1

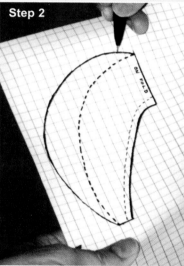

Step 2

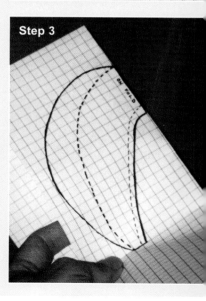

Step 3

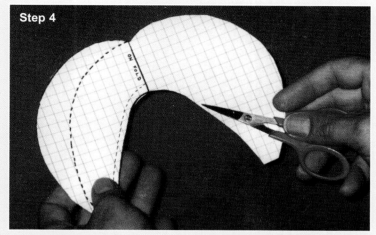

Step 4

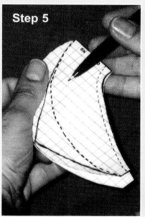

Step 5

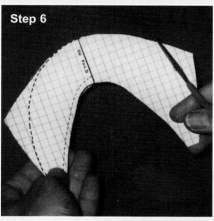

Step 6

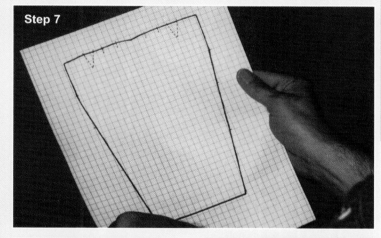

Step 7

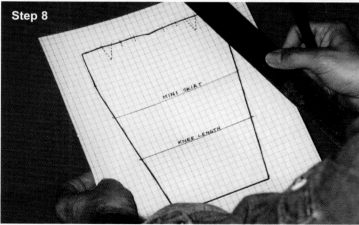

Step 8

half and **(see step 4)** cut it out. When you unfold the graph paper, your collar will have two equal sides. **(see steps 5-6)** As you can see, you can play around with as many collar shapes as your imagination lets you. It's the same with skirts. **(see step 7)** If you have a long skirt pattern, the important part of the pattern is where the waist is sewn to the bodice. **(see step 8)** Once again with graph paper, ruler and pen and you can make the skirt into a mini or midi length, or whatever you like. Just have fun with your patterns. They're not as scary as they look.

Jennifer Hughey: Try out commercial patterns before you cut them on your good fabric. Some need a little alteration. A good idea is to make the pattern out of paper towels and baste it for a test-fit to the doll. You can alter the pattern as needed right on the towels.

Jim Faraone: Good point, Jennifer, and for the life of me, I can't understand why most commercial patterns today have such a bad fit on the dolls. These patterns are designed for specific sized dolls, so you'd think that with all the company's professional pattern makers, they could make a pattern that fit perfectly the first time around.

William Stewart Jones: Make your thin paper patterns stronger by ironing them onto a stabilizer like Iron-On Pellon. It's easier to do this before you cut them out the first time.

Chrissy Stewart: You can combine pieces of patterns to get multiple looks and outfits. I often have to alter a pattern to get the look I am trying to achieve. For instance, you can use a seam in the front, form fitting "top/shirt" pattern to make various bodices.

Jim Faraone: Being a pattern "masher" is great, Chrissy, and it's also fun taking the bodice from one pattern and mixing it with the skirt of another pattern, or switch around sleeves and collars. Don't be a virginal pattern user. Have fun mixing the pattern pieces up.

Sheryl Majercin: Barbie® doll patterns can be scanned into your computer and printed at 126% larger to fit the Gene® doll.

Tricia Hill: I like to transfer patterns that I repeatedly use onto the back of fine sandpaper. Then I can just lay the pattern (rough side of the sandpaper down) on the fabric and draw around it with a fabric pen. That way I can cut it out without having to pin.

Shirley R. Heater: I also found other things to transfer patterns onto to keep them from shredding. You can transfer them onto the clear plastic fronts on doll boxes or x-ray film.

Barb Alexander: When you want to make an outfit for a doll, and do not have a pattern to follow, just lay the doll on a piece of paper and draw around the outline of the doll, holding the pen straight. The resulting outline will be a bit larger then the doll's body, but this is good as you need the space for seams. Then, when you cut out the pattern, allow about a ¼in (.65cm) more all around for the seam area. Then lay the pattern on fabric and cut and sew.

Jim Faraone: With regular patterns I found that enlarging a Barbie® doll pattern by approximately 125% on an office copy machine it will fit a Gene® doll. Then by reducing a Gene® doll pattern by approximately 80% it will fit the Barbie® doll. Now of course, patterns do vary so some adjusting will be needed to fit the doll properly.

Lynn Smith: Jim, I have some tips on resizing 18in (46cm) girl doll patterns to fit 4¼in (11cm) dolls.

Jim Faraone: Great Lynn! Go for it!

Lynn Smith: The proportion of 18in (46cm) girl doll bodies are very close to that of 4-¼in (11cm) Little Kelly© dolls and friends—both dolls have a child-like figure. There are plenty of patterns available for 18in (46cm) girl dolls but that's not the case with the little ones. To solve this problem, I decided to reduce the 18in (46cm) doll patterns using the same method I used to reduce patterns for people to fashion doll size. An 18in (46cm) doll fashion pattern is reduced on a photocopier (or using a scanner and computer). A sample garment is made from this miniature reproduction and some paper towels. The paper towel garment is used to fine-tune the fit of the photocopied pattern. Any necessary adjustments are then transferred back onto the 4-¼in (11cm) doll size pattern.

Supplies and Equipment: 18in (46cm) doll pattern, scissors, ruler or measuring tape, pen or marker, photocopier with an 11in x 17in (28cm x 43cm) window, or if you have a flatbed scanner and printer hooked up to your computer you can scan, resize and print instead of using a photocopier. You also need paper, heavy-duty paper towels, 4-¼in (11cm) doll to use for fitting, tape, needle and thread. When choosing a pattern, keep in mind that simple designs work better. Small details, linings, interfacing and such will most likely need to be eliminated. Layers of ruffled fabric can be replaced with purchased ruffled trim. Waistbands can be made using narrow, doublefold seam binding or ribbon. Select fabrics that are easy to work with, and when possible use fabrics that don't need to be hemmed or faced on the edges. I like using faux-suede instead of velvets, and felt in place of wool.

Preparing the 18in (46cm) doll pattern: In order to fit on a standard size photocopier found in most office supply stores, large pattern pieces and sheets must be divided into sections measuring no more than 11in x 17in (28cm x 43cm). If you are using a scanner to scan the pattern pieces, divide any large pattern pieces to fit the window of the scanner. If you have to divide a single pattern piece, use symbol, number or letter codes along the cut edges to make it easier to match up the pieces again later. I often tape my pattern pieces to paper. If I am using a photocopier to reduce my patterns, I join two 8-½in x 11in (22cm x 28cm) pieces of paper to form an 11in x 17in (28cm x 43cm) sheet. It's not necessary to do this, but I find that it helps to keep the pattern pieces neat and flat while transporting them to and from the office supply store and makes it much easier to position them in the window of the scanner or copier. *Reducing the pattern pieces:* The goal here is to reduce the pattern to 4-¼in (11cm) doll size by reducing it to 20% of the original size (30% for hats). If you are using a scanner for this step just scan, resize to 20%, match and rejoin any large sections you had to divide to fit the scanner window, label the images (pattern name, number and new size) and then print a couple of copies of each pattern piece. It's a bit more complicated using a photocopier. The copier I use would only reduce as small as 50%, so to get to 20%, it must be done in three steps. Copy all your pattern pieces at 50% to create copies that are 50% of the original size. On the back of these copies label them "50%". If you have to divide any pattern pieces into 2 sections for copying, rejoin the 50%-size copies before continuing. Copy all of the newly created half-size pattern pieces at 50% to create pieces that are 25% the size of the originals. On the back of these copies label them "25%." Copy all of the 25%-size pieces at 80% to create pieces that are 20% the size of the originals. Label these sheets on the front "Reduced to fit 4-¼in (11cm) dolls." Add the pattern name and number if it doesn't show up on the copies. Make an extra couple of copies to use for fine-tuning the fit. *To reduce hat patterns:* Copy the original pieces at 50% and then copy those half size images at 60% to achieve pattern pieces that are 30% the size of the originals. You are taking a copy of a copy of a copy of an original and reducing the size each time, so you will lose some clarity of your image. I find it helpful to use the "photo" or "image" mode on the photocopier and I usually set my copies a bit darker than what the auto control selects. Make sure your pattern edges and markings are clearly defined. On the first pass you can reduce 11in x 17in (28cm x 43cm) to 8-½in x 11in (22cm x 28cm) size paper. The 11in x 17in (28cm x 43cm) originals will be placed sideways on the photocopier, so make sure the 8-½in x 11in (22cm x 28cm) paper in the tray is also placed in the same direction. After the first pass you will have the same number of copies that you had of the originals. If you place two of the half-size copies side-by-side (to form one 11in x 17in (28cm x 43cm) image area) you can fit all the second run pieces on just half that number of 8-½in x 11in (22cm x 28cm) sheets of paper. For the last pass through the copier, I print from 8-½in x 11in (22cm x 28cm) sheets of paper onto the same number of 8-½in x 11in (22cm x 28cm) sheets of paper. The ¼in (.65cm) seam allowances were reduced to less than 1/16in (.15cm) when the pattern pieces were reduced, making them almost nonexistent. Add new ¼in (.65cm) seam allowances to your pattern pieces as required. **(see photo 1)** The resized pattern sheet is pictured at a reduced size. These are some of the pattern pieces I used to create the outfits pictured. **(see photo 2)** I replaced the belt with a piece of bias tape so I didn't add a seam allowance to that pattern piece. I also didn't add allowances to the hemlines. That can be done a bit later on. I used my scanner, photo editing software, and my printer to create these resized pattern pieces, but you can do the same thing with photocopies and a marker. *Fine tuning the fit:* Trace the pattern pieces onto a piece of sturdy paper towel. This will be used to make a sample for further fitting. Tape or hand baste the pattern pieces along the stitching lines, overlapping the edges of the paper towel by the ¼in (.65cm) seam allowance and basting any tucks or darts. Check the size by fitting the paper towel garment on a doll. Keep in mind the weight and give of the fabrics you will be using to construct your doll garments. Other considerations include the bulk of the seams and any garment that might be worn underneath. Make any adjustments that may be necessary by marking them on the paper towel pattern. Lengthen or shorten the sleeves and adjust the hemline. Remove the paper towel pattern from the doll and transfer any pattern changes back onto the flat pattern pieces. Once the adjustments and changes are transferred back onto the paper pattern, the pattern should be ready to use. If you're in doubt about the accuracy of the adjustments or the fit of the pattern, make a second paper towel sample garment using the newly adjusted paper pattern pieces and repeat the fitting process. If you want to make nice reusable copies, use some liquid paper and a fine tip marker to clean up the lines on your pattern pieces. Make new copies of these pieces. I used this method to resize the outfits pictured here. **(see photo 3)** The cape, jumper, shirt and tights are resized from Butterick® 5110. The jumpsuit is made using Simplicity® 7688 and the hat is made using Simplicity® 8541. From fine-tuning the fit on the cape, I discovered that the hood was too small. I increased it approximately 50% (I mentioned this previously that hats only need to be reduced to 30% of the original size, so this adjustment makes perfect sense.) I also changed the darts in the hood to gathers. I moved the welt pockets a bit towards the sides to better line up with the little doll's hands. (Instead of making welt pockets I made machine bound buttonholes.) I also shortened the sleeves slightly on the shirt. Phew! LOL!

Photo 1

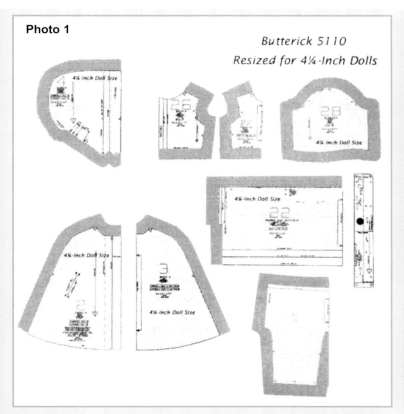

Butterick 5110
Resized for 4¼-Inch Dolls

Photo 2

Photo 3

Jim Faraone: Great tip, Lynn, and thanks for sharing that with all of us!

Jennifer Hughey: I have a technique to modify people-size patterns for the Barbie® doll and it works well. On the pattern instruction sheet, there is a diagram of the pattern pieces for the outfit. I scan this and enlarge by 300%, and usually it is pretty accurate. The Barbie® doll's waist is smaller than a human, and her bustline is bigger, so you have to alter that a bit, but for the most part, it works.

LaDonna Moore: When I copy or design patterns, I use quilting plastic (used for quilting templates and found in the quilting section.) It's very flexible and doesn't tear, it keeps from cutting up your patterns and when I get done with my templates, I put them in a zip lock bag and label it.

Charlie Dale: When it comes to patterns, especially those that are mass-produced, I make the entire garment out of an inexpensive muslin first so I can make any and all changes so that the garment fits perfectly. I find that any pattern, even those that fit human scale are off to some degree. I find I save a lot of time making the adjustments to cotton and then cutting the actual material from my now "perfect fit" cotton pattern. I then transfer all those pieces to paper.

William Stewart Jones: Patterns from historical costume books can be enlarged or reduced on a copy machine to fit fashion dolls. Use a standard bodice pattern to approximate the size. Then pin fit a muslin sample pattern.

Sharon Brendemuehl: I draw my patterns out on interfacing when I design clothing. This way I can place them on the doll and check the shape and length. Interfacing is soft so it folds around the doll's body and does not tear easily.

Jennifer Urbaniak: Use your imagination at pattern making and do something freehand. Sometimes it is easier in the beginning to test the waters on your own than to follow a pattern.

Shirley R. Heater: Taming the pattern monster can be a challenge. I keep a master list by source (McCall's®, Simplicity®, etc.) as well as a list of "wants" that I carry with me. My original patterns are filed numerically by source for easy access, but like others, I don't use my original patterns. I either trace or make photocopies of them to use. I have displayed some of the vintage patterns so I can enjoy the artwork on the envelopes.

Sarah Worley: When you come up with several ideas at one time, it's helpful to place the material, pattern and notions for each design in its own separate zip-lock type bag. When you have them cut out (I always cut out several before I actually start sewing) you can return them to the same bag to await being made and finished. If you plan to use the same pattern for more than one outfit, you can put a note in each bag that will use that pattern. I also found that my kitchen counter to be the right height to help prevent back fatigue which can occur bending over a table or the floor when cutting out patterns.

Jim Faraone: I do almost the same thing with my patterns. When I cut up a pattern, I put the pieces to a particular outfit into a small manila envelope and on the front of the envelope I tape the picture (or sketch) of the outfit to which the pieces belong. That way I don't have to rummage through a whole pattern package looking for the pieces of a specific outfit. It sure does save time. I also trace the pattern pieces on tracing paper and put those in the envelope because they last longer than the tissue pattern pieces.

William Stewart Jones: One of the easiest ways to copy a garment (doll or human size) is to use a tracing wheel and waxed paper. You can see through the wax paper, so place the wax paper on top of each section of the garment, and run the tracing wheel along the seams. Then add seam allowance to each piece. Sometimes, if the detail is tricky, you can press a piece of aluminum foil over the area and it will show bumps and ridges where the seams are. Then copy those.

Jim Faraone: Do remember that commercial patterns are copyrighted and are not meant to be used for sale. As a matter of fact, some new patterns coming out have "For Home Use Only" printed on them. One suggestion is that you cut down on buying patterns and just buy a few of the basic patterns. You can use these basic patterns to redo into your own patterns (as I explained previously), which should be safe to use. Use marketed patterns as a visual reference to help you learn how to make your own patterns. It's not as difficult as it looks.

Lynn Smith: You're right Jim! Purchasing a pattern gives you the right to make up that garment for personal use only (for yourself or as gifts). Without special permission from the pattern publisher, you may not use purchased patterns to create items to sell and you can't just make small changes in a pattern and then call it your own. Resizing patterns in that way seems to fall into a bit of a gray area. In this case, the pattern is being used to create something other than for what it was intended—clothes for 4-¼in (11cm) dolls. In addition, several major, not minor changes, are usually made to adapt the patterns to a much smaller size. Still, I tend to use this method only when creating a one-of-a-kind outfit or gift item. If I want to mass produce or distribute a pattern I draft my own pattern using the original only as a visual guide, like Jim mentioned, much the same way garment manufacturers legally make knock-offs of runway fashions or gowns worn by celebrities. Keep in mind that a copyright doesn't have to be registered to exist. A copyright applies by virtue of the fact that material is published by the author or designer. If you draft your own patterns, include the © symbol and your name. If you are using a published pattern, respect the rights of the publisher and designer.

Jim Faraone: Amen to that Lynn!

Sewing Tips

Ah, the roar of the sewing machine as it glides across your fabric. There is nothing more satisfying than listening to the hum of the motor knowing that you are the one in charge....or are you? The sewing machine can be a friend, a cranky and stubborn friend at times, but still a friend. I have heard from so many that they are afraid to approach a sewing machine. Sewing machines are fun and there's nothing to be afraid of. A basic machine with just a straight stitch is fine for getting you started, but there's nothing wrong with hand sewing either if that's what you prefer to do. With hand sewing, just practice sewing small stitches so your outfits have a clean and professional look. Learning the tricks of the trade can make life so much easier at the sewing machine.

Jim Faraone: I know that when I use certain patterns, there are always one or two pieces that aren't easy to sew on the sewing machine. **(see step 1)** One is connecting the sleeve to the armhole and I'm sure many of us have had that experience of catching the material in the machine trying to go around that tight curve. **(see step 2)** What I do is line up the edge of the sleeve to the edge of the armhole and sew that section by hand using small stitches. **(see step 3)** To get make it even, I usually begin to hand-sew one end going about halfway up to the center line. **(see step 4)** I then line up the other end and **(see step 5)** hand-sew it, once again going about half way up to the center line. **(see step 6)** Then I can easily pleat the extra material at the center of the armhole

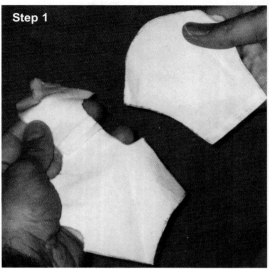

Step 1

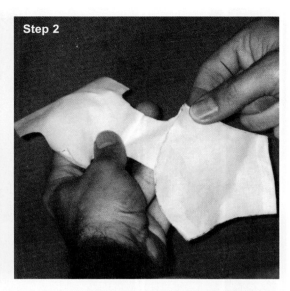

Step 2

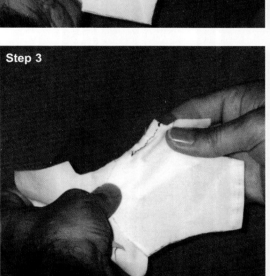

Step 3

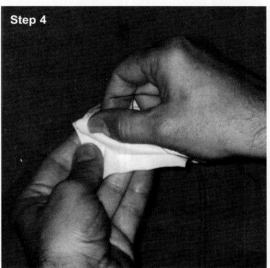

Step 4

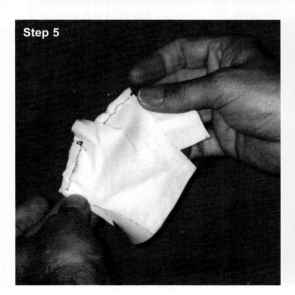

Step 5

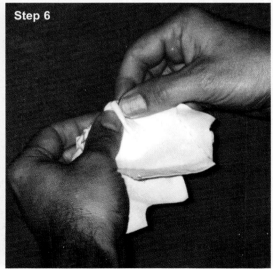

Step 6

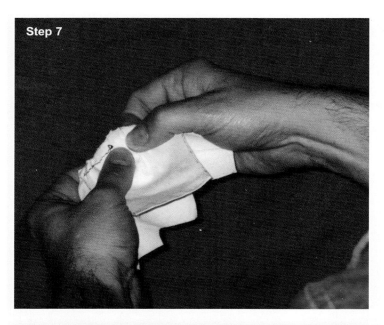

Step 7

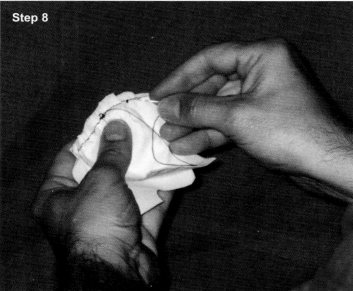

Step 8

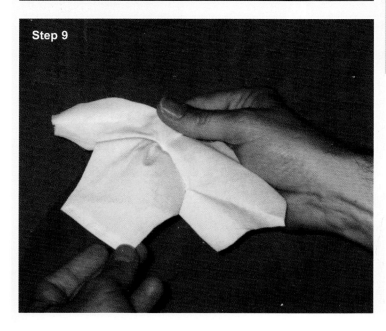

Step 9

(see step 7) and **(see step 8)** hand-sew the center connecting the two end stitches that I did earlier. **(see step 9)** Now your sleeve is inserted without any snags. Maybe this takes a little longer than machine sewing the sleeves in place, but like I said earlier, you have to find what works best for you.

Leslie Hampton: If you do not have a serger, the "Tiny Little Serger" from Walmart® works well if you go over the edges twice. This is very cost effective for beginners like me.

Joyce Marie La Fave: I always pre-soak dark fabrics in a cold water solution with ¼ cup of salt added to set the color and prevent the doll body from staining.

Elizabeth "Beth" Kinsley: When sewing thick layers of fabric, lengthen your stitches and it will sew more easily. When sewing on small trims or zippers, use a small piece of scotch tape to hold it in place until you get it sewn. When sewing a seam on material that has been cut on the bias, use a seam ripper to guide the material into the sewing needle. This will prevent stretching of the material. To prevent unraveling, take a small paintbrush and brush the edges of the cut material with Tacky Glue®. This will keep it from unraveling and also if you need a really small hem, you can turn the hem under and iron. Be careful not to smear the glue on your iron.

Jim Faraone: Good ones Beth! Also, when sewing real fur or leather, lengthen your stitches so it doesn't cut through the pelt of the fur or the leather. For sewing, I set my machine between 0 and 1, but when working with real fur, I'll set my machine on 2 for longer stitches.

Tess Barton: Machine stitches along the hem of a nice outfit are very unattractive. If you look at most of your own clothes, especially eveningwear, the hem is not visible. You can

roll the hem and hand stitch it. When doing sleeve holes and other tricky hems, use bridal tulle. Pin it to the outside of the garment and stitch along where you would like it to be hemmed. Then turn under and press. You can stabilize it in place very easily with a few small hand stitches. You will have a nicely finished smooth hem without the extra bulk and no ugly stitches.

LaRaine Weishar: In order to keep delicate/filmy fabrics from being pulled into the sewing machine, it helps to place a piece of tissue or waxed paper between the machine and the fabric. Typing paper can also be used, however, it will take more pressure to rip it off after sewing and might distort the stitches. Waxed or tissue paper will usually separate and fall right off. As sewing through paper tends to dull the needle rather quickly, it is important that the machine needle be changed often. It is a very good idea to change the needle whenever you start a new project that involves delicate fabrics.

Lynn K. Johnson: I use thread fuse and ¼in (.65cm) wide pre-cut stitch witchery for beautiful, no-thread-showing hems.

Lim Shor-wei: I have found that it is worth paying for the highest quality fabric and materials I can afford when I am sewing. Even for fabric costing $20 or more a yard is worth buying because you usually don't need more than half a yard for a doll. It works out to be quite affordable and it makes all the hard work of sewing worth the final outcome. Similarly, I've compared beadwork and sometimes the person who used crystals and rhinestones made a more striking outfit even though the beadwork is not as good as the person who used seed beads. Even for seed beads and sequins, there are differences in quality. I would recommend using the best quality you can find. The difference in the sparkle does affect the final look of the outfit.

Jennifer Urbaniak: I use old clothes, prom/party dresses around the house for fabrics on which to practice my sewing skills. Use the money you save to purchase proper tools. Also, be patient! It isn't easy sewing for such a small client, but it will come. Try looking at ready-made doll clothes to get an idea of how things are put together. Try to avoid both difficult and expensive fabrics when you are first learning. I wasted plenty of money both buying and using fabric I wasn't ready to use as far as my skills were concerned.

Lim Shor-wei: That's true Jennifer, for beginning sewers, start with cotton and other thin, crisp fabrics like dupion silk. These are easier to work with because they don't slip and slide. These fabrics also don't fray easily. Keep slippery and slinky fabrics for later. The worst to work with are the cheap polyester fabrics. From my personal experience, when I first started sewing, I thought I'd save money by buying these shiny fabrics to practice sewing because they were cheaper and they're pretty. But they caught and tore easily, as well as slipped and slid, making my first time sewing a nightmare.

Carolyn Marnon: If you are afraid of the sewing machine, fabric glue can work for making fashions. It does take time for the glue to dry, so you have to be careful. I have actually used hot glue in making an entire wedding gown dress for a doll once and have still not seen any bad effects from the glue. That fashion is at least 3 years old now and still looks good. Don't be afraid to experiment and use what works for you. Another idea if you don't sew is to use clothes that are already made. You can embellish them and make them into your own fashion designs. There are a lot of simple fashions that can be found at the dollar stores especially around the winter

holidays. You can add beads, sequins, ribbons, lace, appliqués, tiny doll buttons, fringe, or whatever else strikes your fancy. Check out all the aisles at the fabric and craft stores and let your imagination go wild. What about gluing on tiny pom-poms? Would a small button be the start of a great belt? Craft or fabric paints can embellish a plain outfit. Don't think it can't be done because you might be just the one to do it.

Aurora Mathews: Use Fray-Check® for edges of fine fabrics and always take your time. Also, learn everything your machine can do.

Lim Shor-wei: Fray-Check® is very useful not only for edges, but also if you trim too close to a seam for your liking, you can put Fray-Check® on to strengthen the seam.

Jim Faraone: I use Fray-Check® as well, but I sure can make a mess with it.

Zena Myall: Well Jim, when I use it, I squeeze it onto a Q-tip® and gently run it around the edges. This avoids dripping the liquid where you don't want it. If you drop it where you do not want it, dip a Q-tip® into rubbing alcohol and gently rub the area and let dry. This doesn't always work, but it's worth a try before you have to start over.

Rachel Steinberger: When I can't get thread the exact shade as my fabric, I choose a slightly darker color over a slightly lighter color. Most seams are pulled in slightly by the stitches and are always a little shadowed. The darker color will look more natural in the shadow than a lighter color thread. In addition, most manmade fabrics can be melted a little bit along the edge using a candle or lighter to prevent raveling. This works particularly well with polyester and relatively well with acetate. Just make sure to test the method on a scrap of fabric before doing it on the dress you've just spent

hours and hours sewing. Ask me how I know this—never mind, you've probably guessed! :-)

Debbie Jane Cates: When using craft glue on fabric, use a curling iron to set the glue. The heat will dry the glue much faster and will give a better bond. A regular iron also works, but keep it on a low setting and if you are using it near your doll, be careful of the vinyl.

Pamela Bachmayer: Don't use Fabric Tac® to apply metallic trim to metallic PVC ribbon. It

will cause a chemical reaction that will seriously destroy the finish of the PVC ribbon and ruin your design.

William Stewart Jones: Chiffon and sheer fabrics can be hemmed by **(see step 1)** stitching a line of straight stitching about ¼in (.65cm) from the edge, **(see step 2)** then trim away the fabric, close to the stitching, and **(see step 3)** stitch again over the line of straight stitching with a fine zigzag stitch. With washable fabrics, it helps to spray starch the fabric, stitch, then rinse out the starch.

Step 1

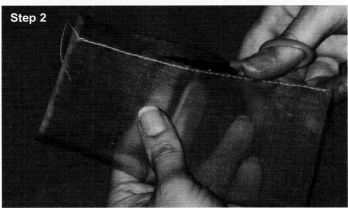
Step 2

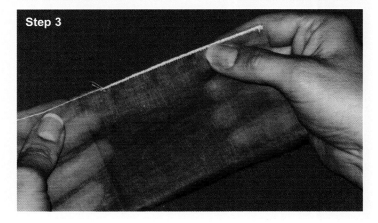
Step 3

Pamela Bachmayer: I find that fabric stiffener is great in getting difficult folds to stay in fabrics. Diluting the fabric stiffener can result in various degrees of stiffness. (Highly diluted, it can give the appearance of sizing without being stiff.) Once dried and stiffened, you can reshape the fabric at any time by heating the fabric with a hair dryer. This will soften the fabric to be reshaped. The fabric will reset and be stiff again. Results may take a couple of hours, so test first on a separate piece of fabric to make sure that the heat does not affect the fabric itself.

Cynthia Luna-Hennes: When you're doing a lot of hand sewing, beading. etc. on a dress that is already sewn to the body, first remove the doll's head which makes the sewing easier and you don't have to worry about messing up the makeup or hair style. Also, I'll sometimes have 2 different heads with 2 different hairdos waiting to see which one will look best with the finished dress. Sometimes even different hair colors. It works pretty well as long as the skin tone on the body matches the face skin tone. I always have several good hairdos on doll bodies waiting for the right dress style. When the dress is finished, I just decide what head looks best with the dress, and then switch heads.

Jennifer Hughey: When sewing, watch the scale of trims, fabric patterns and gems. A good way is to eyeball them against the doll's hand, and think how large the item would be next to your own head. It will give you an idea of the scale.

Sheryl Majercin: I find that plastic snaps can be trimmed smaller and they aren't as noticeable on the outfit. Buckram! I can't say enough about buckram. It can be used for hats, shoes, purses—

anything you want to have dimension.

Jim Faraone: I agree with you Sheryl. Buckram is wonderful for lots of things including stand up collars and head pieces and so much more.

Tricia Hill: Jim, mine's a long one, but can I still post it?

Jim Faraone: As long as it helps us learn about our craft, it doesn't matter how long it is. We're all listening...or is that reading? LOL!

Tricia Hill: First, to prevent fraying of fabrics, I use a product called Fray No More® which stops fraying of fabrics, hems and seams. Like others mentioned earlier, for a very lightweight facing/finishing for armholes, neck holes and hems, I cut my own "tulle" (nylon netting) in the same color as the garment. I cut on the diagonal ¼in (.65cm) in width and just stitch along where I want my finished edge to be on the right side of the fabric. I then press the edge over with an iron and top stitch or do my final embellishments with beads, trim, etc. along the finished edge. I find that sequin fabrics are easy enough to cut, but to sew may be more difficult. Some fabrics come with the sequins already glued onto the fabric (you can test this by trying to lift the edge of the sequin off with your fingernail.) This type of fabric can be sewn by removing the sequins along the sew line. Just heat the fabric up by using a hair dryer. Use caution when doing this. Hold the hair dryer a safe distance from the fabric or it may melt. In addition, you should use VERY low heat. The sequins should easily lift off. I've also found that a warm iron (using a pressing cloth over the fabric) will work. This might also remove other sequins that you do not want removed so use extreme caution with this method, too. With linings, I like to cut 2 of

each of my pattern pieces for linings (usually of the same fabric). By cutting double you are able to sew both right sides together leaving one edge for an opening and then turning the 2 pieces and voila, it's lined. Leave shoulder seams open and finish after the garment is turned. This makes for a very professional finish. If the fabric you are using is slightly bulky, try using lightweight lining fabrics (silks, satins) for the lining and just cut as you would the actual piece. This also gives a great effect if the lining is done in a contrasting or complimentary color.

LaRaine Weishar: If you wish to do machine embroidery on small pieces, in order to avoid the bulk of a fabric stabilizer, it is best to use an embroidery hoop. You can either trace the pattern piece on to the fabric and cut out after the embroidery is done, or baste the piece onto a very fine fabric such as tulle or cheesecloth. Place this into the hoop upside down. This will leave the wrong side level with the hoop and the right side will be inside the hoop. Tilt the hoop to go under the foot and you will have the flat surface to embroider, plus you can hold on to the hoop, giving you more control.

Deborah Fagan: To make a mannequin so you can piece together a design, I use an extra broken necked or thrift store doll. First, drill a hole in the bottom of the body. Then, drill a hole in a square of plywood. Take a wire (coat hanger, etc.) and cut it to the proper length. Place the wire in the hole in the body and in the wood. Now you have a doll without the stand to create lumps and bumps around the waist.

Tricia Hill: Cutting faux fur, DON'T!!! LOL! No really— just tear along the weave if possible. If making a stole, tear off your piece and sew along your seam. Then after turning

your fabric (assuming this is lined) take a large needle or tweezers and start pulling the fur threads out from the seam. Also, when cutting material, it's best to invest in a very nice pair of scissors if at all possible. I use a ginger scissor and a smaller embroidery scissor for those fine cuts and at the seams when finishing. For straight edges I use a quilters rotary blade and a straight edge.

Jim Faraone: When cutting faux fur, my friend David Simpson draws out his pattern on the pelt of the fur. Then with an Xacto® knife, he carefully cuts out the pattern on the pelt. This way he just cuts the pelt and does not clip into the fur.

William Stewart Jones: I use iron-on bonding web for millinery and appliqué work. I've found that old bonding web sometimes is hard to separate. If you have trouble separating the backing paper from the iron-on bonding web, put it in the freezer for a minute and the paper will peel away easily. This will also work with hot glue. You can peel it off a lot of non-absorbent surfaces by chilling it.

Shirley R. Heater: I use silk pins for pinning. I also use sharp needles for hand sewing and a leather thimble, which is flexible and fits over your finger like a glove. With darts, sew from the outer edge to point of the dart for better control of the shape. Use a piece of scrap fabric as a starter piece when machine sewing. This will result in a smooth transaction to the garment pieces and allow easy stitch locking (whether by your machine lock stitch or by making 2-3 backstitches) without the machine "grabbing" your fabric and mangling the start of your seam. The starter piece should be the same thickness as the garment piece you are sewing. For two thicknesses, fold the scrap in half; for four thicknesses, fold it over again. Place the scrap toward the back, under your needle about ¼in to ½in (.65cm to 1cm) from the folded edge and begin sewing. When you reach the edge, stop with the needle down, raise the presser foot and butt your fabric next to this. Lower the presser foot and continue sewing. Some fabrics leave pin marks. What to do? When cutting out a pattern, here are a couple of suggestions. Lay the pattern piece (or template) on the wrong side of the fabric and pin around the piece in an outline form. Then use a dressmaker's pencils and draw around the pattern piece. Lift off the pattern and simply cut out. Cut inside the pencil marking, cutting away the markings. Another method is to transfer the pattern to freezer paper. Press the shiny side down on the fabric and cut around it. The freezer paper easily peels off. It's always a good idea to test on a scrap first. When sewing, place pins only in the seam allowance. You can eliminate "on fold" pattern pieces by making a new piece with the mirror half. Some smaller pieces are especially easy to distort "on fold" so cutting out flat is better. With one complete flat piece, you are also able to cut two at a time.

Jim Faraone: Good one, Shirley. I also use the old graph paper to open up the "on fold" pieces. I just lay the "on fold" part on the line of the graph paper, trace it with a pencil, then fold the graph paper in half and cut the piece out, so when I unfold the graph paper it's one whole piece.

Shirley R. Heater: That's nice, Jim, but I wasn't finished. :-)

Jim Faraone: Oops! Sorry! LOL!

Shirley R. Heater: If you have a fabric that ravels badly and are not sure whether to use a seam sealant, test it on a scrap first. There are various types of sealants. One may be more

liquid and will run or bleed quickly—another may have a bit more consistency and not run as much. Some fabrics, such as lames, both pin mark and fray easily. Add a wider seam allowance and treat with sealant, which can be trimmed closer after it dries. Now, if you're lining a garment, use lightweight silky type fabric or tulle. Hand-finish these so that raw edges and seam allowances are inside or between the layers for a clean look. Make the inside look as good as the outside. Now I'm finished, Jim. LOL!

Rachel Steinberger: The easiest way to make a knot to begin a seam for hand-sewing is to wrap the thread around your forefinger twice, roll the thread off your finger and pull it tight. The easiest way to make a knot at the end of a seam when hand-sewing is to insert the needle for a tiny stitch, wrap the thread four times around the sharp, protruding end of the needle, pull the needle through, and tighten the stitch. The easiest way to make a knot while machine-sewing is to back track (ie: stitch backward over and then forward again) for the first and last 3/8in (.9cm). The easiest was to make a knot in the doll's hair is to give it to a cranky 5-year-old. LOL! I sew my outfits directly and permanently onto my dolls, so sometimes hiding the end of the thread is difficult. The best way to hide it is to tie the knot and then take a very large stitch under a more-loosely fitted area. If the gown has no loosely fitted areas, then I find an inconspicuous spot. Then I pull the thread as tight as I can and gather the fabric as much as possible and cut the thread very close to the fabric's surface. Then I pull the fabric taut and stretch it a little, which pulls the end of the thread inside. Easy, fast and works like a charm. It can also be done by sliding the needle inbetween the top fabric and the lining.

Want to make an easy clown ruff? Use rick-rack (either baby, medium or jumbo, depending on what size you want. Cut a very long piece and then sew a running stitch along one side (one set of points) of the rick-rack. Gather them tightly and place it around the doll's neck.

Barb Rausch: A fitted garment made from sheer, slippery, stretchy, loose-woven or fragile fabric will need a lining. But there is a way to make a lining that will ensure a more correct fit as well as make the garment fabric much easier to handle. For the lining, choose a FIRM taffeta in an appropriate pale to medium-light color. (This technique will not work on a dark color taffeta). Using a light box, trace your pattern pieces onto the taffeta with a fine-point, ballpoint pen. Use a ruler for the straight lines and a small draftsman's curve for the curved lines. Trace ALL cutting and stitching lines and other necessary markings. Being sure to leave an "excess" of about a ½in (1cm) all around each piece and cut out the lining pieces. Place the lining on the reverse side of the garment, pen lines UP. Pin the lining pieces to the garment fabric placing the pins close together in the "excess." Including the "excess," carefully cut out each two-layer piece. With thread that matches your garment fabric, use a fine needle and small stitches to hand stitch the lining and garment fabrics together along ALL stitching lines including the stitching lines of darts. Remove pins. Cutting along the original cutting lines of the pattern, cut out each two-layered piece. Assemble the pattern pieces according to the original directions. If the pattern pieces are small, it is usually easier to do it by hand.

Pamela Bachmayer: For machine sewing or embroidery onto very fine fabrics such as tulle, use a water-soluble

webbing/stabilizer and set your machine for very light fabric. Work slowly! Once stitching is complete, follow the manufacturers directions to dissolve the stabilizer. Make sure that all the stabilizer is dissolved or it will leave dark patches on your fabric. Don't attempt to use tear away stabilizer on very fine fabrics such as tulle. Even the lightest weight stabilizer is heavier than the tulle and the tulle will tear away with the stitches instead of the stabilizer.

Linda Lehmann: I have my instructions for "Boning the Bodice" that I'd like to share.

Jim Faraone: Now that's something even I don't know about, so go for it Linda.

Linda Lehmann: Well, first you need a cover from a margarine container. Then cut a strip of fabric or lining 1in (3cm) longer than the longest part of the front bodice by 2in (5cm) wide. So, for example, if the stay is 1-½in x ¼in (4cm x .65cm), the fabric would be cut 2-½in x 2in (6cm x 5cm). Turn in a shallow ¼in (.65cm) seam allowance along one edge of the fabric strip. The ¼in (.65cm) is turned to the wrong side of the strip and is creased sharply. Place the fabric strip right side down on the tabletop with the folded edge towards you. Slide the plastic stay between the folded seam allowance and the wrong side of the strip. Center the stay between the short ends of the strip and force the edge of the stay against the sharp crease of the fold. Grasp the plastic stay and the fabric layers surrounding it. Turn the stay and fabric layers one turn. This wraps the stay in the fabric. There is approximately 1-½ in (4cm) of scrap fabric beyond the wrapped stay. Crease the fabric folds with your fingers. Topstitch 1/16in (.15cm) from the folded edges of the fabric layers and stay. Stitch through the fabric layers and the plastic stay. Trim away the excess scrap fabric on the long edge of the stay. Now to trim the excess fabric along the short edge of the stay. Fold the excess fabric over the ends of the stay by locating the stay ends with your fingertips. Turn the fabric over the stay and crease with your fingers. Trim the folded fabric end to ¼in (.65cm). Now to sew the stay to the garment. The combination of plastic and fabric layers make the stay slightly thick. It's important the stay is at least ¼in (.65cm) away from the waist seam and neck edge. This reduces the bulk and keeps the stayed area flat and inconspicuous. Place the wrong side of the stay to the wrong side of the garment. Center the stay over the seam. Fold the end seam allowances toward the wrong side of the stay. Using a hand-sewing needle and matching thread, hand stitch the stay to the seam allowances of the seam. Try to catch only the fabric covering of the stay as it's stitched in place.

Sharon A. Lawson: The best over-all glue that I have found for gluing trims to fabric, flat-backed rhinestone or fabric to the vinyl of the doll is Beacon® Fabric Tack. It grabs quickly, dries quickly, is washable and dries crystal clear.

Zena Myall: When making a veil, or a wrap using fine tulle or netting, to get a slightly wavy edge, finish the edge with a small zigzag stitch on the sewing machine, and as the machine pulls the fabric through, gently pull on the fabric as it feeds through. This will cause a slightly wavy effect for a little more body to the veil.

Carol Jones: When sewing on sequins and beads, I use clear thread. It is virtually undetectable and does not take away from the shine and sparkle of the sequins and beads.

Andrea Densley: When I work with sheer, fraying fabric like chiffon I seal the cut edges as soon as the pattern piece is cut out. I like to use Fray Block™

by June Tailor. Just let the edges dry before handling. To finish seams on sheer fabrics or for tiny finished seams, I use the traditional French seam or the following method. This method works easiest on straight seams. Sew the seam using a small stitch length. Sew the seam again, INSIDE the seam allowance, 1/8in (.31cm) away from the first stitch line. Fold the seam allowance back on itself as if you were trying to match the second stitch line on top of the first one. Topstitch through all the layers in a narrow seam next to the fold. Trim the remaining raw seam allowance close to the final stitching.

Barb Rausch: I actually prefer hand sewing except when stabilizing the edges of fabrics that easily unravel.

LaDonna Moore: I agree with you Barb. You should use whatever kind of sewing that you're comfortable with. I love to hand sew also, so I can take it with me and work on it at any given time.

William Stewart Jones: When sewing velvet, put a piece of tissue paper between the layers and baste them together. This will prevent the layers from "creeping." Tear the tissue away after the seam is sewn.

Lynn K. Johnson: Finely woven materials like cotton are dolly's dream fabric, but who wants to live on "Green Acres" when the "Park Avenue" style is more appealing. Slinky, loose weave materials require stabilizers and a single throat plate. Use a serger empowered with three threads to do a lot of major seams. Before you cut out the material, spray with starch and iron to make the fabric good and stiff. The starch makes the fabric more firm and hence easier to cut out and sew. I use fabric glue sticks in hard to pin areas before sewing to baste hems and attach trims. Place the garment under the machine needle and

sew in place. Machine-stitched hems really look klutzy, so bond the hem up with ¼in (.65cm) wide bond tape (Stitch Witchery® type product pre-cut to this width on a roll) or thread fuse product. To use the bonding thread, press up the hem and sandwich the bonding thread between the wrong sides of the hem and heat press. These hems are quick, easy and best of all no machine stitching to ruin the look of the garment.

Charlie Dale: Everything I sew is either at a ¼in (.65cm) seam allowance or smaller when I sew seams or hems by hand. When I sew a seam by hand, I take the needle through the entire side of what I am sewing down and only a few threads of the material it is being sewn to, so no stitches can be seen on the right side of the fabric. This stitch is called a Blind Stitch. I also roll my hems as tiny as possible which gives everything I do a Haute Couture feel. When something is lined or partially lined, I like using coordinated lightweight ribbon as the lining as it reduces bulk in the garment and I press everything including all seams so the garment lays right. I also make absolutely sure that the way the seam falls at the top is the way the seam falls at the bottom.

Tracie Hutcherson: Using smaller machine stitches adds stability to the seams. They are stronger and less likely to pull apart on you.

Jim Faraone: I use small stitches myself and adjust the stitch length knob on my sewing machine between the 0 and 1. I think I said that already! LOL! I think I said that in book 4 also! Senior moment I guess! LOL!

Becky Kelly: When sewing I use a quilters foot for my machine. These feet are exactly ¼in (.65cm) wide, with the length marked at ¼in (.65cm) intervals. This helps me keep my seam allowances at an even

width without having to mark the fabric itself. They can be found where most quilting supplies are kept in fabric and craft stores. Also, when making a sharp turn, I always leave the needle in the down position, lift the presser foot, turn the article of clothing, put the foot back down and continue sewing. This gives a sharp, crisp point with little fuss. Make sure to cut the point off the excess fabric if turning a piece right side out after lining. This helps reduce the bulk in the point.

Jim Faraone: Clipping those right angle points is wise before turning your piece right side out and pressing. Also with curves, it's a must to clip the curved edges all along the edge so when you turn the piece right side out and press, you will get a smooth look to it.

Jennifer Hughey: This may sound basic, but it can't be said enough. WHEN MAKING CLOTHES, IRON ALL YOUR SEAMS THOROUGHLY!!! CRISP SEAMS MAKE FOR PRETTIER GARMENTS, ESPECIALLY ON SILKS OR SATINS!

Jim Faraone: Thank you for screaming that out Jennifer! I think the artists in Europe heard that one. LOL!

Sarah Worley: Lining material for sheer fabrics can be cut out the same as the outer material. It can be stay-stitched around the edges and used as a single piece of material. The lining can also be put together and sewn, right sides together, to the hem of the skirt. When turned to the inside, your garment is automatically hemmed.

Chrissy Stewart: I like making the clothing as realistic as possible. Sometimes lining makes this possible. I use Fray Check® on all my edges so they stay "clean" looking on the inside. This cuts down on the "bulk." I make sure I try to keep the hems small scale for

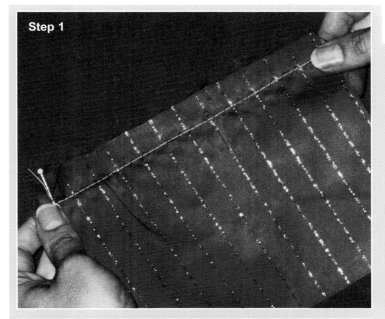

Step 1

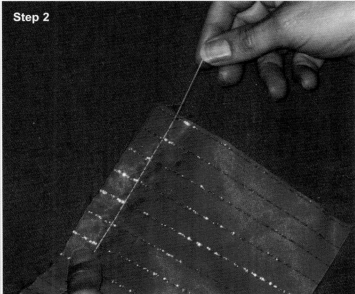

Step 2

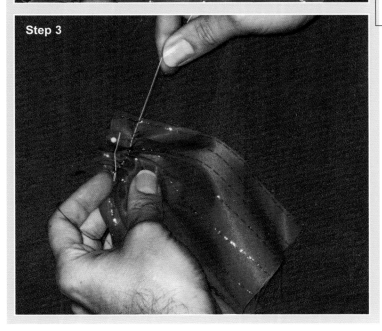

Step 3

the doll on which I'm working. This keeps the clothing realistic.

William Stewart Jones: With gathering fabrics, **(see step 1)** zigzag stitch over a piece of heavy carpet thread or woven fishline. **(see step 2)** Then use that heavy thread to gather the fabric **(see step 3)**. It's much easier than trying to pull a regular thread sewn in a long stitch. I don't like the look of a machine hem, so I make a skirt of regular fabric and a lining fabric, gathering them both as one and sew the hem by hand to the lining. Or I fuse the hem with a ¼in (.65cm) strip of fusible web to the single layer fabric. The fusible I like is self-stick like double stick tape, which makes it easy to fold and stick the hem. Then press it.

Pamela Bachmayer: Embellishing your outfits is part of sewing as well. Hand crochet edgings can be lovely ways to finish off your outfits. Also, for machine or hand stitching and embroidery, if the area you are working on is too small, you may not be able to fit the fabric piece onto the hoop. Outline your shape onto a larger piece of fabric. Do your stitching or embroidery onto this larger piece of fabric, then cut it out for use in your design. When cross-stitching tiny designs onto your fabric, use variegated thread for more color choices without having to purchase lots of colors.

Jim Faraone: When sewing straight skirts, taper the back seam going toward the hem. This will give your doll a longer, sleeker look. On straight evening gowns, always end the hem of the gown at the instep of the doll's foot. Having trouble hemming chiffon? Try using ready-made scarves for full gathered skirts since they already have a nice rolled hem. To make an easy hemmed/lined circle shirt, just cut two of the skirt patterns and sew them together. Turn it right side out

and press and it will give you a clean lined hem to sew onto the bodice.

Linda Lehmann: I have instructions on how I do a fine edge finish to my outfits. You'll need to spray starch the fabric prior to hemming and use a size 70/10 needle. Use the finest thread you can find to match the outfit. Set your machine for a small zigzag stitch. The basic settings are 1.5 wide by 1.5 length. Fold and press the fabric along the finished line of the hem. You should turn back at least ¼in (.65cm). Place the fabric right side up under the presser foot and line up the fabric correctly under the needle and stitch the length of hem. Trim the hem to the stitching line and then press the hem.

Jim Faraone: I have the habit of running my sewing machine like a motorboat. I guess I just have a heavy foot. So to solve this problem, I just place my pedal working foot on top of my other foot, which helps me to press lighter on my sewing machine peddle. Now I can even count the stitches I am doing when making the tiny gloves for dolls, instead of having the material fly through machine and hitting the wall.

Barb Rausch: Hey Jim, is it okay to post about my original pattern for eliminating waistline bulk from full-gathered skirts and petticoats? I have some illustrations to go with the directions, so can I post those also?

Jim Faraone: That would be fine Barb. Sometime visuals really help an individual.

Barb Rausch: Okay. This is my tip on how to eliminate ALL waistline bulk in full-gathered skirts with the use of a drop waistline. (For sewers experienced in using their own pattern. This requires hand sewing.) **(see diagram A)** Depending on your petticoat or skirt fabric, use a light box and a fine-point ballpoint pen to trace this pattern onto firm cotton or stiff taffeta. Leave an excess of about ½in (1cm) all around and cut out the piece. Lay it on the reverse side of your garment fabric and pin them together through the excess, placing pins closely. With thread that matches your garment, a fine needle and small stitches, stitch the two layers together along all the seam lines. Cut out the two-layered pieces along the original cutting lines. If you have a commercial pattern for a full-gathered skirt or have drawn your own, make sure that it is marked as follows, particularly the notches along the waistline edge. At the hemline edge, you may wish to shorten the hem 3/8in (.9cm) because the drop waistband adds 3/8in (.9cm). **(see diagram B)** Gather the top edge of the skirt fabric to fit the bottom seam line of the drop waistband. Matching notches at center front, sides and center backs, hand stitch the skirt to the waistband. Turn the assembled skirt over to the right side. **(see diagram C)** On the right side, very close to the bottom edge of the drop waistband, top stitch with small hand stitches through all layers. If the skirt is to be joined to a bodice, assemble them now, and complete the garment. If there is no bodice, carefully clip the waistline seam allowance, turn to the inside, and top stitch by hand through all the layers, close to the edge. If a waistline facing is desired, use the drop waistline pattern to cut one from suitable lining fabric. By hand, hem its outer edge ¼in (.65cm) deep and press. Placing the right side of facing waistline to the right side of garment waistline, stitch together along the waist seam. Carefully clip the seam allowance turning the facing to inside. Top stitch with small hand stitches close to the edge of waistline. Complete the placket and skirt as desired.

William Stewart Jones: I always dye the monofilament fishline that I use in the edge of ruffles so it matches the fabric.

A. Drop Waistband

This pattern is sized for the classic Barbie® doll figure. It is a <u>CLOSE</u> fit.

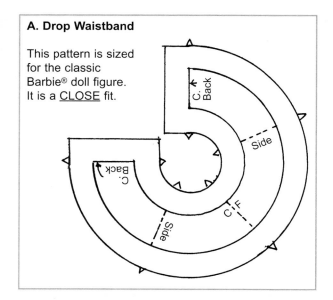

C. Attaching Gathered Skirt Fabric to Drop Waistband

View from Right Side →

Top-Stitching

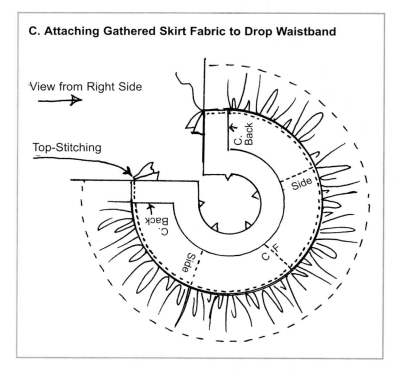

B. Your Gathered Skirt Pattern (not to scale!)

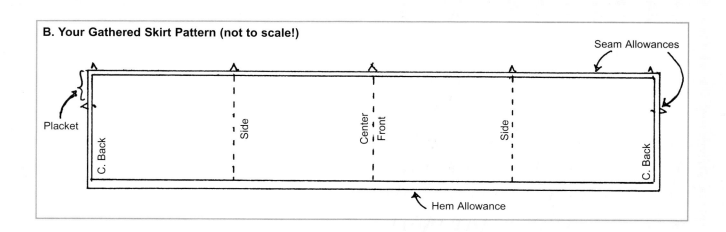

Seam Allowances

Placket

C. Back — Side — Center Front — Side — C. Back

Hem Allowance

Accessorize Your Dolls

Accessorizing your doll has always been a big thing with me. It drives me nuts (or is that nuttier?) to see a doll, although beautifully done, lacking accessories. Accessories really make a doll shine and stand out among her peers. I always find that each doll has its "ugly" stage. This is when your doll is all dressed, yet it seems that something is missing. Once you begin to add the accessories like jewelry, purses, stoles, shoes, etc., that doll changes from its "ugly" stage to a thing of beauty. Taking the extra time to create delightful accessories is well worth the time and effort.

Anke Scharfenberg: When I create necklaces and other jewelry for my dolls, I look for old earrings that I don't use anymore and use those for necklaces or pull them apart to use pieces from them. Small earrings also work great on fashion doll heads.

Jim Faraone: Yes, Anke, some of the larger fashion dolls like the Kitty Collier® doll can use human pierced earrings. Though at times the earring holes on some of the smaller dolls are just too big, here are a few tips that will work to make the earrings fit snuggly. **(see step 1)** Take those twistie ties with which the Barbie® doll is hooked into her box, and with scissors, make a small cut all around the twistie to loosen the plastic coating from the wire. **(see step 2)** When you feel you have it cut through just the plastic, slide your scissors to the tip to remove just the plastic coating. **(see step 3)** You can then insert the post of your earring or an eye pin into the tubing to get a tighter fit into the doll's earring hole. If that doesn't work, **(see step 4)** try taking an eye pin and with your needle nose pliers, bend the pin in half and **(see step 5)** pinch the wire closed. This will give you double the thickness of wire to insert. Now, if that doesn't work, **(see step 6)** take your earring post or eye pin and wrap some tape around the end of it. **(see step 7)** Once you have the thickness that you will need to fill the hole snuggly, cut off the excess tapes and **(see step 8)** it's ready to insert into the doll's ear hole. If that doesn't help, try working with another doll. LOL!

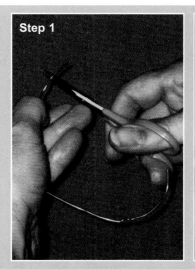

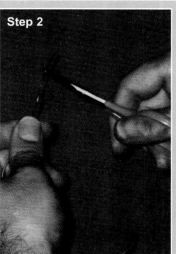

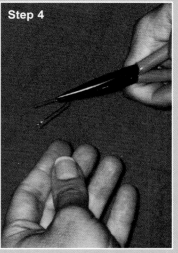

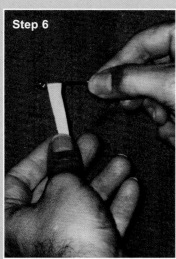

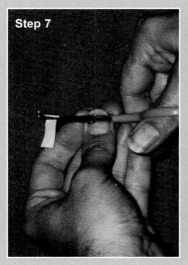

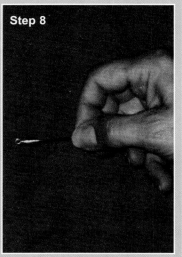

Linda Lynch Holman: You can use old rings as necklaces. You can just slip them around the doll's neck. It will give a kick to many designs.

Jim Faraone: Adjustable rings gotten in those kid charm machines also work great around a high ponytail to give a tiara effect around the base of the ponytail.

J'Amy Pacheco: Jim, I have a long list of tips on how I do my special shoes. Do you think the group would be interested in hearing about how I create them?

Jim Faraone: Is the Pope Catholic? LOL!

J'Amy Pacheco: Never underestimate the impact shoes can have on an outfit. Rather than going to the factory-made route, consider customizing shoes to compliment the outfit. You can paint them in coordinating colors, or even duplicate the pattern of your fabric in paint. With a good adhesive (I use Liquitex® Acrylic Gel Medium) you can even attach beads, pearls, rhinestones, ground glitter or feathers. For that extra-special look, create a purse or a pair of sunglasses to match. Before painting shoes, purses or sunglasses, make the entire exterior surface rough using an emery board. This step helps the paint adhere to the surface and helps prevent peeling and chipping. Don't forget the bottom of the shoe and the inside of the heel. A black or gold bottom and heel tip can have a dramatic effect on the overall look. To hold shoes while painting, cut a small square of cardboard, make a small roll of tape, stick one side to the cardboard, and stick the shoe's base to the other. It's easier to work with the shoes if you put only one on each square. If you slop paint on the tape or cardboard, use a small sharp knife to cut the paint drips once they are dry. Don't pull, or you may pull the paint off the shoe. Paint the top,

sides and back of the heels first, and let them dry thoroughly between coats while still on the cardboard. If you're going to attach beads or stones, leave the shoes attached to the cardboard. Apply a varnish sealer and allow it to dry. When you're completely finished with the top and sides, carefully remove the shoes from the cardboard. Then paint the bottoms, the inside of the heel and the heel tip. Dry these by hanging them upside-down on a toothpick stuck into a block of Styrofoam®. Don't forget to seal it with varnish. Avoid getting paint inside the shoe, or on any part of the shoe that will touch the doll's foot. You never know which doll will end up wearing your customized shoes. Create unusual textured patterns on your shoes by using an artist's quality modeling paste. I once started out trying to make grapes, and ended up with a shoe bridge covered with flowers and leaves. For a less-textured pattern, squeeze a few drops of artist's matte medium onto your palette and let it thicken for about 15 minutes. Then add colored paint, and dab onto the shoe. Look for shoe ideas in catalogues and magazines. Tear out pictures that look interesting and then experiment with different craft supplies to achieve a similar look. My first customized shoe was a replica of an antique shoe I discovered in a Christmas catalogue from the Metropolitan Museum of Art. My favorite shoe design was based on one I saw in an advertisement for a Whitney Houston CD. You never know where you'll find great shoe ideas!

Carolyn Marnon: I have made earrings by using regular post and dangle earrings. You can repaint the earrings that are already in the doll's ears if you are so inclined. You can also fashion your own earrings using bits and pieces of wire and various beads and jewels. Necklaces can be made by stringing beads, making designs using wire, or by fashioning

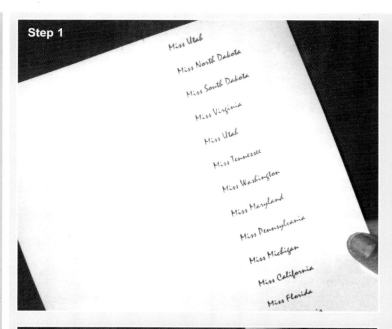

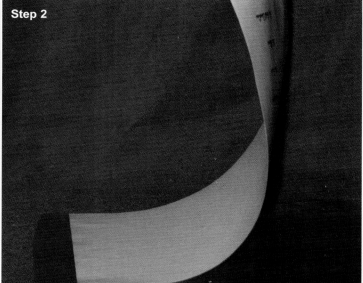

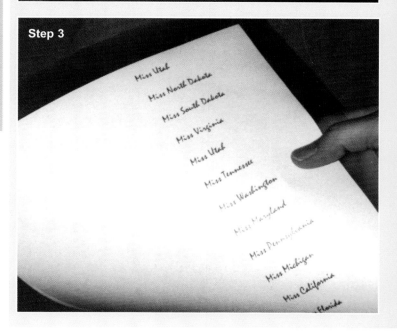

Step 4

Step 5

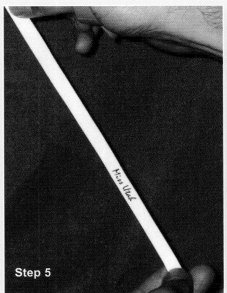

Step 6

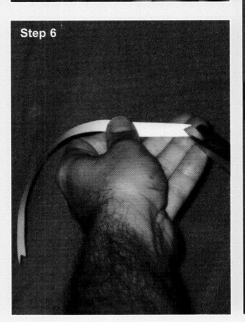

Step 7

them out of ribbon and lace. It is even possible to paint a necklace on your doll much like a choker would be. I have also twisted gold wire into belt buckles and then used ribbon or leather cut into a thin strip to make belts. I have made headpieces for my dolls using earrings. You can find some great looking earrings (headpieces) at discount stores like Big Lots® or Family Dollar®. The clip-on earrings can just be clipped into the doll's hair at whatever angle you choose. I once made a sash for a doll using ribbon from those spools of ribbon that had the picot edging. I draped it over the doll's shoulder and angled it to the length I wanted. I glued the edges together and then cut it at the sash angle. I used tiny rub on letters to spell out what I wanted the sash to say. It became the perfect "Firecracker Queen 1997" sash.

Jim Faraone: I made easy sashes also that said "40 Isn't Fatal" on my dolls for the Barbie® doll's 40th Anniversary. What I did was just **(see step 1)** go to my computer and in small type, I kept listing "40 Isn't Fatal" down a row. I must have gotten a good 50 "40 Isn't Fatal" sayings on one page. **(see steps 2-3)** Then I printed up the page and covered the entire page with clear contact paper. After trimming the overlapping clear contact paper, **(see step 4)** I cut the paper into strips like banners **(see step 5)**, clipped the ends **(see step 6)** and **(see step 7)** glued them onto the dolls. The clear contact paper makes the paper look like a satin ribbon and it's quick and easy to do. I also did this same technique when I was putting the "Faraone Originals" wrist tags on my dolls.

Lori Strawn: The easiest earrings are pearl-topped pins, and they come in lots of colors. Just cut off most of the pin (leave a bit to stick into your doll's ear), add some glue and insert into the ear.

Stefanie Baumler: When painting or enhancing shoes with glitter, rhinestones, etc., stick a pin into the heel or sole of the shoe and then stick the ball end of the pin into a block of Styrofoam®, you can paint the entire shoe without having to touch it and it dries nicely that way as well. I have also used very small rhinestone earrings for rings for dolls. They usually come on a card with several pairs together, sometimes with several different colors on a card. Check in the children's section for smaller jewelry made just for kids. Just use a wire cutters to cut the majority of the post off leaving just enough to insert into the hole in the doll's hand. Use a small dot of super glue to hold it in place.

Laura Fern Fanelli: Remember that after you finish your doll, that it's important to take into account her stand. With just a little more thought and fantasy, her stand can be decorated with the appropriate materials. You're only limited to your imagination.

Pamela Bachmayer: If you buy the smallest jump rings you can find and you still think they are too big, you can still use them. Make them the size you need with a pair of needle nose pliers. Just open the jump ring and use the very tip of a pair of round nose pliers to form a loop on one end of the jump ring but do not close and do not trim. Thread the two items you want to attach together on the jump ring and slide them into the small loop you previously formed. With your needle nose pliers, close the small loop end. Use wire cutters to trim off the excess length of the jump ring. Look in the child's jewelry section of any department store for fine chains and small charms, etc. that are often appropriate for dolls. One necklace will make several necklaces, earrings and purse handles.

Imelda Sanchez: To get a perfect fit on a stocking, what I do is make the stocking as the pattern states. I then powder the legs of the doll I am going to dress in these stockings and slip the stocking up the leg inside out. I look for any gaps in the seam to the leg. Where there may be a gap, I place a pin flush against the leg. I then remove the stocking and resew the seam along the same stitch and adjusting when I come to the place where the needle is. Trim close to the stitching. When the stocking is reversed it should fit snug on the leg with no gaps.

Leslie Hampton: A loom used to make Indian bead jewelry works wonderfully to make beaded purses. They are available at any craft shop and a drop of super glue on the edges will hold the purse together.

Joyce Marie La Fave: To make a snood for the Gene® doll, cut an 8in (20cm) diameter of net or any similar stretch type fabric and slip stitch around the outside edge about ¼in (.65cm) with a contrasting or matching embroidery floss. Leave 3in (8cm) ends on each side for the ties and you could also add a ribbon, rose pearls or other trims if you like.

Jean MaDan: The best paint I've found for plastic shoes is Rustoleum® spray paint. I put a straight pin into the bottom of the shoe to hold it, and put on a pair of rubber gloves so that I don't get the paint on my hands. It dries VERY quickly so you don't have to stand and hold the shoes for long. To make holes in the plastic shoes to sew beads on, I heat up a needle and it slides right into the soft plastic at the toe. To keep shoes from falling off without using glue, I use a tiny piece of double sided tape inside the shoe.

Jim Faraone: That double sided tape that men use inside their toupees work great too because it's very thin. No, I don't know about that because I wear a toupee, I earned every bald spot I have and I'm proud of them! LOL!

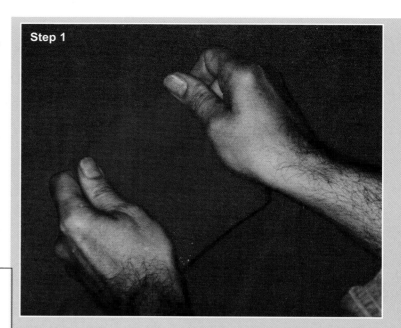

Step 1

Step 2

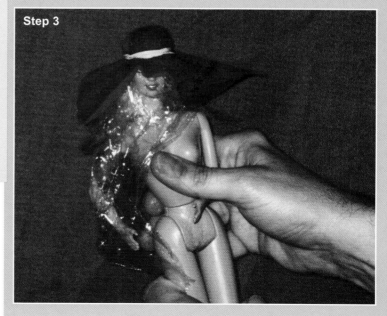

Step 3

Step 4

Step 5

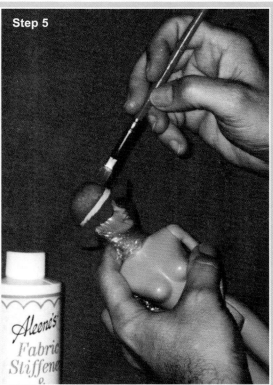

Step 6

Becky Kelly: Instead of using head pins or pins with a loop on the end for earrings, I make my own. I use round nosed pliers to create my own loop from jewelry wire that I keep on hand. After attaching the earrings to this loop, I cut the wire and double over the end before inserting it into the doll's head. This keeps the earrings snug against the head and they do not fall out.

Sarah Worley: Wide-brimmed hats can be made using the 3-¼in (10cm) cardboard ends of ribbon spools. The center can be cut out to fit the doll's head/hair. I've found that a small medicine cup works well as a stencil for that. Fabric can be sewn and glued onto the cardboard, and the edges can be covered with ribbon, cording, or glitter glue depending upon the design.

Dorothy Fannin: For an easy hat, take a square piece of felt, **(see step 1)** soak it in water and pull to stretch on all sides. **(see step 2)** Cover a bald fashion doll with plastic wrap and twist it around the base of the neck. **(see step 3)** Drape the felt over the doll's head and pull the felt down to just above the eyes and wind a rubber band around the felt to hold it secure. **(see step 4)** Fan out the felt on the outer sides of the rubber band and carefully cut all around the felt to make the brim. **(see step 5)** Then dilute Aleene's® Fabric Stiffener with water (don't overdo the diluted glue and make the hat too wet as it will sometimes leave a white mark) and use a soft brush to just brush the diluted glue onto the hat starting at the crown and working down. Then brush the brim. Let the hat dry overnight. When the hat is dry, remove the rubber band and pull the base of the crown to fit your doll's head. Trim any uneven parts of the brim and decorate your hat with braiding, flowers, or whatever strikes your fancy. **(see step 6)** Here is one of my dolls with her brand new hat Jim!

Jim Faraone: Wonderful, Dorothy! Can we get some more hat tips?

Dorothy Fannin: For making a pillbox hat, instead of spreading out the brim, clip the felt under the rubber band and let dry. After it's dry, remove from the head and trim to the size crown you want. Using Sobo® glue, add braid or whatever to the bottom of the hat.

Jim Faraone: Cool, Dorothy and I'm sure if you want to add a different top to the hat, you can always add a big flat button or bottle cap to the top of the doll's head before stretching on the wet felt for a different look. Brainstorming with everyone is great!

Dorothy Fannin: For other brims, you can once again cut the felt under the rubber band and cut a circle from the felt the size you want. Cut out an inner circle just a little smaller than the bottom crown. Brush some Sobo® glue around the base of the crown and slip the brim over the crown. Press to the outer edge of the crown. Let this dry and the seam can be covered with ribbon or braid. Here's a shot of some of the hats I created.

Jim Faraone: Here is another hat tip using those **(see step 1)** little felt sailor hats you see in the craft stores. First **(see step 2)** cut off the brim of the sailor hats leaving a bit of the crown of the hat on the cut brim. **(see step 3)**. **(see step 4)** Turn the brim upside down and sew the little flap of the crown to the crown of the hat. **(see step 5)** This will give you a fun bowl shaped hat. Now, if you cut the circle of the crown into an even smaller circle once the brim is cut off and then sew the long strip of the brim around the crown, it will give you a tighter fitting hat and you can cut the extra length of brim into strips for a "feathered" look. Or **(see step 6)** you can just use the center crown you cut out and apply fur and trim to make a hat for a special occasion. **(see step 7)** You can make a variety of hats for your dolls by just using your imagination.

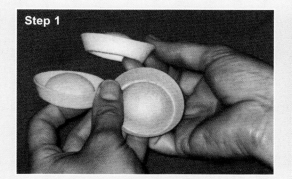

Step 1

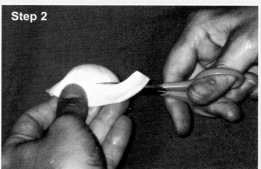

Step 2

Step 3

Step 4

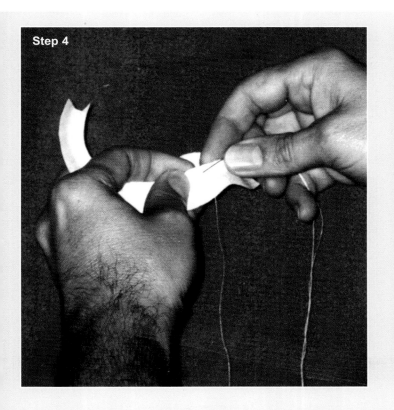

Step 5

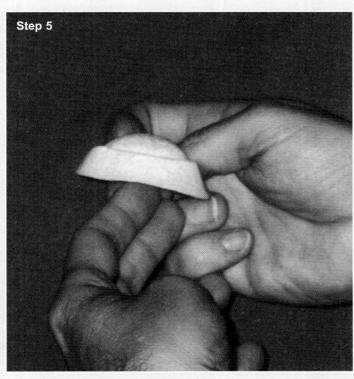

Step 6

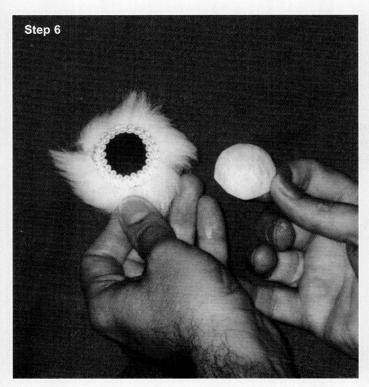

Step 7

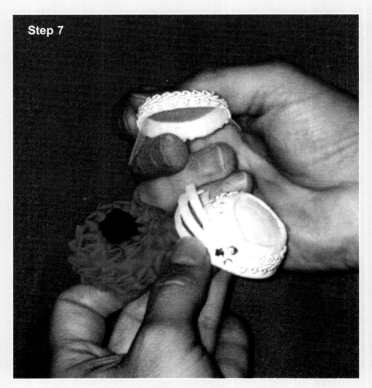

Pamela Bachmayer: Plastic canvas comes in very small mesh sizes that you can cover or stitch for accessories.

Ella Trumpfeller: You can use leather watchbands or leather shoelaces for belts.

Sarah Worley: Trim edges of hems with small flowers. These flowers can be easily sewn on if the stem is completely trimmed off and a heavy needle is used.

Sharon Brendemuehl: I love using pig suede leather for bodices and boots on my dolls. It is very thin and easy to work with. It does not fray so there is no need to hem. Holes can be punched into it and wire or fancy threads can be threaded through the holes.

Tracie Hutcherson: When working with jump rings, twist the ends to opposite sides, so the ring starts to look more like a spiral. Don't pull the ends apart because this bends the ring and weakens it as well as compromising the shape. To create an earring dangle or necklace pendant, first place your chosen beads on the head pin. At the top of the last bead, bend the pin so there is a ninety-degree angle. (This centers the loop in line with the beads.) Clip the excess so there is approximately 3/8in (.9cm) length. Using round nose pliers, twist the remaining length to form the loop. For removable necklaces and bracelets, form a hook and eye closure using eye pins and/or wire. Make one side of the closure the loop, and bend wire or an eye pin into a U shape to form the hook. Spring rings that are small enough for dolls can be difficult to find.

Pamela Bachmayer: This is how I make easy tiaras and crowns. **(see step 1)** You'll need a variety of beads, eye pins and wire of the same gauge, crimp beads, trim, wire cutters, needle nose pliers, round nose pliers, scissors, needle and matching

thread. **(see step 2)** Create several tiers/points for your tiara/crown: Add beads in your pattern to a purchased eye pin or make your own from wire with your round nose pliers. You will need to make the eye smaller on the eye pin so that it fits the tiara better. After the beads are arranged on the eye pin, use your needle nose pliers to put a crimp bead after the last bead to hold them in place. Cut off any extra length of wire with your wire cutters. If long enough, the extra length can be used for shorter pieces along the tiara. Make several tiers/points for your tiara. I make one long one for the center with smaller ones on each side. Make sure they match on each side. You can put as many points on the tiara/crown as you want or even make them all the same size. **(see step 3)** Measure and cut a length of wire as long as you need it for the base of the tiara or crown. Place a crimp bead on one end to prevent beads from falling off. Add beads to the piece of wire, adding your tiers/points along the way. You will generally need to place 2–3 beads between each tier/point. You may need to experiment a bit to get your tiers/points center on the wire. Do not bead the entire length of the wire or it will not bend into shape when you are finished. Leave 3–4 beads width empty at the end of the wire. Attach another crimp bead on the end to secure the beads. Your tiers/points will swing freely around the wire; don't worry about that, as you will secure them in the next step. **(see step 4)** With matching thread and sewing needle, sew the base wire of your tiara/crown to a piece of trim or lace. Sew the stem of each tier/point to the trim as well to secure it and prevent it from moving. Trim off excess trim. **(see step 5)** Bend the tiara/crown to fit the doll's head and use straight pins to secure in place. **(see step 6)** Now your sophisticated lady is ready for dancing the night away with her Prince Charming.

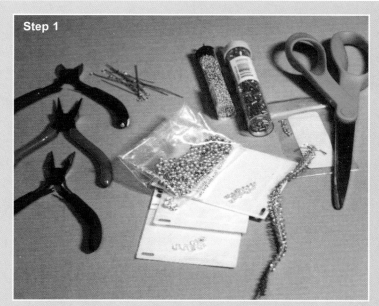

Step 1

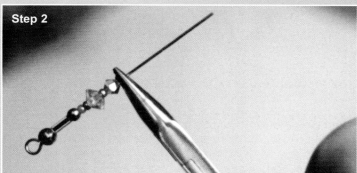

Step 2

Step 3

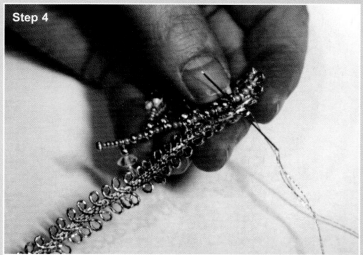

Step 4

48

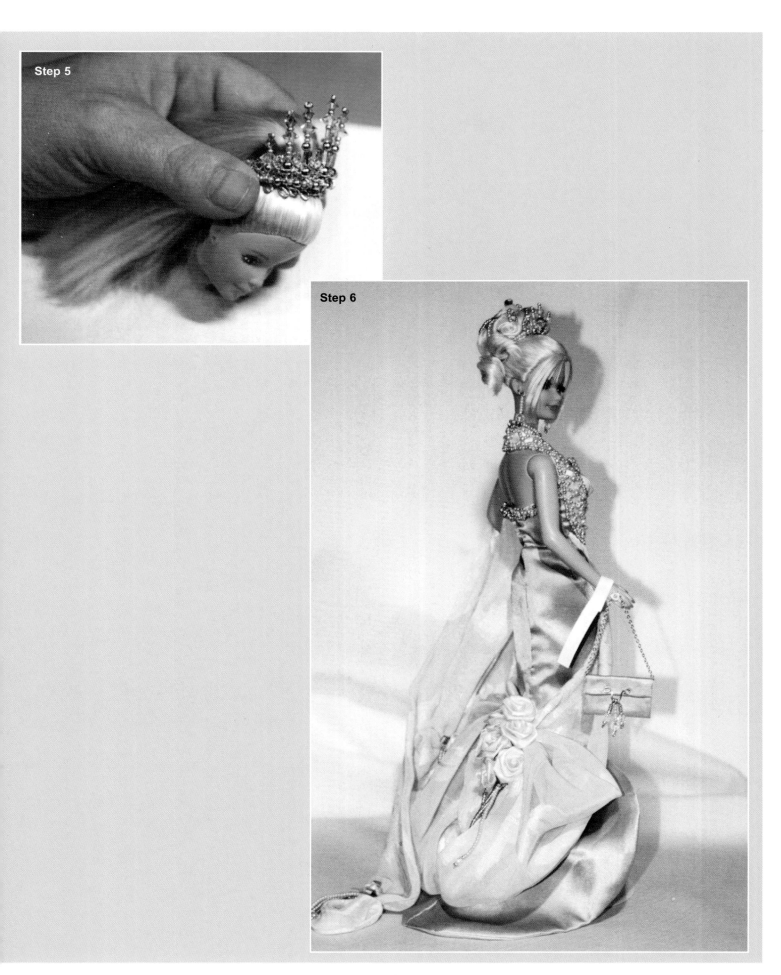

Step 5

Step 6

49

Chrissy Stewart: Scale is very important and you don't want to put earrings that are too large in the doll's ears. This takes away from her realism. In addition, when using beads, try to keep them to scale on the doll. Details are very important when making clothes. I try to add as many details as I can to the entire outfit to complete the look I want. This means jewelry, trinkets or whatever would have gone with the outfit or costume. Hooks and eyes work great for bodice eyelets and shoelace hooks.

Barb Rausch: Jim I have another technique with patterns I'd like to share with everyone.

Jim Faraone: Great, Barb! Send it on through!

Barb Rausch: This is for making a "picture hat" from narrow 3/16in (.45cm) millinery straw, but it's for experienced hand sewers. You will need extra fine millinery needles, very stiff nylon netting in a color that matches your straw, and a fabric marking pen in a color that will show up on the netting. With the fabric marking pen, trace this diagram onto the netting. **(see pattern tip below)** Leaving about ½in (1cm) excess all around, cut out the netting diagram. Do NOT cut out the center circle yet. With matching thread, machine stitch with very small stitches along both dotted lines to stabilize what will eventually be cut edges. With the milliner's needle and matching thread, starting at the outer cutting line. Sew the straw around and around, slightly overlapping each row over the previous one as you work towards the inner circle. Go completely around the inner circle leaving ½in (1cm) of extra under the inner row of straw. Stitch in place. Carefully cut away the excess netting form the outer edge and inner circle. Trim the hat as desired.

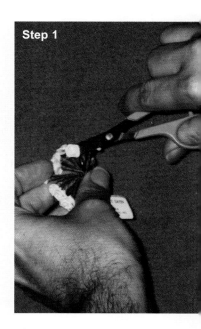

Step 1

Jim Faraone: To enhance the vintage type mules (shoes), **(see step 1)** buy those small bouquets of flowers and cut one off. **(see step 2)** With a needle and thread, thread a flower on double thread making sure you caught the beginning end of the flower so it doesn't unravel and pull through leaving a good length of the thread on both ends of the flower. **(see step 3)** Coat the front strap of the shoe with craft glue and **(see step 4)** insert the needle under the front strap. **(see step 5)** Tie the flower to the front strap. **(see step 6)** After tying the knot about 5 times, clip the thread close to the knot. The glue will hold the flower in place, yet if the glue gives, the flower is still secured with the knotted thread and will not fall off. You can actually trim your doll's shoes with a number of things including sequins. **(see step 7)** Take a decorative sequin and place your double threaded needle through the bottom of the sequin and out the top. **(see step 8)** String on a small seed bead. **(see step 9)** Then take your needle and go around the seed bead and back into the hole of the sequin **(see step 10)**. Now you will have a stable ornament/sequin with equal lengths of thread on both sides of it to tie onto the front of your shoes. **(see step 10)**

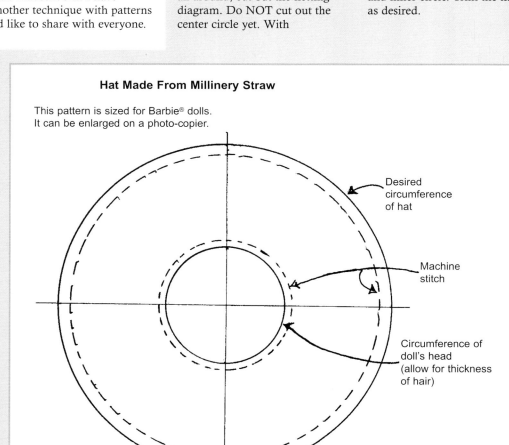

Hat Made From Millinery Straw

This pattern is sized for Barbie® dolls.
It can be enlarged on a photo-copier.

Desired circumference of hat

Machine stitch

Circumference of doll's head (allow for thickness of hair)

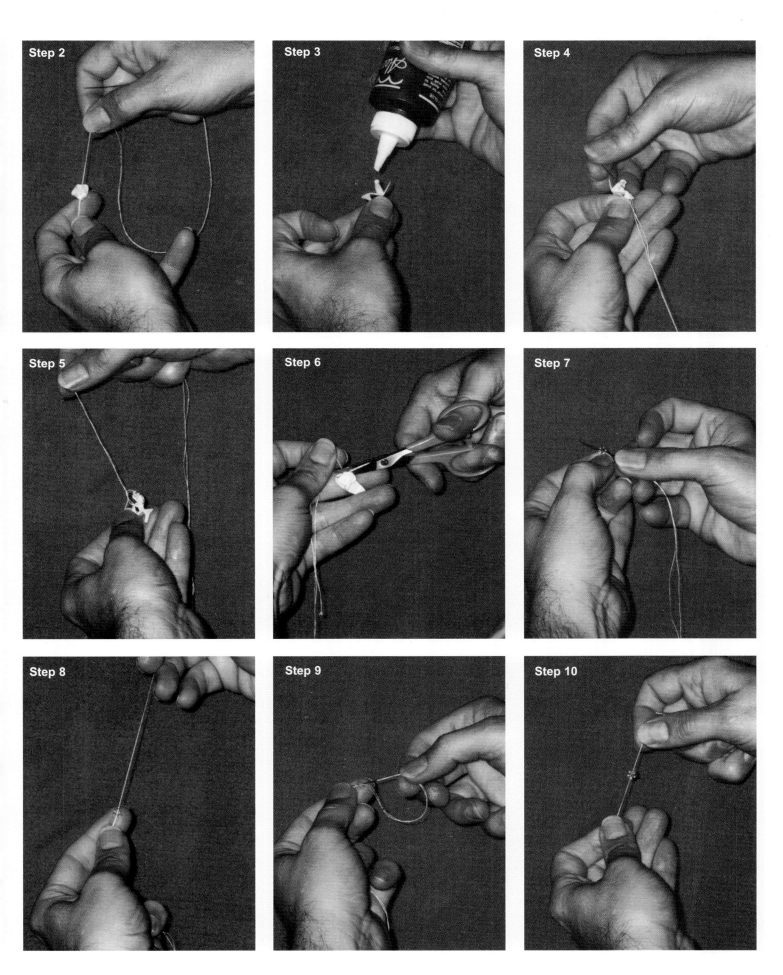

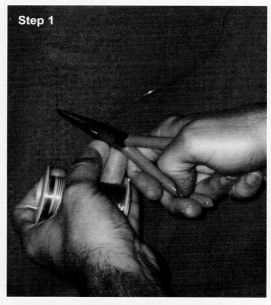

Step 1

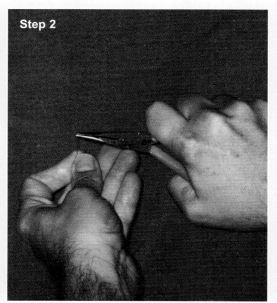

Step 2

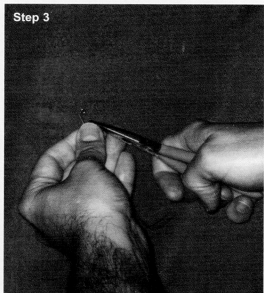

Step 3

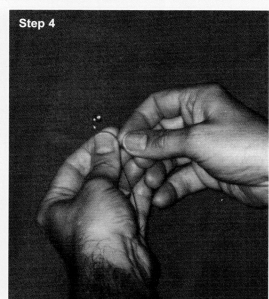

Step 4

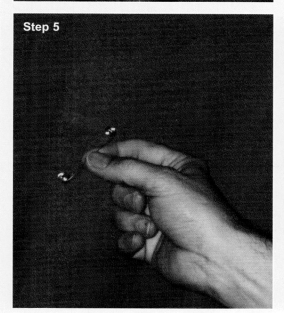

Step 5

Step 6

Pamela Bachmayer: You can easily add interest to your fashion doll jewelry by shaping wire **(see step 1)** into interesting shapes for medallions, etc. **(see step 2)** Use round nose pliers to form perfect loops and spirals. **(see step 3)** Once looped you can then loop it around more with your fingers **(see step 4)**. **(see step 5)** You can loop both ends and **(see step 6)** twist it around a doll's neck to make an interesting necklace. Needle nose pliers can be used to straighten out unplanned bends and flatten wire shapes as needed. Keep in mind how you plan to use your shape and how you will be attaching it so that you can add loops where/if you need them. Use wire cutters to cut off excess wire when you are finished so you don't need to worry about cutting the exact size before you start. Use crimping beads to secure ends when necessary. You may add beads in the middle of a twist as you are forming it (beads may not want to go beyond twists and bends already formed). The possibilities are endless. Use any size wire that achieves the effect you want. Remember that earrings may require mirror images.

Debra Jo Van Dyke: I have used artificial flower tips as earrings or rings. Another alternative is to whittle down parts of a "turned" end fancy toothpick. I have seen these carved toothpicks at some Oriental import stores and the Cracker Barrel® restaurants. Use a craft knife to score around and break off the lower knob and carefully pare down the stem with a craft knife until it will fit in the ring or earring hole. By cutting them shorter, you can use these toothpicks for fancy hair sticks.

Bunny Dedes: I have a great tip for the Barbie® doll ear holes that are too big hold new earrings. Just remove the plastic earrings by clipping, do not pull plastic earrings out because this makes the hole bigger. If using real earrings, I found that wrapping the metal post around no-sew tape cut to the exact length of the post works well. Slowly peal the white backing off the no-sew as you slowly roll the post around the sticky part of the tape. It's kind of like curling your hair except the post is the curler and the tape is your hair. The two sided no-sew tape will be stuck to the post as well as building up the post to make it large enough for the Barbie® doll's ear hole. It also keeps the earring from coming out without glue. This technique makes a nice clean job with no glue marks.

Loanne Hizo Ostlie: Bunny, what a great idea. I have

another tip for large earring holes. When I use store bought earrings, I bend the posts in half and shove them into the hole. It makes them fit to a tee!

Tracie Hutcherson: I use some leftover items from my days as a nail tech. For rings, I insert a headpin up through the palm of the hand, then place a crimp bead as close to the back of the hand as possible. Once it's crimped, I use ultra-glitter nail polish to simulate a gemstone. The polish was intended to use in a technique called satined glass. For custom-made jump rings in any size you need simply wrap your wire around any round object that is the correct diameter (a pencil, a metal

rod, etc.). Slide the wire off and cut down one side. Voila! You have jump rings that are already open and ready to use.

Jim Faraone: Some try and look for different kinds of stretchy, thin materials for making gloves. Try looking in the women's lingerie department. You can buy women's panties in wonderful colors and designs, including leopard print. By purchasing the largest pair available, you can get numerous pairs of gloves from them.

Dorothy Fannin: Hey Jim! How do you make those necklaces with the "loops" in them?

Jim Faraone: That's simple, Dorothy! **(see step 1)** With a double threaded needle, knot the thread onto your clasp. **(see step 2)** Thread on the number of beads you want using some larger beads in the center of your necklace and knot the thread onto the other end of your clasp. **(see step 3)** Without cutting your thread after you tied your knot, go back through the beads that you already strung. **(see step 4)** When you pass through your first larger bead, **(see step 5)** thread on the desired number of beads you want for your loop. **(see step 6)** Then go around and back through the larger bead to create you loop and out of the next large bead.

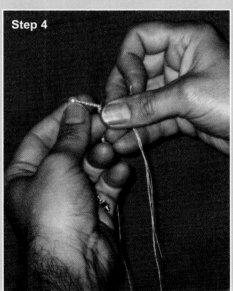
Step 1

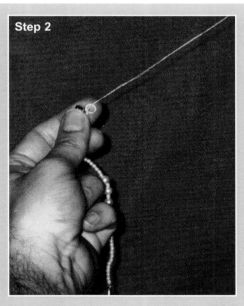
Step 2

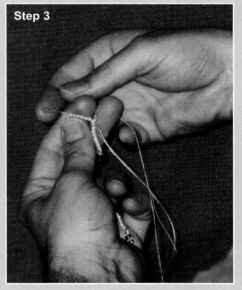
Step 3

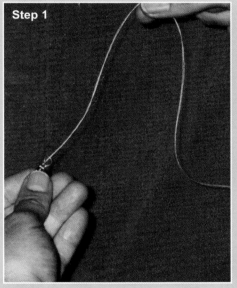
Step 4

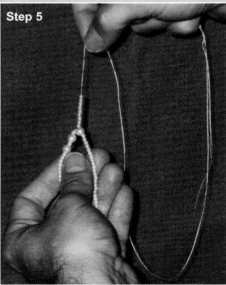
Step 5

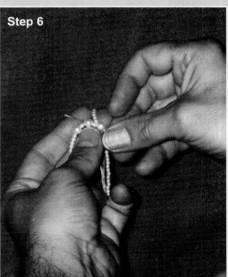
Step 6

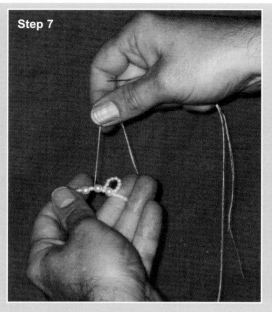

Step 7

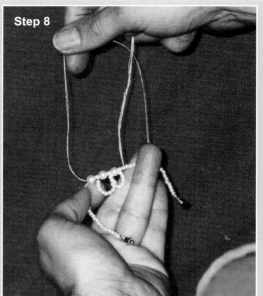

Step 8

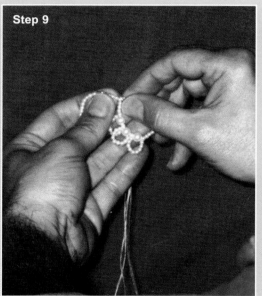

Step 9

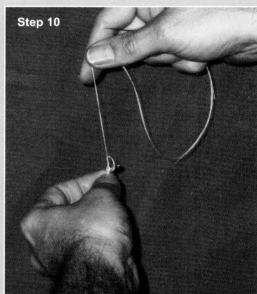

Step 10

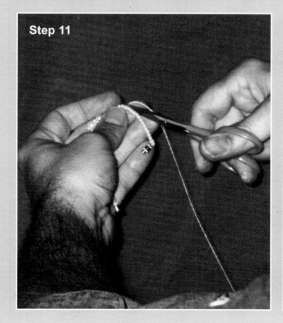

Step 11

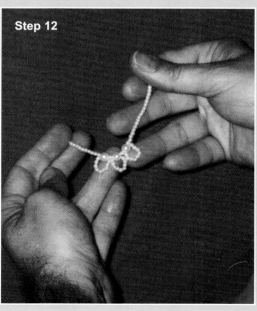

Step 12

(**see step 7**) This will form your first loop. (**see step 8**) Repeat steps 4, 5 and 6 until you have all your loops in place. (**see step 9**) Now continue rethreading the rest of your beads and (**see step 10**) once again knot your thread at the clasp. (**see step 11**) Once again, go back through about half your beads and snip the thread. As a little safety precaution, put a dab of Jewel-It glue on your knots and let dry. (**see step 12**) You now have a necklace full of loops to adorn any fashion plate.

Creating the Unusual

Sometimes we all get into a rut and our creations start looking alike. Then it gets worse and everyone's dolls start looking like one another's and blending together. Then it gets even worse when some artists start copying the creations of someone else. Then there are those few dolls that stand out in a crowd because the designer tried something different and unusual. That's what creating is all about—experimenting and coming up with styles and techniques that no one else is doing.

Deborah Fagan: For that singed look on fabrics, I found that using incense, instead of just a lighter is less of a fire hazard and more controllable.

Natalie Tetzlaff: I do just about the same thing, Deborah. To achieve a tattered look for my fantasy creations (fairies, elves, etc.), I singe the fabric as well. To singe without igniting the entire garment, I use an incense stick that has been lit and is now slowly burning. Matches lit for a few moments then blown out make nice round holes. You can also drag the match along the fabric to tatter and tear it.

Sharon A. Lawson: For dying fabric trims, those made of 100% cotton dyes more easily and thoroughly than acrylics or other blend trims. Acrylics and other blends usually will take of different shades of color. Use acrylic paints mixed with water and fabric medium. Fabric medium is found with the acrylic paints in most fabric stores. Paint the mixture on the trim with a small stiff paintbrush. This method is better than dipping the trim into the mixture. If you dip the trim into the mixture and lay it out flat to dry, the paint will bleed to the outer edges of the trim drying darker than the center of the trim. The trim will dry with more even coloring by painting it on with the brush and not allowing it to get too wet. Let the trim dry for 12–24 hours. Iron the trim to set the color so it won't rub off or stain other materials.

Andrea Densley: Here's a way to do a tie-dye fabric. You will need is a clear squeeze bottle such as the kind used for hair perms and hair coloring, acrylic paint, water and string or rubber bands. Use a different bottle for each color needed. Fill the bottle about ¼in to ½in (.65cm–1cm) with acrylic paint. Add the same amount of water to the bottle making a 50/50 mix and shake. **(see step 1)** Wet the fabric to be dyed and **(see step 2)** tie tightly with the string or rubber bands. Fabric may be gathered in tiny bunches for a circular effect, or pleated and banded for a more striped look. **(see step 3)** (Okay, so I didn't have any squeeze bottles but a wet brush will work! LOL!) Squeeze out drops of paint into the fabric and let colors bleed out into the dampness of the fabric. Let the fabric dry several hours or overnight, then press the fabric with a hot iron to heat-set the paint.

LaDonna Moore: To add featured breasts to your dolls, add a small seed bead to the end of each breast with fabric tack glue, let dry and then paint with acrylic paint.

William Stewart Jones: The way I make chain mail armor like on the legs on my "Atilla" is using knitted fabric, wrong side out. For the "Atilla," I glued the cotton knit sweater fabric onto the doll's legs with thick white glue. After it dried, it was painted with flat black paint, then the surface was burnished to smooth it, then lightly painted with silver paint. It is important to select a fine

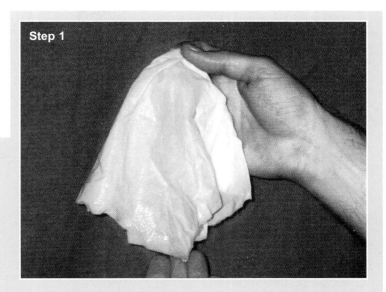

Step 1

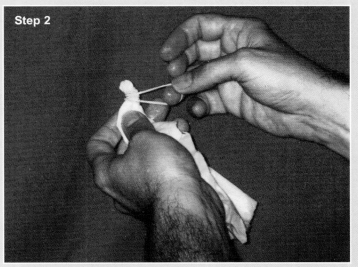

Step 2

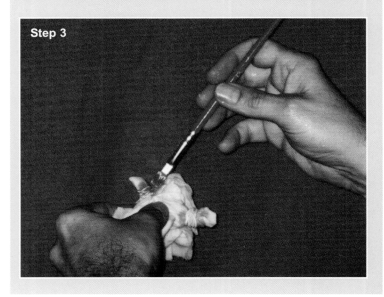

Step 3

knit in scale with the dolls, and smooth fibers like rayon or cotton work better than wool or acrylic because of the fuzz.

Carolyn Marnon: On one doll, I used Soft Flock® by Delta® to cover the body of the doll. You just paint on the colored glue and then spritz the flocking from the bottle over the doll. Be sure not to pat it down right after spritzing or the fibers don't work well. I gave the doll a liberal dose of flocking to make sure I had all the areas covered. You can always go back over the doll if you missed a spot. Let it dry for the recommended time on the package before shaking the excess flocking off. You can then shake the flocking off over a piece of paper and replace the leftovers back in your flocking bottle. I have also used the flocking to cover a pair of store bought doll shorts. They were the wrong color for what I wanted. I just painted on the correct-colored glue, flocked and let dry. I had a pair of shorts I wanted and didn't have to fight with the sewing machine to make them. It is important to keep the flocking off the velcro. The velcro doesn't work well once the flocking gets embedded in it.

Natalie Tetzlaff: Look for new and unusual material for your one-of-a-kind creations. Hair can be replaced with beads, yarn, raffia—just let your imagination go. Craft stores are a great place to find new materials. Instead of regular fabric, try making an outfit from craft moss or fake flowers for a fairy.

William Stewart Jones: Synthetic fur can be colored and tinted with permanent artist felt pens like Prismacolor® pens. These come in shades of browns and grays as well as the standard color palette. I have samples that have been in the sun for over a year with no fading. These can also be used on synthetic hair for subtle changes in hair color.

Linda Lynch Holman: When making vampire teeth, I use modeling paste. First, I paint the doll's mouth. Then using a toothpick, I place a small dab of modeling paste where the fangs are desired shaping the fangs with the toothpick. I let it dry overnight and then paint. There—vampire teeth with a 3-D look!

Aurora Mathews: You can make paper fingernails. **(see step 1)** First cut them out like fingernails to fit the Gene® doll or Barbie® doll. **(see step 2)** Coat them underneath from the cuticle to the tip of paper with a good clear-drying glue and let dry. **(see step 3)** Pick the nail up with a toothpick and **(see step 4)** attach it to the doll's fingers with the glue and let dry. **(see step 5)** Coat under the nail tip and top of paper with a good acrylic varnish and let dry. **(see step 6)** Then use metallic acrylic paint to color the nails.

Anke Scharfenberg: You can use very pretty ribbon on your doll if you want to create fairy wings. Or if you are good at crafting with wire, you can form the wings with wire and pull an old (or new) stocking over it. It looks even better if you use a colored pair of stockings. Finally, apply metallic acrylic paints to decorate.

Ella Trumpfeller: The supplies I use for making my cat ears are: polymer clay, straight pins, superglue, paint, paint brush or color markers, oven and doll. Mold the polymer clay into triangle "ears" and push a straight pin into the small flat side of the triangle. Bake the ears for 10–12 minutes. When you are ready to attach them, either paint the ears with acrylic paints or use the color markers. Then apply superglue to the straight pin and the base of the ears and push it into the vinyl head of the doll. Hold it just long enough for it to adhere. You can use the same molding of polymer clay to form a pregnant belly on your doll. Press it over the doll's tummy to

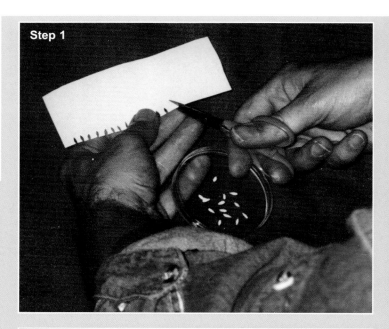
Step 1

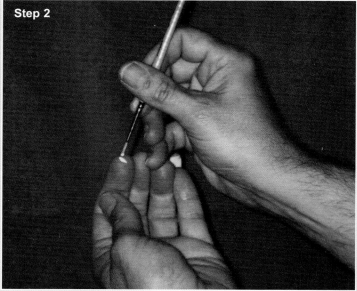
Step 2

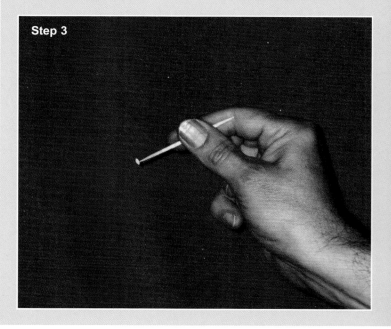
Step 3

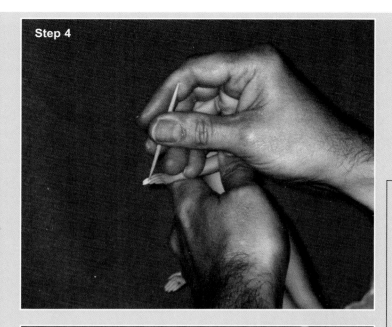

Step 4

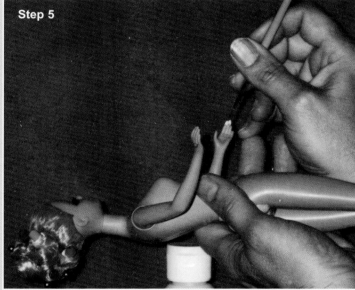

Step 5

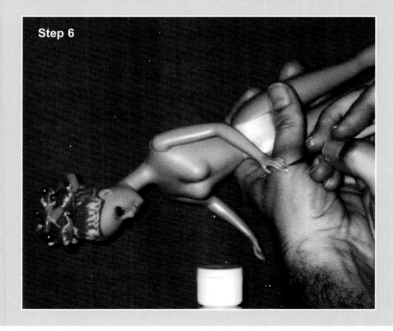

Step 6

shape the flat side and then bake it. Apply superglue to the belly and attach to the doll. I usually cover that with a piece of material just to secure it in place. The same could be used to make breasts for a male doll in making a Drag doll. I would also cover them with a handmade "bra" so that they are covered.

Linda Lynch Holman: To make my dragon lady fingernails, I use clear colored drinking straws cut ¼in to ½in (.65cm–1cm) lengths. Then I cut these into tiny slivers and shape into a fingernail. Using tweezers and a silicon glue, I stick the fingernail sections onto the doll's fingers. Let them dry overnight and paint.

Pamela Bachmayer: Using different cake tips and the triangle papers that cake decorators use to make the disposable bags/cones for holding icing have achieved some interesting textures with modeling paste. The paste must be thick enough to hold the shape of the tip, but thin enough to squeeze through the tip. Practice with thickness before using. Use the very small tips to prevent paste from getting too thick on the doll. Insert the tip into the bag/cone before adding the paste. Use scissors to cut a small hole in the tip of the paper bag/cone just large enough to clear the tip. I use a rubber band at the top of the cone to prevent the paste from coming out the top of the bag/cone. Bags can be put into a zip-lock bag for brief periods of time if needed to keep from hardening during use. Wash tips well before and after use (before it hardens!.) The triangle cones can be tossed away.

Ella Trumpfeller: I have another way I make cat ears on my dolls. I purchase mini bumblebees or butterflies that are made on wires and covered with nylon from craft stores. Just carefully twist the wings to cross the wires and then cut them with wire cutters. You will have a nylon-covered wire with

a small stem of twisted wire at the base that will be used to insert into the doll's head. Drill a hole into the vinyl of the head where you want to place the ears. I usually separate the hair and slice between the rows of hair with an X-Acto® knife. Then I place a drop of super glue onto the wire at the base of the "ear" and insert it into the hole. After the glue is dried, you can shape the ears.

William Stewart Jones: I frequently sew fine wire into the edges of fabrics to allow me to shape it.

Kathleen Forsythe: I use paint, fabric paint and then acrylic paint to create the illusion of rhinestones.

Jim Faraone: I've done the same thing, Kathleen, with my BMAA entry of "Queen of the Black Widow Spiders". I wanted the spider web design on the sheer fabric to have a beaded look. I took silver metallic acrylic paint and began dotting the spider web design. Once this dried, I then took a metallic pearl white acrylic paint and dotted the center of the silver paint to give it a 3-dimensional look. It worked well though it was quite a tedious job. The big kicker is that now that same spider web material comes out with the dotted beaded look!!! LOL! I heard that some use the Tulip® paints to create 3-dimensional designs on their outfits.

Kathleen Forsythe: For my Cher feather dress, I used an old pair of stockings. I cut it out to be smaller than the actual dress. Then I stretched it as I sewed it by hand till it fit the doll. I used fabric paint to draw the lines and things on the dress and used crystal acrylic paint to make it shine. Then when it came time to put the feathers on, I sprayed it with glue, stuck a nail in where I wanted the feather and put the feather in place. I sprayed it with glue again. Since the glue is already sprayed on, I work very fast to get the rest of the feathers in place. Then I seal it with glue spray again and let it sit. The paint for the lines that I did previously also hid the part of the feather that is inside the dress.

Kathy Van Camp: I have used non-yellowing clear nail polish for tears on my dolls. You can also use a product called Treasure Crystal Cote® for making tears on your dolls.

William Stewart Jones: I also like using wire for hair. My "Titiana," BMAA winner 1999, has hair made entirely from fine spool wire. Each strand was inserted into a hole made by the previously rooted hair, from the outside in, and out the neck. Then after I'd threaded about five strands, I twisted them together, trimmed the ends and pulled a bunch back up into the head tight against the scalp. This tends to stiffen the wire and make it more easily styled. I used the same technique for the "Candleabra," but put bugle beads onto each wire. Both of these techniques are time consuming, but not difficult. The wire can be colored with paint, coated with textures, glued and sprinkled with glitters, curled, kinked, smoothed!

Sandy Cunningham: White stockings can be painted with watered acrylics to match the color of your outfits. Soak the stockings in the watered down color and let it air dry on a paper towel.

Jim Faraone: Creating a sheer illusion dress is always fun. An illusion outfit is an outfit that looks like it is see-through. Basically, all you have to do is find a sheer fabric to use and some fabric that matches the skin coloring of your doll. **(see step 1)** You cut out your pattern pieces with the flesh colored fabric. **(see step 2)** Then baste on your sheer fabric to the flesh colored fabric. **(see step 3)** Trim the excess sheer fabric. Then sew your outfit pieces together by machine to create an illusion of fantasy! **(see step 4)**

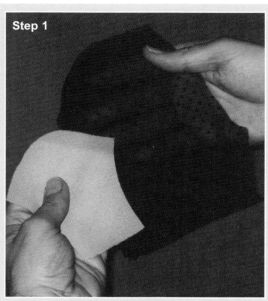

Step 1

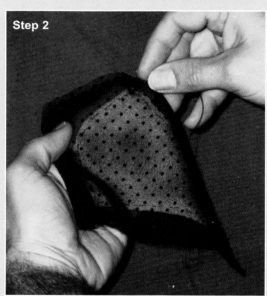

Step 2

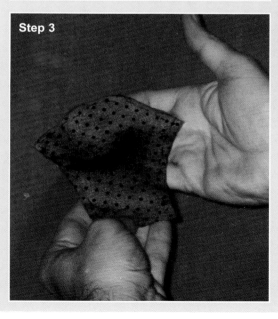

Step 3

Step 4

Sculpting and Remodeling Your Doll

Taking your dolls even a step further and truly altering their appearance can be a rewarding experience. A little chop here, a little slice there and definitely some addition somewhere else will give your doll that distinct, unique look. It may be time now to play plastic surgeon and get out those scalpels and cut away.

Juan Albuerne: The only tool needed for modeling is a cuticle pick. You can do anything with it. Cover the point with a fast drying glue or gel (cyanocrilate type). Let it dry and then sandpaper it till you get the chosen shape. This way, you can get different shapes for different purposes. It works better than any modeling tool that you can buy. Modeling is not easy work. Many times you can close a mouth, retouch a nose and so on. I don't like to use glue to make this. I always prefer the modeling paste. You must use small amounts of the paste and model it with the pick a little wet. The modeling pastes that I use are Duro® or Milliput® (two components paste). The first one is green; the second one is gray or white. The main problem when you use them to remake a part of the face (except lips) is that you must match the face color. Once you paint it, don't varnish the color. You only have to smooth the color (well dried) with your fingertip. You'll see that the color becomes a soft sheen.

William Stewart Jones: I like to joint the arms by cutting them apart, removing about ½in (1cm) from the elbow joint and inserting a piece of heavy copper wire. I drill a hole in the cut end of the piece and glue in a short length of copper wire. That allows me to bend the arm in various positions. Then I fill the joint with spackle and sand and paint to match. If the joint is to be covered by a costume, I usually cover the joint with thin fabric. I also do this with the doll's legs. I use aluminum armature wire or heavy copper wire and super glue or "527" glue works well. This only works with long sleeve clothes. I also sculpt the faces of the hard vinyl dolls like the Tyler Wentworth® doll, the Gene® doll and the Carlos® doll. For a fantasy eye, I carve and sand down the brow bone so I can paint a more exotic eye. The sanded vinyl can be smoothed by rubbing it with acetone.

Gael Singer Bailey: I think we all like to play plastic surgeon, Bill. When I play in the Dr. Frankenstein School of Plastic Surgery, I use a dremel tool to sever the arm or arms at the elbow. Then with a soldering iron turned on, I insert it into the upper arm and melted a hole about ½in (1cm) deep, then do the same with the lower arm. Then depending upon whether I want it to have a bendable arm or stationary arm, I choose my wire to connect the two pieces. I used my hot glue gun to connect the wire into the arm. If you wish to move the arm you can cover the slight opening with flesh colored plastic dressing tape. Then the doll must always wear long opera gloves or long sleeves. If you wish to position her arm permanently, you can use a variety of products to fill the space. I use the same acrylic nail stuff used for sculpting nails. It is the greatest stuff. Just position the arm and fill the space. File and buff when dry. I use the nail acrylic to build up noses, chins, change eye shapes and add finger nails. You can also slightly fill in large earring holes. I even added it to a Barbie® doll's feet to make her into a ballet dancer on point and then all I had to do was cover her feet with satin for ballet toe shoes.

Becky Kelly: For my hand-sculpted mermaid tails and other tails, I prefer I use "air dry" clay in order to get the length and suppleness. To keep this type of clay from cracking after it is dry, I create an armature of the tail shape I want. Then I build the tail around it. The armature can be made from any wire, but I prefer the smaller gauge wires available in the jewelry section of most arts and crafts stores. This can also be done with polymer clays as well. After modeling the tail and allowing it to dry for at least 24 hours it is time to decorate it. I mix an acrylic texture gel with the paint color of my choice. Be sure to mix it thoroughly. Then I apply it to the tail with a spatula (I use my fingers!) I dab it on to give the tail a rough finish, but patterns such as swirls, whirls, etc. can also be created. Then, before the gel sets, I add glitter, sequins or other glittery objects to the tail surface. Let the tail dry for another 24 hours and the final step is to apply a clear acrylic varnish to seal it.

Gael Singer Bailey: To separate fingers I use my dremel with cut off wheel #409. You have to steady your hand or you may amputate a finger. Just take the dremel and cut between each finger. The vinyl will be like sawdust, but just brush it from between the fingers with a stiff brush. I use a firm toothbrush. If you need to smooth between the fingers, use extra fine sandpaper folded in half.

Deborah Fagan: I made a mermaid that was more of a sculpture than a doll. In other words, if you're going to reposition the doll, I used paperclay, and sculpted the tail of the mermaid. It turned out pretty realistic.

Jim Faraone: I have taken slightly bent armed Barbie® dolls and straightened them out. **(see step 1)** Using an X-Acto® knife, just slice at the inner elbow almost half way through the vinyl. **(see steps 2-3)** Put the arm in boiling water for 3 seconds and bend the arm

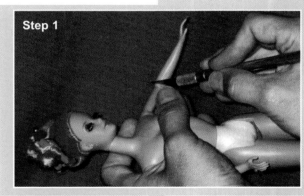

Step 1

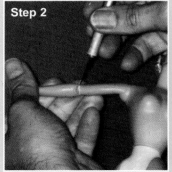

Step 2

Step 3

Step 4

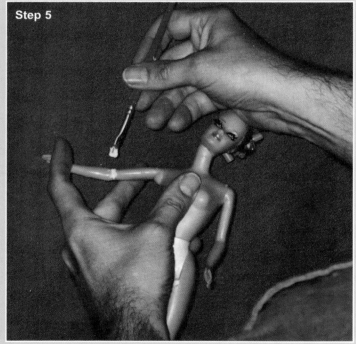

Step 5

You can bake the items you made from this in an oven at 200 degrees until they're hard. Then you can preserve the pieces once done with a clear acrylic varnish.

Susan Yslas: With a little help from a special Internet friend, I learned to make my version of a Centaur. I found a white horse about 18in (46cm) tall from the thrift store for a dollar. I took the horse out into the garage and went directly to the scroll saw where I cut off the head of the horse at the neckline. OUCH! Don't worry—it didn't feel a thing! :-) There is usually an indenting line and you can cut right on this line to get a perfect cut. I then took a Barbie® doll and popped off her legs (ooooh get the hubby to do this because it was really hard for me to do). I stuffed the body of the horse with crumbled newspaper almost all the way to the top of the opening. I set the Barbie® doll in the opening and when she sat with her waist above the opening, I sealed the body in the horse's body (all the way around) with Das Clay®. It is an air-drying clay and I let her sit for about 24 hours until she was good and dry. I curled the tail of the horse using the boil method and then customized the Centaur to my theme.

Linda Lynch Holman: To close the gap between the Barbie® doll's lips, you can fill it in with modeling paste and reshape.

Kevin Kilmer: I've done that, Linda. When I want to change my open mouth dolls into closed mouthed dolls, I first remove all the paint from the face of the doll using the standard non-acetone nail polish remover. I let this dry and then wipe over the area with a damp cloth to remove any traces of the polish remover. Then I use a brand modeling putty for plastic car models (TESTORS®.) I take a very small amount and work it into the open part of the mouth and fill the open area in completely. Let this step dry for a couple of minutes so the area becomes tacky. Then take a

small object, ie. a pin or other similar small object, and make the indentation for the part of the mouth and work from the center out to the outer lip area keeping your work as smooth as possible. Continue shaping the lip area until you are satisfied the lips are now closed and not looking open. Then let it dry completely. I usually let it dry overnight to insure that the added putty is completely dry. Finally, I take whatever color I am using for the lips and paint them in the shape I want. I then line the lips and voila, a closed mouth doll from an open one!

William Stewart Jones: I give many of my dolls a "breast reduction" by sanding the bosom down. Period costumes, especially corseted ones, need a smaller flatter bosom.

Jim Faraone: Want that stubble look on your male dolls? **(see step 1)** Just take a straight pin and begin poking it into the doll's face in the beard area. Once you made enough pin holes, **(see step 2)** take some diluted brown acrylic paint and "wash" the doll's face. **(see step 3)** Wipe off the excess paint and you'll see that the paint remains in the pin holes creating that "scruffy" look on your doll. Now, if you want that full beard look, flocking found in craft stores is always fun to use. Following the directions on the flocking kit, **(see step 4)** use the flocking adhesive to apply your beard onto your doll. **(see step 5)** Apply the flocking fibers as directed on the bottle and let dry a few hours. **(see step 6)** Once dried, gently tap you doll's head to remove the excess flocking and you have a Dapper Dan with a full growth of beard! **(see step 7)** Flocking is really a lot of fun. Remember those molded hair tips I gave in my 4th book featuring the added on buckram pieces and beads? Well, there's no reason that you couldn't flock the hair onto the doll once you have your first thin coat of modeling paste dried on its head.

straight. **(see step 4)** Run it under cold water to set it. Dry off the doll and **(see step 5)** fill the hole in her inner elbow with modeling paste and let it dry overnight. You now have straight arms on your doll and you can hide the area with gloves or a long sleeved outfit. For a little extra support, once the modeling paste is dry, you can put a band of duct tape around the sliced section.

Joanna Bond: You can make parts for your dolls with oven-baked clay, but if you want to sculpt directly onto a toy, you must use air-drying clay so you don't risk melting the plastic.

Jim Faraone: Salt dough clay can be made in the oven to make pieces for your dolls. It's just 1 cup of flour, 1 cup of salt and 1 cup of water. Just mix it all thoroughly and refrigerate.

Step 1

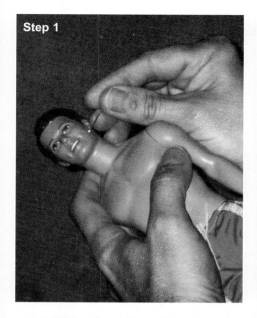

Step 2

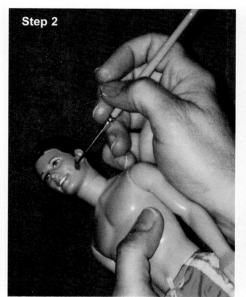

Step 3

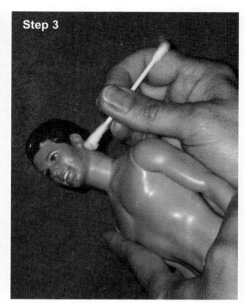

Step 4

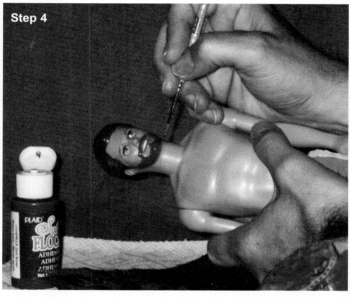

Step 5

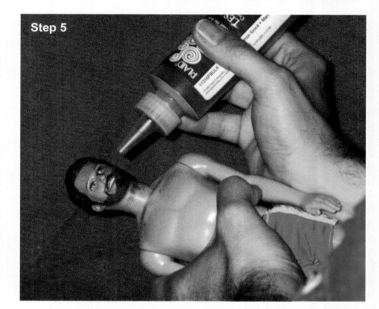

Step 6

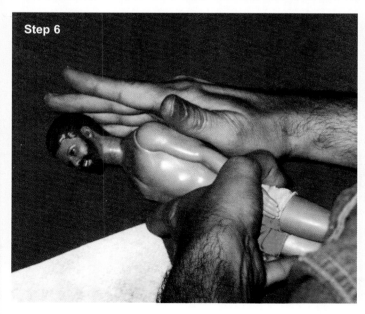

Step 7

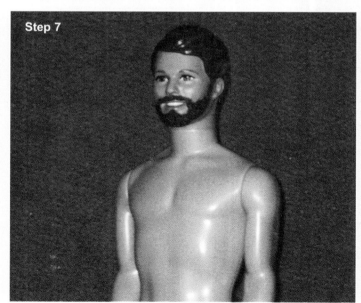

Restoring Well-Loved Dolls

Restoration is a must for those who enjoy working with well-loved dolls. These dolls are found at thrift shops, rummage sales, flea markets or maybe in your own attic or basement. These well-loved childhood playmates will need special attention to get them back in shape before you start creating with them. As with most doll collectors, they enjoy adopting these down-on-their-luck dolls and I've seen many go from down right nasty to gorgeous, rejuvenated beauties. Let's bring those dolls back to life.

Jim Faraone: For those of you who have bow-legged dolls or dolls with crooked ankles, just try placing the legs/ankles in boiling water for about 5 seconds, straighten them out with your hands and then run them under cold water while holding them straight and that should help get everything back into shape.

Patricia Palka: I developed this technique when I restored vintage Barbie® dolls. To make the eyebrows symmetrical, I first trace off the original eyebrows on a comparable mint doll (be it Bubble Cut, American Girl, etc.), using non-tear tracing paper. I then darken the lines, making sure to maintain this original shape. I place this tracing under glass, and using a stencil burner, I create a stencil of the eyebrow pair on a sheet of stencil plastic (available at craft stores). I also notch out where the nose is located to stabilize the stencil when I apply it to the face (allowing it to fit like a pair of sunglasses). I then cover the doll's hair and body for protection, place the stencil over the nose, and airbrush the color on. Using a stencil plastic creates a reusable template. It's an involved process, but with practice, you are guaranteed to have a perfectly matched set of eyebrows every time.

Carolyn Marnon: If you have to cover up eyelash skin pricks, I don't see why you can't use flock (Delta® Soft Flock) in brown or black or a mixture of black and brown to cover up the holes. You just paint a thin line of the colored glue mixture that comes with the flocking onto the lash line and spritz on some flocking. Let it dry and it could be a nice effect.

Nikki Avery: Lots of vintage ponytails (#5's) and bubble cut Barbie® dolls have a "greasy face." A problem caused by different vinyl used to make the Barbie® doll's heads in the early 60's. Some dolls are a bit shiny and others are plagued by "grease" oozing out of the facial/scalp area. The doll's "greasy" appearance can be improved with a treatment that can last 6 months to a year. Just remove the head using the proper method for vintage Barbie® dolls. Wash the hair to remove any grease residue in the hair. While washing, fill the head with water and gently clean inside and out with a Q-tip®. I like to use dishwashing soap like Dawn®. Let it dry completely and then using a Q-tip® dipped in rubbing alcohol, gently swab the face AVOIDING the original paint areas. (If I am working on a ponytail doll, I like to pull the hair back into its ponytail to keep hair away from the face.) Swab inside the head with alcohol. Let this dry. Then use a makeup brush (eyeshadow sized) or a clean paintbrush and dip it into baking soda. Knock the excess baking soda off of the brush and gently dab over the doll's face and neck opening (as if applying powder). The baking soda will help absorb the oil. Use another clean, dry brush (without baking soda) and go over the face once to brush away the extra. I place a small pouch inside the Barbie® doll's head filled with baking soda. White mesh material is

great for this or very thin cotton fabric with a few tiny holes punched on the pouch. Pouches should be replaced about every year or so. This method will take away the greasies for a while depending on the amount of "greasy face" your doll has. Treatment can be repeated when needed.

Natalie Tetzlaff: To remove hot glue that I found on a few dolls from a neighbor's daughter, I cut the fabric off as much as possible, but I wasn't able to remove it all. I used my fingernails to lift the edges as mush as possible and peeled off what I could. Some of the glue will peel off, especially lower-quality brands. Since there was no glue on the head, I removed it and placed the affected areas in boiling water for 10-15 seconds. Then working on one small area at a time, peeled as much glue as possible. If it will not peel up using your fingernails, you may need a scraper. I use an X-acto® knife with a flat scraping blade. Work gently, as warm plastic is prone to cuts. Work the scraper under the glue as mush as possible without pushing it to the point of breakage (NOT fun to remove) and gently lift. Re-dip into the hot water as necessary, and re-heat the water as necessary. It may take a while, but it works.

Kim Burie: I buy a lot of used dolls and collectibles, and sometimes they come to me smelling less than appealing. Febreeze® works well to take out musty or smoky smells in dolls and doll clothing, even doll boxes. When I am worried about spotting or staining an item with the Febreeze®, I spray it onto a piece of paper toweling and place both the item and the paper towel inside a resealable plastic bag. Over time, the smell does come out. Ink marks can be lightened and often removed by covering them

with a benzoyl peroxide based acne cream. Maximum strength works best, and whatever you use, it should be the cream form (not lotion) and it should not be the tinted form. Light ballpoint pen marks may take a week or two, but darker permanent markers can take a few months. I usually put a thick coating of the cream in the area that is stained and put the doll in a closet and forget about her for a while. Every once in a while I will check to see how the process is going. If I scrape any cream off, I replace it with more. I have also successfully treated dolls with minor green ear using this method. I have heard that this is tricky on TNT and mod era dolls because their vinyl may fade along with the marks, so for that reason, I don't recommend it on them.

Joelle Cerfoglia: I use acne cream also. To remove the stains of ink from the vinyl, I use the acne cream Benzac C10®. I put some on the stain and expose it to the sun for two to three hours. If there is still something there, I repeat the operation.

Kathy Van Camp: For ink stains, I first wipe the stain with alcohol with a soft white cloth, which will remove the surface of the stain. Then I put on Oxy 10® and put the doll in the sun on a windowsill. This technique works more quickly. Then I continue putting on a fresh coat of Oxy 10® until the ink disappears. It gets fainter with each application. Replace the Oxy 10® when it dries. The time it takes to remove the ink depends on how long the ink has been on the doll. The longer the ink is on the doll, the deeper it goes into the vinyl and the longer it takes the Oxy 10® to remove the ink. Vinyl is slightly porous and that is why it absorbs stains. You can cover up the doll if you want and just leave the treated area exposed to the sun in order to protect the doll. Also, only use white cloths to cover the doll and to wipe off the Oxy 10®.

Angel Mitchell: For ink and stain removal I use Clearasil®. I simply put it on the doll and put it in a sunny window (covering all parts of the body and head with a paper towel). Change the Clearasil® every few days till the ink is gone. Remove-Zit® will also remove ink but more precaution should be used and the directions need to be followed exactly or damage can result. This is also good for the dreaded green ear. For skin pricks they can be shrunk at times by immersing the affected part in hot water for 10 seconds and allowed to cool. This doesn't work all the time, but I've had good results on the older dolls.

Zena Myall: I've tried everything from Clearasil® to Remo-Zit® to try and clear up green ear and remove permanent ink marks from vinyl dolls and nothing has really "worked" until I found this new stuff called "Grunge Gone®." To my knowledge, the lady who sells it is not on-line, but I told her if it works, I will advertise it for her because that's the way I am. Anyway, I am currently using it on a vintage bubble cut with terrible green ear. I've put it on one ear only and in just one week, it is half as dark as the other side. I also used it on a doll with an ink mark on her cheek. It is at least half-faded already.

Kim Burie: Loctite® Super Bonder Instant Adhesive glue can be used to repair neck splits. Other super glues may possibly work as well, but Loctite® was recommended to me by a professional restorationist, so that is what I use. Put the head onto the body and apply the glue to the edge of the vinyl that needs to be rejoined. Press the edges together and hold until they are dry. Use a fine sandpaper to

smooth the edges and remove the excess glue. Be aware that if you remove the head from the body again, the split will reopen and you will have to do the repair again. The glue can also be used to repair rips and splits in the leg vinyl in the same manner. To repair pinpricks in the face, put a dot of glue on the hole and let it dry. Again using fine sandpaper smooth out the area. This technique might also help with bite marks although I have not tried it yet.

Anke Scharfenberger: When the head of your doll shakes all the time (you may have a very friendly doll but it doesn't look very elegant). :-) You can put some tape around the pin in the doll's head or you can carefully remove the pin. For smashed or bitten hands and feet you can try to remodel it by holding the hand/foot in boiling water.

Jim Faraone: To get rid of musty smells on your dolls, place kitty litter into the bottom of a plastic container. Then lay the doll or clothes on a piece of foil on top of the kitty litter and seal the container. Leave this for a few weeks and the kitty litter should absorb the odors. Also, if you have tiny paper products that go with your dolls and they are slowly being eaten by those invisible bugs, just place the items in a resealable plastic bag along with a dog's flea collar. Seal it up for about a month and you should see the decay of the papers end.

Kathy Van Camp: Usually any strong cleaners/soaps can be used to clean vinyl. However, products containing ammonia and chlorine can set some stains. A soft toothbrush can be used to get into small places. Baby oil put on a doll and wiped off will help restore old, dry vinyl and restore moisture. It helps to put this on after you clean a doll with alcohol or strong soaps since they tend to dry out the vinyl a little. A doll restorer also told me to use Johnson Kitchen Wax®, but I haven't found the stuff to even try it yet. She said that's what

she uses for older vinyl. Be careful of petroleum-based cleaners though.

Carol Jones: If you have a doll with a wobbly head (usually due to taking the head off to root hair or eyelashes and stretching the vinyl), try taking the head off, use a hair dryer (cover the doll's hair with your hand or a towel so that it won't melt), and work the vinyl neck opening together by pinching it. I usually blast it with a hair dryer, then pinch it together all around, blast, pinch, and so forth until it is a tiny bit smaller. This usually occurs when the head was not heated enough when it was taken off of the doll. This method also works well with loose arms and legs.

Lynn K. Johnson: I stored some Barbie® dolls in the basement for a couple of years and discovered one had developed gangrene on one thigh. Observed that the green was part and parcel of the plastic and didn't want to bother with stain and removers to lighten the green. Since this is a relatively easy spot to cover with clothing, I decided to send the patient to the plastic surgery table. This method is drastic, yet it gets the green out without the concern of a re-appearance. Take a craft knife and cut the green out. There is no need to make a deep incision. A shallow scrape to completely remove the green is all that is necessary. Fill the hole in with plastic modeling compound for plastic model making, and let dry. Lightly sand the rough surface with fine grit sandpaper and mix liquid acrylic paint to match the body color and seal it with a matte fixative.

Jim Faraone: Restoring flea market and garage sale dolls to create fashion doll makeovers can be challenging and fun. But if you want to restore a vintage doll in your collection, I would first seek out a professional in restoration rather than experiment yourself.

Crocheting

Crocheting outfits for dolls has come a long way since our grandmothers and great-grandmothers crocheted those little outfits for our baby dolls. Yes, we all remember those bathrooms in the 50's and 60's with crocheted dolls sitting on just about everyone's toilet tanks hiding the toilet tissue. Let the experts share with you just how far this technique has come over the years.

Kim Burie: The key to success with crocheted fashions for dolls is the fit. Take the time to work out a gauge swatch before you start the pattern. If your gauge is off, keep trying (using different hook sizes) until it's right. Only after you have the gauge right, should you start the pattern. When you work on a gown, keep your doll right beside you and try the dress on her after every few rows to make sure your gauge is still true, and make any adjustments in your crocheting pattern as necessary. I have very easy tension, and I still find I have to make adjustments at times. It is better to constantly check this than to make the whole dress only to find it doesn't fit properly in the end. Blocking a gown when it is finished really makes a big difference, and is definitely worth doing. I do not use any sort of starch or stiffener since I don't know what the long term affects of those products will be (I have heard they can sometimes yellow over time), and most of my crocheted fashion doll costumes are sewn directly onto the doll, and so they can't be easily cleaned. I put the dress on the doll, put the doll on a sheet of Styrofoam® insulation, spray the dress lightly with water and use rust-proof pins to hold the edges of the dress to the foam. I also use the pins to hold any trims in place. Those get pinned to other parts of the costume. To shape sleeves of other dimensional parts, I stuff them lightly with plastic wrap. After this is all dry, I remove the pins and the doll costume is nicely finished and shaped.

Barb Alexander: I use rayon thread for a lot of my design work so here is my tip for using it in case anyone might be interested. When crocheting with rayon thread, as it is very slippery so wrap it about 3 times around your little finger for control. If you lay your work down, put a small safety pin in the last loop to keep the thread from unraveling, as the rayon will work itself loose and come un-done. When designing with crochet thread and you have no pattern to follow, make your foundation chain and then as you work each row, put it to the doll and be sure it is looks the way you want it and that it fits. Count stitches carefully so each side of the outfit balances out. Otherwise it is very easy to get one side longer or wider than the other side.

Pamela Bachmayer: Use sewing thread to crochet to scale for the Barbie® doll. Double strands of sewing thread also work wonderfully for the Gene® doll. Do not use a crochet hook that is too small or the stitches will be too tight and difficult to work with. The result of the fabric will also be stiff. For really quick work, and a pretty and loose weave, use the larger size hooks such as a G or F size hook. The fabric will be very flexible and not look like crochet stitches at all. This is very effective with metallic threads.

Stephani Knutson: Jim, can I share an original dress pattern based on a dress made by my aunt?

Jim Faraone: You sure can, Stephani! That would be wonderful!

Stephani Knutson: Let me give you all some abbreviations first. ch=chain, sc=single crochet, dc=double crochet, tc=treble crochet, st=stitch and beg=beginning. To increase, 2 dc in one st. **Bodice:** Starting at the waist, ch 28. **Rnd 1:** dc in 4th ch from the hook and in each st across. (26). **Rnd 2:** ch 3 (counts as first dc from now on), turn. dc in each st across. (26). **Rnd 3:** ch 3, dc across increasing every 5th dc (remember to count beg ch 3 as 1st dc), dc in last 6 dc. (30). **Rnd 4:** ch 3, turn. dc across increasing every 5th dc, dc in last 5 dc. (35). **Rnd 5:** ch 3, turn. dc across increasing every 5th dc, dc in last 6 dc. (41). **Rnd 6:** ch 3, turn, dc in next 15 dc. 3 dc in next dc. dc in next 6 dc. 3 dc in next dc. dc in last 17 dc. (45). **Rnd 7:** ch 3, turn. dc 17, 3 dc in next dc, dc 8, 3 dc in next dc. dc in each remaining dc. (49). **Make arm holes: Rnd 8:** ch 1, turn. sc in the next 5 dc, ch 15. Skip next 17 dc, sc in next 4dc, chain 15, skip next 17 dc, sc in next 5 dc. (44). **Rnd 9:** ch 1, turn. sc in the next 5 sc, dc in each ch, dc in next 4 sc, dc in each chain, sc in last 5 sc. (44). **Rnd 10:** ch 1, turn. skip next 5 sc, (tc, ch 1, tc, ch 1) in each dc across. Slip st in last sc. Fasten off. **Skirt:** With bodice waist at top, join thread to first space of bodice row 1. **Rnd 1:** Ch 5, tc, ch 1 in same space as joining, (tc, ch 1, tc, ch 1) in next and each ch 1 space across. (tc, ch 1, tc) in last ch 1 space. (50 tc). **Rnd 2:** ch 5, turn. (tc, ch 1) in each ch 1 space across. tc in last tc. Join to 4th ch of beg ch 5. (50 tc). **Rnd 3:** Repeat Rnd 2. (50 tc). **Rnd 4:** ch 6, turn. (tc, ch 2) in each ch 1 space across. Join to 4th ch of beg ch 6. (51 tc). **Rnds 5-9:** ch 6, turn. (tc, ch 2) in each ch 2 space across. Join to 4th ch of beg ch 6. (56 tc at end of rnd 9). **Rnd 10:** ch 6, turn. *(tc, ch 2) in each of next 2 ch 2 spaces. (tc, ch 2, tc, ch 2) in next ch 2 space. Repeat from * across. (tc, ch 2) in last ch 2 space. (tc, ch 2) in same space as beg ch 6. Join to 4th ch of beg ch 6. (76 tc) **Rnds 11-14:** ch 6, turn. (tc, ch 2) in each ch 2 space across. Join to 4th ch of beg ch 6. (80 tc at end of rnd 14). **Rnd 15:** ch 4, turn, dc in next ch 2 space. *ch 1, dc in next tc, ch 1, dc in next ch 2 space. Repeat from * across. ch 1 and join to 3rd ch of first ch 4. (160 tc). **Rnd 16:** ch 3, turn. dc in each stitch across. Join to 3th ch of beg ch 3. Fasten off. (320 tc). **Finishing:** Sew 2 snaps on either side of back opening to fasten.

Vicki Young: When selecting crochet threads or yarns to use for crocheting fashion doll-size outfits, I recommend threads/yarns equivalent to size 10 or smaller. This ensures that the crochet stitches are scaled down, which makes the outfit finer and more delicate looking. If you use thread larger than this, the outfit can tend to look bulky, fat and unfitting. Don't be afraid to experiment with different threads other than just cotton. I have found some threads (e.g. eyelash, metallics, nylons, etc.) that give the outfit an exciting and unique finish. Try crocheting with different techniques (e.g. pearls, beads, pom-poms, buttons, sequins, etc.) I think stringing materials such as these onto crochet thread and crocheting them right into the gown can give a very unusual and elegant finish. I think it many times looks nicer than if you would have hand-sewn them onto the gown afterward. Sometimes stringing beads onto crochet thread can be difficult because it is not easy to find a needle whose eye is large enough with crochet thread, yet small enough for the bead to pass over. When this occurs, I use a small (approximately 4in [10cm]) wire instead of a needle. I take the wire, fold it in half, and begin twisting the two ends together tightly, leaving a small loop at the folded end which acts as an eye. Then thread the crochet thread through the eye loop and begin stringing beads. After I finish a crochet piece, I always fray check the first and last crochet stitch. This adds an extra prevention against your crochet stitches unraveling. Sometimes I want my fashion doll to hold an item in her hand. To attach the crocheted accessory (e.g. purse, umbrella, muff, etc.,) I start by threading and knotting a needle with matching thread. I fit the accessory into the doll's hand and take a small stitch from the back of the accessory close to the hand. I pull the thread up through the accessory to the front and through the ring finger of the doll (the doll may have a ready-made hole, but if not, just create one with your needle.) I then string on a small, matching pearl or bead and pass the needle back through the ring hole (the pearl/bead should catch on the front of the hand and appear like a ring's stone. Pull tightly and pass the needle back through the accessory from front to back and knot off. The accessory is attached with no threads showing. In addition, the doll now has a matching ring for her finger. I have seen many nicely crocheted outfits and accessories that do not appear finished or professionally made because they are crumpled or wrinkled and have not held their shape. One thing I cannot emphasize enough is to finish your crochet work by shaping your outfit. You do this by using a blocking or stiffening product. You can find these products (which can be diluted to be different strengths by adding water) in any craft or fabric stores. I usually dress the doll in the crocheted outfit before I starch it. Once the doll is dressed, I stand the doll on a 12in x 12in (31cm x 31cm) piece of plastic-wrapped cardboard that I then place on a lazysusan. Then I shape the entire outfit and, if necessary,

pin the skirt to the cardboard. Once the entire outfit looks just like I want, I use one of the following techniques to stiffen it. Inside a spray bottle, I mix the stiffener with water to the strength that I want. Then I can carefully spray the outfit where I want the stiffening to hold the shape, or I mix the stiffening solution inside a bowl and use a small sponge to dab the area I want stiffened. I then let the doll's entire outfit dry overnight. Another way that I keep the doll's floor length skirt in shape is to place the doll in a pillow form, sized and shaped to the skirt. This provides an additional foundation under the skirt and also eliminates the need for a doll stand. Pillow form patterns can be found in the crochet section of your craft or fabric stores.

Jim Faraone: If you're really interested in learning about how to crochet (or in Beth's case knitting,) there are many books on the market that will get you started. Learning a new craft is always an enjoyable experience, which leads you down the road to creative excitement.

Barb Alexander: Jim, would it be okay if I also shared? It's one of my copyrighted crochet patterns from one of my pattern books I create? It's for a swimsuit, sarong, cover up top and scrunchie.

Jim Faraone: That would be great, Barb. We all appreciate that!

Barb Alexander: This one I call "Beach Time Fun". **Materials**: 150 yds size 10 crochet cotton, variegated pink; 150 yds 10 crochet cotton, white; 4 small

snaps; small rubber band about ½in (1cm); 50 3mm silver beads, these are used for earrings, finger ring and scrunchie; steel crochet hook size 7 or size needed for gauge. **Gauge:** 9 dc = 1in (3cm); 4 dc rows = 1in (3cm). **Swimsuit:** Starting at the waist for the swimsuit bottom portion. **Row 1:** With pink, ch 26, sc in 2nd ch from hook and each remaining ch across, ch 1, turn. **Row 2:** Sc in each st across, ch 2, turn. **Row 3:** 2 dc in next st, * in next st, 2 dc in next st; repeat from * across, ending with dc in last st, ch 1, turn. (40 sts). **Row 4:** Sc in each st across, ch 2, turn. (40 sts). **Row 5:** Dc in each st across, join with sl st in top of beg ch-2. **Note:** You will now be working in rounds instead of rows. **Rnd 6:** Ch 1, turn, sc in each st around, ch 2, turn. **Rnd 7:** Dc in each st around, join with sl st in top of ch-2, turn. **Rnd 8:** Ch 1, sc in each st around, join. **Rnd 9:** Ch 2, dc in each st around, join. (40 sts). **Rnd 10:** Working now in rows for crotch, st st in each of the next 2 sts, ch 6, skip next 15 sts, join with a sc in next st, ch 1, turn. **Row 11:** Sc in each of the next 2 sts of rnd 9, ch 1, turn. **Row 12:** Sc in the 6 sts of rnd 10 across crotch piece catching both loops, sc in each of next 2 sts on rnd 9, ch 1, turn. **Row 13:** Sc back across crotch piece, sl st in same st as last ch-1 made, cut thread and finish off. **Top of Suit:** With right side of bottom towards you, join with sl st in first ch st of beg ch-28. **Row 1:** Ch 1, sc in same st as joining, sc in each st across, ch 1, turn. **Rows 2 to 5:** Sc in each st across, ch 1, turn. **Row 6:** Sc in each st across, 2 sc in last st, ch 1, turn. **Row 7:** Sc in next 7 sts, (2 sc in next st, sc in next 3 sts) 3 times, 2 sc in next st, sc in next 7 sts, ch 1, turn. (31 sts). **Row 8:** Sc in next 8 sts, 2 sc in next st, sc in net 13 sts, 2 sc in next st, sc in next 8 sts, ch 1, turn. (33 sts). **Row 9:** Sc in each st across, ch 1, turn. **Row 10:** Sc in next 8 sts, 2 sc in next st, sc in next 15 sts, 2 sc in next st, sc in next 8 sts, ch 1, turn. (35 sts). **Row 11:** Repeat row 9. **Row**

12: Sc in next 8 sts, 2 sc in next st, sc in next 17 sts, 2 sc in next st, sc in next 8 sts, ch 1, turn. (37 sts). **Row 13:** Repeat row 9. **Row 14:** Sc in first st, 2 sc in next st, sc in next 13 sts, skip next st, 10 dc in next st, skip next st, sc in next 13 sts, 2 sc in next st, sc in last st, ch 1, turn. **Row 15:** Sc in next 15 sts, skip next st, dc in next 9 sts, sc in next st, dc in next 9 sts, skip net st, sc in next 16 sts, ch 1, turn (50 sts). **Row 16:** Sc in next 14 sts, skip next st, dc in next 9 sts, sl st tightly in next st, dc in next 9 sts, skip next st, sc in next 14 sts, ch 1, turn. (47 sts). **Row 17:** Sc in each st across to sl st (47 sc), sl st very tightly in sl st, sc in each st across to end, cut thread and finish off. Sew 3 sets of snaps on. **Sarong: Row 1:** With white, ch 29, sc in 2nd ch from hook and each remaining ch across, ch 2, turn. **Row 2:** Dc in first st, *2 dc in next st, dc in next st; repeat from * across, ch 1, turn. (41 sts). **Row 3:** Sc in each st across, ch 2, turn. **Row 4:** Dc first 2 sts tog, dc in each st across, ch 2, turn. **Row 5:** Sc in each st across to last st, sl st in last st, ch 2, turn. **Row 6:** Repeat row 4. (38 sts). **Row 7:** Repeat row 5. **Row 8:** Repeat row 4. **Row 9:** Repeat row 5. **Row 10:** Repeat row 4. **Row 11:** Sc in next 13 sts, 2 sc in each of next 2 sts, sc in each st to end, ch 2, turn. **Row 12:** Repeat row 4. **Row 13:** Sc in next 17 sts, 2 sc in each of next 2 sts, sc in each st to end, ch 2, turn. **Row 14:** Dc un same st as turning, 2 dc in each st across, ch 2, turn. **Rows 15 to 16:** Repeat row 14, at end, cut thread and finish off. **Ruffle: Row 1:** Join pink with sl st top of right side at waist (this is the curved side that has the decreasing sts), *ch 3, sc in post of dc st next row down, ch 3, sc in post of sc st next row down; repeat from * down side until you reach the bottom edge of ruffle, **ch 3, skip next st, sc in next st; repeat from ** across bottom edge of ruffle to left side, ch 3, turn, do not work up the left side of sarong in this row. **Row 2:** Sc in first ch-3 space, *ch 3, sc in next sc, ch 3, sc in next ch-3 space; repeat from * to beginning of row 1, sc in joining sl st of row 1, ch 3, turn. **Row 3:** Sc in first ch-3 space, *ch 3, sc in next sc, ch 3, sc in next ch-3 space; repeat from * to beginning st of row 2, sl st in beginning sc of row 2, sc up left front edge by putting one sc in each sc row and 2 sc in each dc row, cut thread and finish off. Sew snap at waist. **Cover Up Top: Row 1:** With white, ch 41, sc in 2nd ch from hook and each remaining ch across, ch 1, turn. (40sc). **Row 2:** Sc in each st across, ch 2, turn. (40 sts). **Row 3:** Dc in each st across, ch 2, turn. (40 sts). **Rows 4 to 5:** Repeat row 3. **Row 6:** Dc in each st across, cut white, join pink, ch 2, turn. **Row 7:** Dc in each st across, ch 2, turn. **Rows 8 to 9:** Repeat row 7. **Row 10:** Dc in each st across, cut pink, join white, ch 2, turn. **Row 11:** Dc in each st across, ch 2, turn. **Working Left Front: Row 12:** Dc in next 10 sts, ch 2, turn. **Row 13:** Dc in next 8 sts, ch 2, turn. **Row 14:** Dc next 2 sts tog, dc in next 6 sts, ch 2, turn. **Row 15:** Dc in next 4 sts, cut thread and finish off. **Working Back: Row 16:** With wrong side facing you, skip 3 sts on row 11, join with sl st in next st, ch 2, dc in next 11 sts, ch 2, turn. **Row 17:** Dc in same st as turning, dc in next 11 sts, 2 dc in last st, ch 2, turn. **Row 18:** Dc in each dc across, ch 2, turn. (14 dc). **Row 19:** Dc in next st, hdc in next 3 sts, sc in next 5 sts, hdc in next 3 sts, dc in last 2 sts, cut thread and finish off. **Working Right Front: Row 20:** With wrong side facing you, skip 3 sts on row 11, join with sl st in next st, ch 1, dc in next 10 sts, ch 2, turn. **Row 21:** Dc next 2 sts tog, dc in next 8 sts, ch 2, turn. **Row 22:** Dc in next 6 sts, ch 2,

turn. **Row 23:** Dc next 2 sts tog, dc in next 4 sts, cut thread and finish off. Use a tapestry needle and sew front sides to back at shoulder seam. **Ruffle: Row 1:** With pink, join with sl st at bottom right front, ch 1, sc in same st as joining, sc in each st around, work sc in each sc row and 2 sc in each dc row, join with sl st in first sc, turn. **Row 2:** *Ch 3, skip next st, sc in next st; repeat from * across bottom, up the left front, and around the neck, sl st in last st at front right edge, ch 3, turn. **Row 3:** Skip ch-3 space, *sc in next sc, ch 3, sc in next ch-3 space; repeat from * to bottom of right front, sl st in last st, cut thread and finish off. **Scrunchie:** String more beads on thread then you could possibly need. **Rnd 1:** Attach thread around rubber band with a sl st. Ch 1, sc in same st as sl st. Sc all around rubber band getting sts as close as possible to each other. Number of sts will vary according to size of rubber band. Sl st to first sc to join. Ch 1, DO NOT TURN. **Rnd 2:** Sc in same st as ch1, *bring up a bead, ch 2, sk1 st, sc in next st. * repeat between *'s all around. Sl st to first sc to join, Ch 1, DO NOT TURN. **Rnd 3:** Sc in same st as ch1, *bring up a bead, ch2, sc in next ch loop* (being sure that you attach sc on the LEFT side of the bead) Repeat between *'s all around. Sl st in sc to join, ch1. DO NOT TURN. **Rnd 4:** Sc in same st as ch1, *bring up a bead, ch2, sc in next ch loop* (Being sure you attach sc on the RIGHT side of the bead) repeat between *'s all around. End off. Depending on size of rubber band you might want to twist it twice around dolls' hair to hold.

Jim Faraone: Thank you, Barb, and crocheting sure has some interesting codes! Ever think about working for the FBI? LOL!

Stephani Knutson: Whether you are new to crocheting or not, get a good crochet technique book. Start with a simple pattern, which you can find many on the Internet. I prefer to use crochet thread, but many people prefer to use yarn. If you are new to crocheting, a simple yarn pattern may be best. They work up much more quickly. Like Kim mentioned, keep a doll close by and try on the outfit as you go. If you get the bodice done and it is too tight, add fastening tabs on each side of the back opening by single crocheting across the rows, turn and single crochet in each stitch across until the bodice fits. You can create your own unique fashions by using full-size patterns as guides. Many full-size knit or crochet patterns have line drawings of the separate parts that are very close to the Barbie® doll size. Use a small crochet hook and single strands of yarn or cotton thread and follow the basic pattern directions decreasing the number of stitches and/or rows to match the line drawings. Be sure to make the neck opening large enough to go over the doll's head if the pattern does not have a front or back opening. Another way to create a unique fashion is to combine patterns—for example, a bodice from one pattern and a skirt from a doily pattern. Simply crochet the bodice as usual. Then, increase the number of stitches at the waist to match the number of stitches from a row on a doily pattern that looks like a good place to start (usually row 3 or 4) and continue the doily pattern from there.

Tips, Tips, Tips

Most of the time we have freebie days for the group where they can throw out any tip ideas that they may have. Honestly, our Yahoogroup™ list is not as regimented as this book shows and we actually get to chat about anything and everything we'd like on any given day. Questions are asked and questions are answered each and everyday of the year!

Everyone can always use tips, and the more tips you discover, the better. Throwing out ideas is like brainstorming at a business meeting. You never know when one tip will lead to another and the cycle goes on.

Kathy Van Camp: I know a way to make it easier to remove a doll's head. A while back I wanted to replace the eyes in a Chatty Cathy® doll and everyone told me to just take the head off and cut open the eye sockets, replace the eyes and glue the cut back together. I didn't like the idea of damaging the eye sockets, so I took a blow dryer and heated the vinyl around the eyes and popped them right out. To put new ones in, I heated up the eye sockets again and pushed the eyes back in right through the front of the face. I also take heads off of dolls in the same way. By heating around the neck, the vinyl gets softer and stretches so much more easily. It also helps to keep the vinyl from splitting on the older dolls. I tried it on an old Barbie® doll just now and it works really well.

Jim Faraone: Heat does help Kathy. **(see step 1)** On a low warm setting, heat the base of the doll's head with a hair dryer (you should cover the hair to protect it from melting in case you forget and use a high heat on it.) **(see step 2)** Some work the head around till it pops off, but at times I use a blunt object such as a butter knife to gently pry off the doll's head **(see step 3)**.

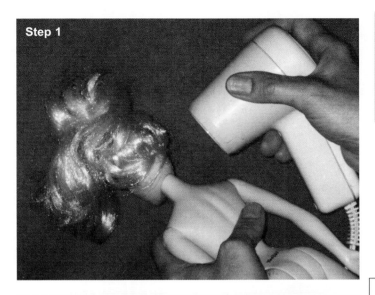

Step 1

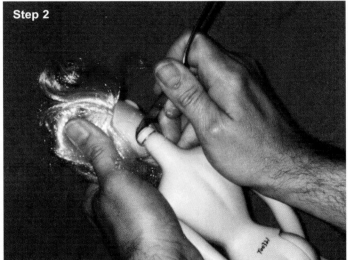

Step 2

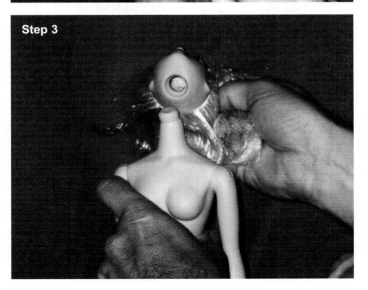

Step 3

Joyce Marie La Fave: Thanks for the tip Kathy and Jim! Until now, I've been just closing my eyes, counting to ten and saying a Hail Mary while removing and doll's head!

Jim Faraone: Another great tip for removing heads when you're not sure what kind of neck knob is involved—just take a flashlight and hold it against the doll's head and at times it illuminates the inside of the head so you can see the outline of what type of neck knob you have to deal with.

Brad Jensen: I found an easy way to remove my doll's heads. I put the head in boiling water (making sure to keep as much of the hair out of the water as possible) and then removing it by working it carefully around the prongs. This works for all dolls since heat seems to be the secret weapon in working with the vinyl.

Zena Myall: I have a tip for removing heads also. For the newer dolls with the butterfly clip inside the neck, I take a very thin, blunt knife and gently slide it up the back of the neck of the doll, inside the head, and then carefully try to find one side of the butterfly clip, push down on it and slide the head off over the knife. I cut the butterfly clips off about halfway up to keep the head from being loose when I put it back on.

Sandy Mahan: Being a senior citizen and keeping my nails real short, I use a mouse pad to hold straight pins and needles. The pointy things can go in only so far so it's easier to pick them out when you are trying to hold something together and only have one hand to use.

Rachel Steinberger: All of us love starting projects, but if you're like me, finishing them is an entirely different matter. To prevent huge piles of half-finished dolls from stacking up in my workspace, I keep a list of all my in-progress dolls. The trick is I never allow more than 25 items on that list at a time. If I have 25 projects going on, then I have to finish one before I can start another project. Like diets, this trick only works if you don't cheat! ;-)

William Stewart Jones: Instead of plugging in an iron, I "iron" ribbon by running it back and forth over a light bulb. Be sure to test first since some synthetic ribbons can melt.

Kert Hoogstraat: When getting ready for a major show, try doing tasks in "batches". Do five basic ensemble constructions, then do the hair for all five dolls and then do the facial repainting, etc. It keeps things flowing and you will achieve a "look" that is unique to that group of dolls. Try to find a signature statement that can be included in every piece you do. Plus, no task is ever wasted. Even if you spend hours on a row of beading only to have it all tragically fall apart, learn the lesson and move on to the next doll.

Sheryl Majercin: Don't wrestle with tiny glass or seed beads. They can be bought on the "hank" at most bead supply stores. A hank is a group of pre-strung beads on a temporary string.

Joanna Bond: Rescue dolls from garage sales, flea markets and thrift stores. You'll be giving an old toy new life and spending less money. Your mistakes may not be as disastrous and you never know what you may find. Don't be afraid to use an unknown or non-Barbie® doll. The Barbie® doll is not only overused, but she's very recognizable. No matter how you dress her or do her hair, the Barbie® doll will still look like the Barbie® doll. If you want to make up a new character, use a different doll or do some creative work to change her looks substantially. If it looks like something that Mattel™ would make, potential buyers might just opt for Mattel™ instead.

Kim Burie: The Internet is an incredible way to meet people who seem just like you, and also nothing like you. Both are good things. I have been on the Internet since August 1996 and I have made so many good friends, and also I have learned so much. If you can't find a local doll club (and you don't want to start one) you can join one on the Internet. If you need to thin out your doll collection (or add to it) you can do it through the Internet. I don't know what I'd do without it now.

Carolyn Marnon: I agree with you Kim. The Internet is a great place to make new fashion doll friends. There are many people out there who are willing to share their tips and ideas so generously. It is easy to learn with such wonderful folks lending their support to the newcomers. There are web pages full of information. If you can't find the information, there is usually someone who knows the answer. All you have to do is ask.

Amy Nardone: Don't be afraid to try new things. How do you know if you are good at it if you never try. Also don't be afraid to ask about tips from other artists. Most of them will be more than willing to help you along. Don't get discouraged.

Steph Gazell: That's true Amy and one should never, never compare the work they're doing with the work of other artists you admire and aspire to. It will drive you CRAZY! Your work will probably never look like theirs even when you are skilled and have lots of experience, so why set yourself up for disappointment from the get-go? Start fresh with your own vision, which for me means creating as you go, and seeing what the face becomes as it is created. This may not work well for seasoned artists, but for beginners, it's less painful than trying to do work as lovely as some of the more experienced artists. Keep it as simple and as clean as possible. Detail will come in time.

Joanna Bond: If you're working with an X-acto® or other sharp implement, and you hear yourself mutter, "I'm going to cut myself," you probably are. Replace the blade if it's not sharp and reset your senses, paying attention to where the blade is pointing, where your fingers are and how fast you are going. Be careful!

Joyce Marie La Fave: I like to use floral plastic sheaves to slip over the dolls while I'm working to protect their face, hair and clothing from dust. This still keeps them easily accessible. The floral plastic sheaves can be acquired at the grocery store in the plant and flower department. They are clear and cone shaped in 2 sizes—one that is perfect for the Barbie® doll and one for 15in (38cm) and 16in (41cm) dolls. These are free depending on how you get along with your local store employees. LOL!

Pat Feick: To make a wooden stand for dolls, craft stores sell small wood plaques and turned dowels. Drill a hole in the stand, insert the dowel, paint and seal. This is a stand similar to the plastic stands that come with a lot of dolls.

Michele Frazee-Jackson: I have recently begun doing some different bases for some of my fantasy creations. Since I haven't learned (yet) how to use power tools, I have found some really nice wooden bases (plaques) at artist/craft stores. These can be painted, stained and decorated in a myriad of ways to complement the doll that either sits or stands on them. For example, a fantasy fairy creation can be displayed on a stand that has a rose garland positioned along with a small basket of flowers. It makes for a nice setting to display the doll.

Vonda Silliman: To make a decorative base for a doll, **(Step 1)** cover a Kaiser® stand with Aleene's® tacky glue. **(Step 2)** Then glue on some moss or a selection of **(Step 3)** decorative flowers, pine cones, ribbons, etc. that can be purchased at any craft store. To save a few dollars, buy these decorations after the holidays when they are on sale.

Jim Faraone: During and after the holiday seasons are a great time for buying unique things for your dolls, Vonda. I especially like the Halloween season. There are lots of little accessory type things that can work well with your dolls. Christmas with all the trims and bows is also a perfect season to find goodies to decorate your dolls. Just set your mind in doll mode and not holiday mode when shopping at those times. Maybe a cheap, rotating music box could turn into a revolving stand for your dolls. I saw some wonderful beaded garland that had beautiful gold beadcaps on all the red beads. The garland was only $8 and there must have been a good 200 bead caps on it. It's $2 just for 4 beadcaps at craft stores.

William Stewart Jones: You can dye lamé, mylar trims and different fabrics in the same boiling Rit® dye bath to tie them all together and help the colors match. Some metallics won't change color, but the fibres woven with them will take the color. One piece of silver and white fabric can become several different colors. You can also dye sequins, pearls, some plastics, and sequin trims so everything matches on your creations or at least "relates" in terms of color.

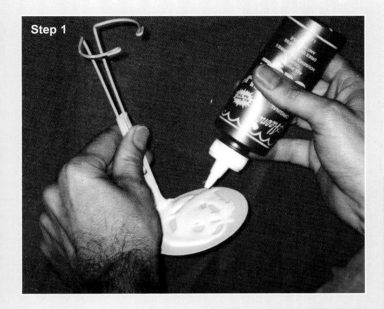

Step 1

Step 2

Step 3

Kim Burie: To pierce the ears of dolls that come with no earring holes, heat up any needle or pin (although I like to use something that is a bit thicker than a sewing needle, like an embroidery needle or a corsage pin) over a candle flame. Poke it through the ear in the desired spot. The heat makes the needle go in so much easier.

Loanne Hizo Ostlie: When doing molded hair, I use Susan Scheewe's Blue Masking Fluid® and paint that all over the face as close to the scalp as possible. After molding the hair, I just peel that off and the face paint is still intact. I also use this product on other areas of the doll that I don't want to get messed up. It's like a protective coat.

William Stewart Jones: Don't reverse the natural order of colors. For example, yellow is lighter than purple, so dark yellow and light purple are probably not good together. To gray or soften a color, mix some of its compliment into it. The compliment is the color opposite on the color wheel.

Dorothy Fannin: I have two uses for old doll boxes. I use the plastic for templates to cut my hat patterns and patterns from magazines. I also clip the doll pictures and name and store them with the fashions in a plastic bag.

Michelle James: Wow, I spent an hour sorting fabric on Monday! I sorted by color, and got my method from the lady at Wal-Mart®. She put the fabric I bought in one of those big resealable freezer bags. I usually buy about ¼yd to ½yd (.23cm–.46cm) so several pieces fit into one bag. It sure is better than what I had before. My fabric was tumbling through one of those huge Rubbermaid® bins and literally overflowing. Now all my scraps are on the bottom, the boas and marabou are all in the middle and the resealable bags with color-coordinated fabrics are all on top. Now my bin looks nice and neat.

Sarah Worley: I also use resealable bags to put material and accessories together as well as pattern pieces for a particular outfit. Those big 2-gallon bags work well for shipping dolls, too. I've found that I can carry a doll to work (for show and tell) in one of the bags and her hair doesn't even get messed up. They're great for transporting as well as storing.

William Stewart Jones: The BEST way to sort your fabrics is to throw them out of the window. Whatever blows away in the wind is too small to keep! LOL!

Carol Jones: For bridals, I tend to buy a lot of white antique lace and tulle. When I need off-white, I dye the white items in tea. You just take a glass, bowl or other container and fill it with hot water. Take a tea bag (don't use a fruity or chamomile tea! Plain old Lipton® in the red and yellow packaging is the best!) and dip it into the hot water a few times to color the water. Don't leave the tea bag in the water! Soak your white items in the tea water for about ten minutes (also depends on how "off-white" you need it). Take them out and rinse well, but do not use soap. Let dry by hanging over your shower door or wherever you can put them so that your cat doesn't try to play with it like mine does. If it is too light, repeat the procedure. If it's too dark, use dishwashing liquid soap and wash well. If still too dark you can usually bleach them out and try again. Most notions will work well using this method. Fabrics work well, but some may not take to the tea, or it might streak because of the creasing when it is put in the tea water. I have used this method a lot and have always gotten great results! Incidentally, this is the method Marilyn Monroe used to dye her veil when she married Arthur Miller!

Boo-Boos

Confess! We've all made those boo-boos while creating and that's normal. It happens! You deal with it and then laugh at your mistakes. If it weren't for mistakes, none of us would have learned what we have. Trial and error always comes with creating and it's nothing to be ashamed of. Without making boo-boos, we'd stand still and not progress and it sure would be boring chatting with one another about our creations. As a matter of fact, be proud of those boo-boos.....I am!

Barbara Fowler: I wanted to make a different doll that involved building up parts of the head and thought sculp-epox would be great. It's a two part sculpting material we use in doll repair so I was familiar with the fact that it attaches well and paints very well. Well, it's like epoxy glue and you need equal parts mixed together well. Usually my husband mixes it because he's more patient than I am. I want to get right into things. He was out of town, so I mixed it and made my additions. Well, I was pretty impressed with myself and it looked great! It's supposed to dry in 24 hours so I checked it the next day and it was still wet. A week later....still wet. A month later.....still wet. So, my advice is to follow the directions exactly and take your time!!!

J'Amy Pacheco: How much damage can a paper towel do? I found out the hard way when I decided to remove the acrylic paint from a freshly-painted set of doll lips. I wet the paper towel, and began to wipe the pink lip paint from the doll's mouth. As the pink paint wiped away, a green tint appeared around the doll's mouth. The more I rubbed, the worse the green tint became. I finally realized (duh!) that the paper towel was printed with a few tiny green flowers, and the ink from the flowers was staining the doll's face.

Carolyn Marnon: One time, I did not put enough attention into choosing the doll for an idea I had. I ended up having to make my own shoes for her. I used a Hula Hair Barbie® doll to make a Candy Corn Confection for a Halloween swap one year. Her hair had yellow, orange and pink streaks in it that were perfect for my idea. I had the doll dressed and all I had to do was add her shoes. I then discovered that these dolls have flat feet. I had to try to make shoes for her and I could only manage to make sandals. This doll taught me never to buy a doll with large flat feet for creating again—unless I plan to have her go barefoot.

Jennifer Hughey: I like using acetone nail polish remover to remove the facial paint on the Gene® doll (her eyebrows have smeared using non-acetone) but I got some on the hard vinyl one time and it really ate the vinyl.

Amy Nardone: I was trying to separate the fingers for a boil job on one of my dolls that I was making for centerpieces for the 1999 Barbie® doll convention and I accidentally chopped off her pinky and part of my finger. I also tried using enamel paints to paint a doll. Big mistake. That was 4 years ago and her lips are still sticky!!!!

William Stewart Jones: Be careful when doing a boil perm. I've melted the hair with the hot edge of the pot.

Scott Shore: It's the same when using a hair dryer, Bill. I really frizzed out one of my dolls in the beginning, but she became my first showgirl. I had to cut off all her hair, and glue gold sequins to her scalp making a skull cap. I also used small pins to keep everything in place.

Jim Faraone: Getting cuts and needle pricks when working on dolls is always a hazard. But have you noticed that whenever you make a bride doll or a doll in a white gown, you are guaranteed to get a cut and get a drop of blood on the white outfit? LOL!

Rachel Steinberger: The first time I tried removing the face paint on a doll, I did exactly what people had told me to do. I used Q-tips® and nail polish remover. Unfortunately, I didn't use enough nail polish remover, so the makeup ended up smearing all over her face. What's more, I was rubbing with the Q-tip® trying to get it off, which was actually just rubbing it in and making a permanent stain. Her face got so dirty that I just had to paint over it entirely with white paint and make her Queen Amidala from Star Wars®! Despite my first disastrous use of nail polish remover on a doll, I decided to try it again. This time I decided to only remove the freckles though, and that part worked great. Unfortunately, I bumped the bottle of nail polish remover and it spilled all over my work surface, including under the doll body and a pair of snipping scissors. In less than 10 seconds, the back of the doll had started to melt and deform (literally, 10 seconds!) I immediately rinsed her off, but her back was permanently scarred with white marks and wrinkles. Maybe I should try this as a way to create cellulite on a doll!

Jim Faraone: Nail polish remover sure can eat things. I taught a class on face painting and bought little plastic cups so everyone could put the nail polish remover in while working on their dolls. Good thing those plastic cups lasted for the hour class, but when I was cleaning up, I noticed that all those little plastic cups were starting to deteriorate and the nail polish remover was beginning to leak! LOL! I guess those little metal artist's cups for linseed oil and things in oil painting is the best way to go.

Natalie Tetzlaff: Remember, if you're creative enough, you can make up for any mistake. Bad hair job? Perfect time to try a short new style, re-rooting, or even molded hair. Paint smear and won't come off? Try something wild, like a total facial repaint, or maybe a tattoo inspired design.

Sharon A. Lawson: I was trying to root eyelashes on a very hard-headed doll. I was trying to push the needle through the eyelid and was squeezing very tightly on the needle and pushing as hard as I could. Finally the needle started to enter, (I thought). When I loosened my grip on the needle to move my fingers up higher on the needle, I discovered the end of the needle with the hair threaded through it had went directly into my finger. Not the doll's head! I didn't even feel it, because I was squeezing the needle so hard. But, as soon as I let loose I felt it!!

Lynn K. Johnson: A customer ordered a devil suit for a Tyler Wentworth® doll complete with cape, tail and horns. Materials I used for the suit was a very stretchy red lycra. I drafted up the suit patterns, cut out the material and sewed it up. The closure I selected was a hook and loop tape for a beautiful sealed back opening. The hook and loop tape was stitched to the suit. I noticed that the hook wanted to grab the lycra, but it wasn't a serious molestation problem. I also used the hook and loop on the belt. I sent the suit and accessories to the customer and got an email back stating that the hook on belt attacked the suit and created a lot of snags. No matter what the customer did the hooks grabbed onto the catsuit and WHAM pulled snags. Imagining the hapless owner in the clutches of a wild hooker on the loose, a simple remedy came to mind with any boo boos, a replacement suit with snaps.

Jim Faraone: When I first started out, an artist told me that with a boil perm, I should boil the water and put the doll's head in the boiling water, turn off the heat and keep the dolls' head in the water till it cools off. What did I get? I got wonderful dolls with 3 foot Afros!!! Frizz City big time!!!

Michele Frazee-Jackson: I had the same thing, Jim. When I first started to learn to customize, I left a doll's hair too long in the freshly boiled water. (I thought if 15 seconds was good, then a minute would be even better). LOL! When completed, she had a really "bad hair day", the permanent turned out extremely fuzzy. Lesson learned: stick to the recommended 15-20 seconds to perm a dolls' hair.

Jim Faraone: I can top that, Michele. I had a friend that wanted to customize me and give ME a perm and thought that if the 30 minutes gave you curly hair then an hour and 45 minutes would give you really curly hair! WRONG!!! Talk about a bad hair day! Oops! Sorry for getting off the topic of dolls! LOL!

Nikki Avery: When I first started rerooting, the only method I knew of was putting hair in from the inside of the head. I was very excited. I had tried it once before and it was hard, but this time I was determined to learn it and be good at it. I sat down at my table with an old Barbie® doll head. I had my needle thread with hair. I thought I would put my first plug of hair into the "bang" area. I pushed the needle through and it came out somewhere in the part line. Hmmmm. I missed. I tried again, this time sending the needle straight through the poor dolly's forehead!! I tried again, and again. You guessed it! I missed the empty plugs EVERY time. Still not entirely discouraged, I decided to try and put some hair in for the eyelashes. I tilted the needle this way and that, all the time wondering where the needle would pop out. I finally pushed it through...right through the doll's eye! After that I decided to find my own way to reroot.

Jim Faraone: Once, I was rerooting a doll's hair and put too much hair into each hair plug and the doll's head actually expanded and distorted.

Kathy Van Camp: When I sew, I always take the thread, lick it and then thread my needle. I was counting out hairs and was so intent on trying to see them to count them, that I put the whole thing in my mouth to wet it before I threaded the needle. I don't know what I was thinking! I had the shorter hairs still in my mouth and it was human hair and I didn't even know whose head it came off of!!! I about gagged! I now have a little cup of water and wet my fingers and run the hair through them to get the entire thing wet. It's easier to thread and then easier to tie the knot if all the hair is wet and sticking together.

Carol Jones: I use a fork (yes, a regular old kitchen fork!) to comb the curls on my doll's hair. The prongs are a good width apart so they don't frizz the hair. I also like to use a flat rubber-tipped cat brush for the straight styles. Well, one day I was doing a boil perm on a Gene® doll and I had just eaten a danish and I set the fork with the plate on the kitchen counter. Well, I was separating the curls with a clean fork, set it down to finger-style, then picked it up again to do a little more separating. I started combing the hair and noticed the raspberry and icing from the danish in the hair! I looked at the fork and realized it was the wrong one!! Now, I put the dirty utensils in the dishwasher or at least in the sink!!

Tracy Lynn Lake: I had done a Rapunzel makeover that I was really excited about. I used full-length straws and wrestled with all of the hair to give her curls. Right before it was time to make the dress, I decided to take her hair out of the "curlers." I had left it there for a couple of days because the kids had distracted me. I used sewing pins to keep the straws in place and had just stuck them into her head as I had with other dolls. This time,

however, not all of the hair was covered with the perm paper and when I started pulling things out, I realized that the colors, particularly red and blue, of the pins had faded into the portion of the curl that they were touching. So don't use the pins with the colored heads even if they are easier to remove.

Scott Shore: I purchased my first Jewel "Flex Waist" Barbie® doll for a makeover. Everything was going along fine. I do most of the sewing by hand, so when I got around to sewing the skirt to the top, I couldn't figure out why it was so hard for the needle to go through the fabric. Well, it turns out that I sewed the fabric directly to the doll's "Flex Waist". The finished product looked good. I always preface my sales with "clothing is sewn directly to doll and should not be removed." In this case, it was truer than ever; the clothing was sewn directly into the doll!!!

Lim Shor-wei: Don't use Clearasil® AND Oxy 10® on the same stained doll spot. I did it for one doll. When I ran out of the Clearasil®, I used Oxy 10®. This resulted in brown oily stains that are embedded in the doll. I think it's a chemical reaction and I can't find anyway to get them out. Also, more isn't always better. Don't imagine that luscious eyelashes and luscious hair on the doll means sticking as many plugs of reroot into as little area as possible. I split an eye and a doll's head doing that. Plus, sometimes disasters can be a path to unique styles if you try to come up with creative solutions to save the disaster.

Sharon Marquiss-Morris: I made a boo-boo when I was gluing a heel onto a boot, which was the final stage, after a whole bunch of blood, sweat and tears. I managed to superglue my finger to the boot. I had to rip the boot to get my finger off. Boo-hoo! Start all over again! Yuck!

Debbi Sherart: When doing a molded hair doll, and wanting to do rooted eyelashes, please don't make the same mistake that I

made. Do the eyelashes first while the head is off the body, then re-attach the head and do the molded hair. I cracked the dried paste when putting the head back on the body.

Harriett Weymon: The biggest mistake I seem to make is being so anxious to see the finished product that I rush the garment construction and miss some minor detail. I've learned to carve out some uninterrupted time, and take my time. I've also learned to follow a basic sewing rule I seem to have forgotten FIT BEFORE YOU STITCH! The Corduroy Cool® dolls have a smaller bust than the regular Barbie® dolls.

Scott Shore: I have another goof! LOL! I was so excited with one of my facial repaints—the blush was just the way I wanted it, lips looked perfect and eyes matched the deep purple of the gown. I had some left over long hair from a Diana Ross doll (circa 1968) I had done, and I very rarely throw anything away that I think I can use later. I used the long hair for some great looking lashes. The doll was stunning. Only one thing left to do—a boil perm. Needless to say the synthetic eyelashes melted and adhered themselves to the doll's face. It took me hours to remove the now melted on lashes, re-do the makeup and then reroot the lashes. I now use only human hair for my girls' eyelashes.

Lisa Howell: I learned not to use fingernail polish on any part of the Barbie® doll. No matter how tempting it is to use them and the fact the colors are great and there's no need for mixing, the paint will NEVER dry. One of my favorite and first makeover dolls was done in fingernail polish, but her face paint has never dried.

Debbi Sherart: My first creation became a fairy when the paintbrush with the black paint slipped. Ooops! I was able to turn her into a pretty wicked looking fairy though.

Funny Situations

We've all had funny experiences in the fashion doll world whether some decide to reveal theirs or not. If one does not have a sense of humor in what they do, then it becomes a JOB and creating should be fun.

Jim Faraone: Every time I go shopping to get new dolls to work on the cashier always announces loudly, "Well, some little girl is going to be very happy tonight!" LOL!

Juan Albuerne: Every time that I finish a doll, I show her to my Siamese cat, Toffee, and I ask him: "Do you like her?" He always says: "Miaaaaauuuhhh." I suppose he means "yes," but one never knows.

Carolyn Marnon: I made a butterfly out of a friend of the Kelly® doll. The butterfly wings I used were bought at the store and had a wire already attached. I needed to hang the doll from a little screw hook at the top of the display shelf my husband made for her so it would look like she was flying over her garden. I was going to use invisible thread to hang her, but I thought I could get away with just using the already attached wire. I attached the wire to the hook and thought I had a nice effect of a butterfly flying over the garden. My husband came around later and looked at the doll. He commented that she looked like she had just been hanged. I guess in my enthusiasm to complete the doll, I failed to notice that she looked like she was in a noose. The wire was removed and now she happily stands in her garden. I will no longer hang my girls. LOL!

Barb Wood: Let's see. I've glued my fingers together and accidentally cut the tips of my real fingernails off. I also burned part of my hair while singeing fairy wings, cut through my sweatpants when cutting out a pattern, sewed an outfit to my sweatpants while attaching sequins to the outfit and even tried to totally remove the face paint from a doll and it didn't work out smearing all over the place. With that, I just repainted the doll's face as a butterfly and it turned out so well I am now painting butterfly faces "on purpose!"

Jim Faraone: I've done the old "sew your outfit to your pants thing" also.

Lori Strawn: I was buying (strawberry blond) hair to reroot a doll. The woman at the register kept looking at me, then the hair, then me again. I could see she was thinking, "Boy, she didn't match her natural color very well." So I had to quickly explain that the hair wasn't for me, it was for a doll. I don't know if she believed me. :-)

Kathy Van Camp: I was surfing the net looking for pictures of showgirls so I could kind of get an idea of the kind of costumes they wore. Well, I did a search and started clicking on all these sites and was getting frustrated because I couldn't find anything good. Well, then I got my phone bill and there was a charge for $26 from AT&T and I have Sprint. I called up my phone company and they told me it was a charge for a pornographic site! GEEZ, was I embarrassed! I tried to tell him that I was just looking for pictures of showgirls for a doll make-over and he just said, "Uh huh!" Well, I know he didn't believe me! Now there is probably some kind of notation on my account that I am a pervert! What had happened was I clicked on this foreign site and they automatically disconnected me and reconnected me without my knowledge resulting in the long distance charge. You would think that would be illegal. I do remember getting on a site with a bunch of German language and some pics of half-dressed girls, but you had to pay to get into the site and I just closed it and went on searching. I didn't have to pay the $26 though. The guy just told me to get the program "Net Nanny!" Can you believe that? My son cracked up!

Barbara Fowler: My mom still teases me about the first doll dress I ever made when I was about 3. My dad had taken off his shoes and socks (good dress ones, of course) for a nap and I took the socks and cut them up for dresses.

Jillian Manning: My friends ask me how I decide on names for my girls and I have to reply that the girls tell me what their names are. When I began gathering dolls to make over, I thought it would make naming easier if I worked in alphabetical order. So the first doll would have a name beginning with A, the second B, the third C and so on. My first girls are from around 1900-1901 so I thought my first lady would be called Annie or Anabel or Alice. But before I was half way through working on her, she had let me know in no uncertain terms that she wasn't having any of those names. Her name was Louisa, thank you very much. Well, it wasn't my place to argue with her. My second girl, Phoebe, is a much gentler and more serene character. She wasn't so forceful about being named, but she still made sure I knew what her right name was. That suits me fine. I don't have to worry about names. I just wait for them to tell me. I'm not sure if this counts as funny or just eccentricity, but perhaps it says something about the way some of our minds work.

Barb Rausch: Whenever I've donated a makeover doll as a convention centerpiece or raffle helper, the item has been won by someone whom I know.

Scott Shore: I am forever losing my good needles, especially the ones I use for beading. After looking everywhere that I can think to look, it shows up on the sleeve of my robe or on my pant leg. Ouch!

Jim Faraone: I've been out shopping all day and later have looked down and discovered not one, but three needles stuck into my pant leg with streamers of colored thread hanging from them. LOL!

LaDonna Moore: I once made a plus size Barbie® doll by adding stuffing, pantyhose and clay. What a hoot she was!

Carol Jones: It wasn't funny at the moment, but I can laugh now. My cat walked across my paint palette once and was leaving little blue pawprints all over my kitchen. It took me forever to get those paws clean.

Joan Champagne: For the most part, I like to be by myself when I am working on a doll so I do a lot of rerooting, eyelashes and hand-sewing in my bedroom on the bed. There's nothing like relaxing on the bed and scraping your leg on a bunch of straight pins because you forgot you used your mattress as a pincushion. It's also not unusual to find a doll that I have been working on buried in the covers somewhere. I never know what I'm liable to find when I have been using the bed as my work area.

Cynthia Luna-Hennes: My cat, Jack, has a thing for my Barbie® dolls. He has ruined more than one by chewing the feet and hands to a bloody plastic pulp. He also has a thing for the Barbie® doll's hair. One time I found him choking on the hair he had chewed off one of my dolls. I thought he was hacking up a fur ball until I saw doll hair on his chin. Well, I saved him from that. Now I have given him his own headless Barbie® doll that he can chew on to his heart's content. I work on my dolls and he works on his and so far, so good. His doll looks like something from "The Night of the Living Dead," but maybe he is thinking of putting it up on eBay™ next Halloween? He also sleeps with this headless, mangled doll and my son says he looks like a lion with his "kill." All I can say is "GROSS." My son says he is going to put red paint on the doll to look like blood. Yuck! I guess that's what boys think is funny, and this "boy" is 33! LOL!

Gael Singer Bailey: I have another animal story. I just finished a Gene® doll with emerald green eyes and long eyelashes. I was just checking her to make sure she was finished, when I looked at her eyes, and they looked funny. A closer look revealed that my cat, Mrs. Murphy had been chewing on her lashes. All I could do was laugh. Everyone is a critic! LOL!

Joan Champagne: I have another funny story! I did a doll called Vermont Weekend and I wanted to photograph her outside in real snow. I think it was in January or February and I spent one afternoon taking a roll of film for this doll. It was cold and I was literally up to my neck in the snow because I wanted the doll positioned on the ground and I had to be level with the doll. When I went to remove the film from the camera, very pleased with myself that I had braved the elements and got, what I thought, were some great photos, I found out that I had neglected to put film in the camera!!

Cynthia Luna-Hennes: My turn, my turn! I have another one! Once, I went out and got brand new acrylic nails put on myself. I was going to try my first attempt at singeing fairy wings that night and I had read to use a lighter to do it. Well, try as I could with the new nails I just couldn't light the lighter. Now, I used an iridescent plastic ribbon and cut it into the shape I wanted for the wings I had been working on, and of course, wanting the wings to look good on both sides, I had to glue the wings together with 527 glue. Since I couldn't get the lighter lit, I was wondering what I could do instead. Then my eyes fell on my gas stove, so I thought I'd be real smart and use the flame on my stove. I got out my long needle nose pliers and turned on the stove. I was thinking how smart I was to improvise this way. With the Helen Reddy song, "I Am Woman Hear Me Roar, if I have to I can do anything" going through my brain, I put the very edge of the fairy wing into the flame. With a huge WHOOSH sound, the whole thing went up in flames. I panicked and dropped the flaming gob of plastic on the top of the stove and then noticed that my acrylic nails were also on fire. I kept waving them in the air as if that would put them out. It only made them flame higher. I thought "drop and roll", but couldn't see how that would help. I noticed my kitchen curtains were open and the thought came to me to close the curtains so the neighbors couldn't see me running around my kitchen with my fingers on fire. Before I could do that stupid thing, I noticed I had dishes soaking in the sink and managed to stick my hands into the dishwater and put my nails out. Right about then, my husband says from the living room, "I smell something funny, what are you doing in there?" I said, "Nothing much, just doll stuff." Then I had to scrape the melted blob of plastic off the top of my stove before he saw it. All I can add to this is please think before you singe, and kids, don't try this at home.

William Stewart Jones: I've often had sequins fall out of my wallet at the grocery store. I leave a trail of sequins everywhere I go!

Amy Nardone: I tend to sequin and bead a lot and in between the couch cushions are the items that I dropped or went flying. Like Bill, the other day at work, pulling out my wallet, a whole bunch of sequins came out with it.

Jim Faraone: I wonder how many of you have done this one? You're painting your dolls and you have a nice glass of soda (or whatever) to quench that designing thirst. You reach for the beverage, take a big gulp and realize you just drank your dirty paint water. I've done that enough times that you'd think I'd learn to move my soda glass .....NOT!!!

Kim Burie: My cat, Charlotte, has a favorite toy. She's always had a thing for carrying off my dolls (usually ones that I have just spent a lot of time on, hair just perfect and all.) I came across one of those soft-bodied Barbie® dolls with the eyes that open and close with cold water. I knew I had no use for her, so I decided that would be Charlotte's Barbie® doll. I opened up her back and filled it with catnip, and re-stitched it shut. She loves her! A word of caution though—cats get seriously ill (and even die) if they ingest too much string or long thin materials like string. I didn't take any chances and I braided the doll's hair so she couldn't eat it. We get some funny comments about Charlotte's Barbie® doll, but nobody is very surprised considering she's MY cat! LOL!

Gael Singer Bailey: Once I had just finished adding a little color to a Platinum Blond Gene® doll's eyes, wearing the Madra® doll's white coat. I went to read my email so I laid her on the floor to dry. I looked over and saw my silky Terrier curled up on top of her and the coat, nice and warm. Her eyes were all fuzzy with dog hair stuck to them, so I had to start all over.

Tools of the Trade

The right tools will always make any project go more smoothly. But, there are also some items that are not actually tools, but work as well as tools of the trade. With fashion doll makeovers, just about anything can become a tool. How many use their teeth on things? Let's not forget spit! LOL!

Jim Faraone: I find that a paintbrush can, not only be used for painting, but for mixing paint and for poking the thumb out of a pair of gloves when I turn the glove right side out. I also use the brush handle when turning any garment right side out and need to poke out the corners. Good to scratch your head with as well!

Steph Gazell: I use a large hang-around-the-neck magnifying glass, which sits against my chest with little rubber feet. It has a cord that you can adjust, so you can place it as far up or down as you please. This is nice for holding a doll under to work with. I also use a plastic tool carryall that I bought at a hardware store for my paints, brushes and other equipment. I work at my dining room table and I need my equipment to be easily removed. So, if you have to clean up each time you work, this is a great solution. They come in a number of sizes and have drawers underneath that are perfect for pliers, pins, toothpicks and other loose tools. The upper area is fairly deep and holds lots of bottles, jars and dolls. A handle is built in and you just whisk it off your table and set it aside. I really enjoy this carrier.

Lori Strawn: Lots of people on the list were joking about having sore thumbs after a day of rerooting. I use a quilter's thumb guard. It's made of plastic and has a groove notched in it to hold the needle snugly in place so it doesn't scoot around. I got it at the local craft store. No more sore thumbs!

William Stewart Jones: For making holes in vinyl, I often heat a piece of wire like a paper clip, with the flame from my gas stove. Then I can just push it into the vinyl. For bigger holes, I heat an ice pick, but wipe the soot off first. I also cut synthetic fabrics with a "hot knife" made for cutting stencils. This seals the edge and prevents fraying. It's excellent for cutting shapes for fairy dresses and wings.

Barb Rausch: For anyone who makes their own patterns, the following tools are indispensable: a very thin (¼in [.65cm] wide) cloth tape measure; thin, flexible transparent rulers (12in and 6in [31cm and 15cm]) marked in 16ths of an inch (.15cm); a very small draftsman curve; small draftsman's templates (circles, ovals in graduated sizes); artist's quality tracing paper; graph paper with ¼in (.65cm) squares; hard lead pencils (5H and 7H); Staedtler® white plastic eraser; and a close acquaintance with 6th grade fractions.

Gael Singer Bailey: I use a couple of different tools that others may not think of using. I use a dispenser for nail polish that manicurists use. It can be purchased from beauty supply stores and they come as plastic or ceramic. It works on the pump principle. You slide the lid over and press down on the top, which has several holes to dispense the remover. It prevents spills and you get just the right amount of remover. Orange sticks (the thin ones) work like Q-tips®. They have a narrowed end and are slanted, so you can wrap any amount of cotton you wish around it for removing tiny boo-boos. I also use wood Q-tips® and they can always be reused by pulling off the used cotton and replacing with just the amount you need.

A toothbrush makes a great hairbrush for your dolls. Plus, the glass containers that manicurists use for acrylic nail products work great for water and they are glass and heavy enough not to spill easily.

LaDonna Moore: Hemostats are good for pulling hair out. (of the doll that is!) Knitting needles are also good tools for turning clothes inside out. My favorite tool is an old ice pick. It's great for pushing out that old earring stub on the doll.

Becky Kelly: I wear a cheap pair of bifocal half-glasses when I work on my dolls. I can look over the top of them to get my paint, and through them while I paint the doll's face.

Nikki Avery: I find that toolboxes make for great craft storage. They are easy to find and often cost less then the special craft storage containers. Many lightweight ones are available with different pull out tray features. School boxes or children's pencil boxes are a cheap way to get organized. They can be used for storing drawing pencils, kneaded erasers and paintbrushes. Cosmetic trays are fantastic for organizing your workspace. They often come with sections intended for lipstick or makeup brushes. These areas can be used for your paintbrushes. The brushes will stand upright to prevent crushed bristles. Some of these cosmetic organizers come with compartments to hold your cotton balls and Q-tips®. What do you do with your old paintbrushes after they have been used on all the doll faces? They don't have to be thrown away. Often these brushes that are split or frayed can be trimmed down to just a few bristles. Sometimes those brushes with just 1-4 bristles can be very useful to work on the tiniest details. Toothbrushes can be used to clean dolls.

They are especially useful in cleaning vintage and mod dolls (toe and finger areas). The best hair combs I have found for dolls is in the pet department. The plastic ones are good to use and they often come with 2-sides—1 side has tiny teeth (perfect for working debris and knots out of the hair). Eyebrow brushes and eyelash combs found in the cosmetic's department of any discount store are useful tools to have. Sometimes you are able to find a combination of the 2 tools in one. The eyelash comb can be used to comb or style a doll's hair (or bang area). The brush can be used for hair or for cleaning.

Elizabeth Anne Dean: I have discovered two tools that have a variety of uses for doing fashion doll makeovers. They are the ballpoint bodkin and the nitpicker. Both items can be found in sewing supply stores. The bodkin is a long, thin piece of metal with a rounded "ball" on one end, and a flat tip with a hole in it on the other end. My favorite use for this device is removing the Barbie® doll's head. I slide the flat end of the bodkin into the head and over one of the hooks in the head. I gently slide the bodkin between the inside of the head and the hook as I ease the head back over the hook. I find that the head comes off quickly and easily using this technique. The other tool, the nitpicker, comes in handy for removing hair plugs in preparation for a rerooting. It is a very thin, sharp hook with a latch. First, using a pair of pliers, remove the small latch attached to the hook. Remove the doll's head, trim the hair close to the scalp and simply use the nitpicker to pluck the hair plugs out from the inside of the doll's head. Both tools work well for reversing sewn materials and pulling elastic through casings.

Michelle James: Toothpicks are great for applying tiny dabs of glue. Plus, small 3-½in (9cm) detail craft scissors are perfect for trimming rooted lashes, as they can get into smaller spots than regular sized scissors. 10/0 brushes are great for repainting eyes and lips.

Elizabeth "Beth" Kinsley: I have used cake-decorating tips to apply the molded hair mixture (acrylic modeling paste) to a doll's head when creating molded hair.

Laura Fern Fanelli: I keep in my doll supplies a wire cutter for pinching off metal. These can be used to shorten the tiny decorative bobbypins from the drugstore to fit your Gene® doll or Tyler Wentworth® doll's hairdos.

Deborah Fagan: I'm in love with my magnifying lamp, the kind that jewelers use for detail painting. I found mine at Office Depot® for around $49.00.

Kim Burie: My favorite tool is a small pair of jeweler's needle nosed pliers. I use these for pulling needles through the head when rerooting and rooting lashes, for clamping items together when they are being glued, pulling out little individual stray strands of hair to be snipped, for making doll jewelry (of course) and tons of other things. Often times they save my fingertips from becoming bloody nubs, and they save my sanity too.

Pamela Bachmayer: For me, a very sharp pair of embroidery scissors is vital to trimming eyelashes, hairstyles, etc. I feel Fiskars® is the best brand to use because they are sharp the entire length and they get into tiny areas.

Pat Feick: Medical supply stores sell Stay's Up®, which can be used to keep shoes, gloves and clothes in place. It is a roll on used to keep patients' stockings up.

Lori Strawn: Looking for more tools to help? Raid the toolbox of your husband/father/brother/cousin/significant other. There are lots of great gadgets to be had. As mentioned previously, needle-nose pliers are ideal for yanking old plugs of hair out of a doll's head before you start to reroot. I use a set of metal needle files to rub and shape dry molding compound. This works particularly well when you use the compound to "close" the mouth of an open-mouthed doll. Just dab some compound over the tooth area and smooth with your finger. Be sure to turn the doll sideways to ensure that you haven't formed one big lumpy lip. When the compound dries, a needle file will help you get your new mouth perfectly formed and smooth. And don't forget to look in the kitchen for tools. I use a handheld battery-powered lighter (used to light gas stoves or caramelize sugar on the tops of desserts) to melt the tips of hair I'm rerooting so that I don't have to knot it. The lighter is easy to use in your non-dominant hand (just squeeze the "trigger" to light) and it has a long handle for safety. Some models can even be locked in an "off" position when you're not working.

Jennifer L. Brown: I have sometimes found that on dolls' heads when I have to denude the old hair for a reroot, some dolls have glue inside the heads making it difficult to pull out through the holes (my preferred method). I have used medical hemostats to get a secure grip on the hair chunks and pulled them out through the neck hole.

Dorothy Fannin: I use an ice pick to push earrings through the head after I clip them off with scissors. I also use aluminum potpie tins to mix paint and modeling paste for colored hair.

Michelle Candace: The potpie tins are a good idea, Dorothy. I use lids from plastic yogurt, cottage cheese or other containers for paint mixing trays. They can be thrown away after use or washed and used over and over again. Fill the cup/bowl part of the container up with water and use it for rinsing your paintbrushes while painting.

Jim Faraone: I use the pop off lid from a spray starch can. Under the lid there are two circle sections. I fill both with water and when the water gets dirty in the center circle section, I start using the water to clean my brushes in the outer circle. It saves time changing the water often.

J'Amy Pacheco: For picking up small beads or rhinestones, nothing beats a piece of beeswax on the tip of a toothpick. Blocks of beeswax are sold at craft stores; just break off a tiny piece, rub it between your fingers to soften and shape it around the toothpick tip. With your fingers, form a small joint with the beeswax. Gently tap the wax on the bead or rhinestone and it will stick. Press it gently on the adhesive you're using to affix the bead or stone and it will come off the wax.

Jim Faraone: Great one J'Amy! I usually take my round toothpick and dab it onto my tongue to pick up the teeny rhinestones. Your way is so much more sanitary! LOL!

Dorothy Fannin: EEEwwwwww!!!!

Jim Faraone: Eeeewww??? Confess, Dorothy. How much spit goes into your dolls? LOL!

Dorothy Fannin: BRB! Just ran out of spit to reroot my dolls! LOL!

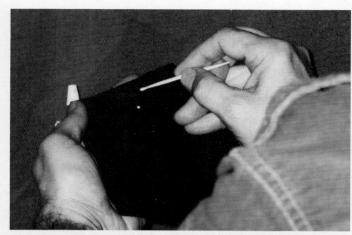

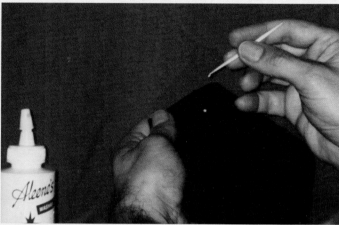

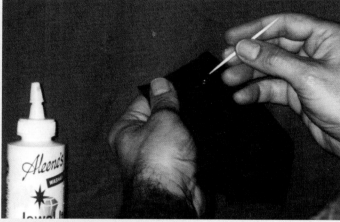

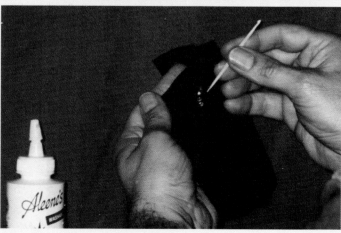

Jim Faraone: Just for spite, I'm showing my spit technique! LOL! **(see step 1)** Round toothpicks come in handy for just about anything. Just dab you toothpick in some Jewel-It glue and dab a small amount on your fabric. **(see step 2)** Then dab a clean toothpick on the tip of your tongue (or use J'Amy's bees wax tip) and dab it on the top of your rhinestone to pick it up. **(see step 3)** Set the rhinestone into the glue and press it down gently with the tip of the toothpick. **(see step 4)** Continue this process until you complete your rhinestone design and let dry.

Pamela Bachmayer: Not to change the subject, but paper plates are useful as a disposable paint palette, and they can also hold beads and various other items. I can see them better on a plate than trying to work out of something smaller. Straight pins are useful for holding stoles and accessories in place during photography.

Gael Singer Bailey: I wear contact lenses and I use extra lens cases for paint. They are great if you want to mix a special color and save it for a while. One side you can fill with water and the other has your special color. I am not sure how long the color will last, but if you get the good cases the paint should last like any other paint.

Kelli "Jinx" Getchell: I use fine metal nibs and holders in place of pins or toothpicks to add fine dots of paint. The holder allows me more control over the placement of the paint and the nibs hold a bit more paint. The nibs are also good for removing paint. I take a little material from a cotton swab, wrap it around the nib, dip the nib in polish remover and then I can remove the paint from a small area. Be careful not to get the plastic nib holder anywhere near the polish remover as it will "melt" the plastic. I also use a child's soft bristle toothbrush to remove stubborn paint from the doll's face. Never dip the brush in polish remover as it might melt the plastic. I apply the polish remover to the doll's face, let it set a second and then scrub it with the toothbrush. I do this by the sink so I can immediately was any polish remover and paint from the bristles of the brush. I haven't had any toothbrush parts melt on me yet, but I did manage to melt the inside of a plastic glass, which is why I now do this procedure over the sink.

Laura Fern Fanelli: I have two tools that I really like. I use a wire crimp tool a lot to cut off the backs of earrings to fit the Barbie® doll. I also use a mini hacksaw for working on Centaurs. The horse's head needs to be removed for these exotic creatures.

Pamela Bachmayer: A computer and color printer are valuable tools for customizing my boxes, certificates of authenticity, wrist tags, labels, etc. Avery Labels® and Avery Wizard® software are great tools as well: The labels are precut to size and are perfect for making smaller labels such as disclaimers. The Avery Wizard® is a free program that allows you to individualize each label, print from a database, etc. with some customization of fonts and colors. Adobe Photoshop® is a program that allows me to crop, resize, sharpen, etc. my pictures from my digital camera. It also has a wonderful lighting effect that allows you to add spotlights to your pictures. I use some of the artistic functions on my Certificates of Authenticity. I couldn't function without this program. ACDSee® is a program that allows me to quickly scan through my uploaded pictures without having to load each one to make a choice for the final pictures. It also is the best program I've found that reduces my finished pictures to a very small size without loosing any significant quality. A paper cutter is a great tool. I use a small Fiskars® brand that I found in the Scrapbook section of my local craft store. I use this on every doll to precisely cut labels, wrist tags, etc. It's quick and simple and gives me nice sharp, even, professional looking edges on my labels.

Creating Your Workspace

Not all of us are lucky enough to have a special room just for our designing purposes. Many of us are cramped into small quarters or have to share our space with others. Setting up a workspace for yourself is very important. This will be your little home away from the realities of the real world. A place to escape into the miniature world of dolls, fabrics, laces, beads and at times one big MESS!!! I thought it would be interesting to hear about the workspaces of other artists and see how they deal and organize their special get-away.

Jim Faraone: Let's see who can beat my "studio," which consists of a drawing board stuck between the wall and the refrigerator in which I have to climb over tons of fabric, beads and such just to get to my chair to work. LOL! **(see photo below)**

Steph Gazell: I like to work with a nice thick white terry towel under my doll. I fold it so it's about 5in (13cm) thick. This is a nice surface for turning the doll to get angles. On the towel, and slightly to the right of the doll, I keep a couple of layers of white paper towels. These I use to wipe my brush and let excess water or paint drip off before applying the brush to my doll. You get very use to having those paper towels there, and it's most annoying to work without them once you've become accustomed to them. I also have an extending halogen lamp with a very bright bulb to work under that is clamped to my table. It does create some heat, but the good clear light is necessary to working with tiny detail.

Michele Frazee-Jackson: As I have a limited space to work in, I use a rolling TV cart to hold most of my "everyday" customizing supplies. It provides 2 "shelves" to hold things and when I need to put it all away, it is easy to roll into a closet or some other hidden place.

Sarah Worley: For beads and sequin storage, I've found the small plastic film containers to be great for storing beads when you have them separated out by color or size. I usually pour them out into a flat plastic lid such as that used for pet food or other food products so they're easy to pick up with my needle when sewing them on. I keep my fabrics in plastic see through drawers and have them arranged according to types. For example, the cotton-types are in one drawer, the silk in another, the sheer in another, etc. Because I live in an area with high humidity, my dolls are kept in enclosed cabinets with a small container of a moisture absorbing material called calcium chloride that I frequently check. It is a mineral salt sold in the grocery or closet area of Kmart® or Wal-Mart® under the name of Damp Rid®. This helps prevent possible mildew damage.

Pamela Bachmayer: I set up boxes for each craft I will use. One box is for my paints, one for jewelry, one for hair, etc. They can be stacked out of the way, but easily pulled out for use with everything I need for that particular part of the project. I use clear plastic boxes with lids and compartments, sized accordingly to the particular craft. For fabric storage, I use large purchased stackable drawers. I label each drawer: Velvet, Tulle, Cotton, Satin, etc.

Vonda Silliman: I use plastic shoeboxes to store my customizing items. Labels help to identify the contents. Bigger, plastic boxes are needed for some things, and I store my fabrics in a laundry basket.

LaDonna Moore: To make my tables that I work on look nice, I get fabric I like and then cover it with a clear plastic tablecloth. It's easy to clean and you still have a nice looking table.

Fran Czosnek: Even though I am relatively new at fashion doll makeovers, I have a tip to share. I have a traveling workspace. I really like being able to work on my dolls just about anywhere. I have developed the perfect traveling workspace area. Things that you will need is a 20in x 30in (51cm x 76cm) foam board, velcro tabs, bead containers (come in sets of 6 and 12), and some containers with lids (Rubbermaid® works well). First decide how big of a work area you would like. Then put your velcro tabs on the bottom of all of your containers. Velcro your containers to the foam board in a way that they are within reach and accommodating to your makeovers. (Leave sufficient room for your workspace). I prefer to use the larger bead containers that are joined together and come in groups of six. **(see photo below)** I use them to hold my sequins and bugle beads. I also have the bead containers that come in sets of 12. They hold seed beads

and other small accessories. Lastly, I use a square sandwich size container to hold scissors, thread, wire, needles and everything else that I may need for my makeovers. I have found that this works really well, and I can take it anywhere. I can watch TV in the living room and even go outdoors to work. I am no longer secluded in the craft room, which sometimes is a blessing!!! Try it. I think you will enjoy your new work area.

Melinda Sprague: I found that a great place to put all kinds of doll things (beads, trims, small feathers, pins, even small spools of thread) is a Bolts and Nuts organizer. They are found in the hardware sections of most stores. Most of them have holes in the bottom of every little bin, but that's also easily taken care of with either a small piece of tape or a little bead of glue to seal off the hole. They come small to huge and usually don't cost half as much as organizers in the craft sections of the store.

Joanna Bond: I arrange my workspace with plenty of tabletop room with most-used supplies within reach and everything else underneath. If dolls are in the way of supplies you need, they will be knocked over repeatedly. Clean up often! I keep a current projects bin (plastic tub with lid), so that if something has to be put away temporarily, it has a safe place to go along with the supplies I am using with it. This is also handy if I just want to move to another room for a while. I have a large bin full of semi-sorted dolls, and a smaller one with dolls I've already earmarked for something in particular. I also have a bin for parts (heads, arms, tentacles, etc.) You can hang doll stands upside-down on the wall in your workspace, and put dolls in them to dry, be gazed at lovingly, or just be ruminated on. They'll be out of the way and safe, but in sight. Things I always keep within arms reach are a paint eraser (looks like a pencil with a pointed eraser at both ends), tweezers, a doll

stand and an old cloth diaper or soft rag.

Kim Burie: I use spice racks, which can often make great paint organizers. Many of them have holes and spaces just right for holding bottles and jars of paint. Garage and workshop organizers work wonderfully for creating. There are the sets with tiny drawers usually sold to organize screws, nails etc. I use them for sorting beads and jewelry findings, shoes and doll accessories, threads, pins needles and any other small item I use when creating that I might otherwise lose in a drawer, box or closet.

Barb Wood: My work area is my den and I have a coffee table set up with my "creating materials" on it, but most of my stuff still ends up on the couch, on the floor, anywhere there is room!!

Jim Faraone: Hey, Barb! Now that sounds like a true work area. I don't think many of us have work areas that are neat as a pin. As you have seen, mine always looks like a bomb hit it! LOL! Of course we do try and be neat and clean it every so often, but another bomb is sure to arrive at least a day after I've cleaned and organized it.

Stefanie Baumler: The plastic containers made to hold embroidery threads make great bead holders.

Kelli "Jinx" Getchell: I see some are like me and you don't have a "special" workroom and have to do your work in the kitchen and store your supplies/finished product wherever you have room. There are a few things you should keep in mind if you have pets. I have four—two cats and two dogs—and they all shed. If you are working with any slow-drying glues, like Elmer's® glue, keep a blow dryer handy. Set it on cool to dry the glue quickly so that you won't end up reeling fur out of the glue. Keep ALL dolls in boxes or totes. No matter how high you put them up on a shelf, the cats can still

get to them. For some reason that escapes me, cats like to chew on the semi-hard plastic of the hands and feet. They also like to eat the hair. The ingestion of plastics isn't good for the cats and it certainly doesn't do the dolls any good either. There is nothing worse then spending hours working on a doll only to have your cat chew off one of the doll's hands. Dogs on the other hand will simply chew up the entire doll. Hands, feet head, body—doesn't matter. They look at them as tasty little chew toys. Never leave the dolls unattended where a dog can reach them. I took a new Barbie® doll with me to my computer one day. I removed it from the box as I wanted to get a good look at it. I liked it so much I decided to order a few more. I set the doll next to me on a small table, well within the reach of both my dogs. I was halfway through ordering, while talking to a friend in chat and suddenly found myself typing "AFK dogs got my doll." My golden retriever had grabbed the brand new doll off the table and ran. After him I went, yelling for him to drop the doll. He ran right into his crate and refused to come out. He was NOT giving up the doll. It took two tries with dog biscuits and me on my hands and knees for me to recover the doll covered in dog slobber. I was lucky, as the dog didn't do any damage to the doll except cover her with drool. Anyway, keep all fabrics and trims in plastic totes if you don't have other storage areas. Remember to put the tops on the totes or close the door to the fabric cabinet because if you don't, you will find a cat sleeping on the fabric. It's really difficult to get the fur out of the fabric once a cat has napped on it.

Jim Faraone: I have no pets here, but for getting fur or lint off an outfit, I wrap my index finger with masking take with the sticky side facing out. Then you can just dab the outfit and the fur or lint comes off onto the sticky tape. If it's delicate material, first dab your own

blouse or shirt with the taped finger to get rid of some of the stickiness and then dab the doll.

Carolyn Marnon: Although I have a studio in the basement to use while working on all of my projects, I seem to always gravitate to the kitchen table. It's where I do my best work. One important consideration is to always have good lighting where you work. If you don't, you can really strain your eyes trying to see what you are doing. I know people who have purchased Ott® lights to work by. There are floor models and tabletop models that provide a great deal of bright light by which to work. Make sure your worktable is clean when you begin. You don't want to ruin something you have worked hard on by accidentally running it too close to that chocolate milk spill or a tiny spot of spaghetti sauce from dinner. You might think it is at the other end of the table, but it's amazing how quickly your items seem to spread out over the entire table—things like fabric, ribbons and trims, the patterns, the scissors, the cutting board, the sewing machine, etc.

Debbi Sherart: I have a few little wooden shelves that stack that sits in the middle of a looooong piece of plywood. On these shelves I have cardboard organizers (like the ones that nuts and nails are in at the hardware store). These boxes fit perfectly inside of these shelves and I can store the paints and tools that I use regularly right there within arm's reach. I also have more shelving that I can shake a stick at which is loaded with various crafts, fabrics and books. HE/SHE WHO DIES WITH THE MOST DOLLS & FABRICS WINS!!! LOL!

Kathy McLeod: I am limited in space so I found a desk that is a table. It pulls out to make a work space of 40in wide x 6ft long and when I need that space, I just push the table in and it's a desk the size of 42in x 28in (105cm x 71cm) deep with drawers. The table rolls up like the old kitchen Hoosier cabinet under the top and out of sight. This is the greatest thing. I found it at a flea market and I have put some shelves on the top of it for added space.

William Stewart Jones: Create a "Morgue!" A "Morgue" is a collection of clippings for reference. I have file folders full of magazine pages, each filed by the name where I could look for an idea. For example— Fantasy, Makeup, Historical, Embroidery, Glitz, 50's Fashion, 60's Fashion, Ideas, Colors, Chinese Art, etc. My color folder has pictures of gardens and flowers, pictures of fabrics, anything that shows interesting color combinations. It's important to put clippings in the place where you would think to look for them, not necessarily where a librarian would put it. When I need an idea, or just when I feel like relaxing in my workspace, I browse through the folder and the ideas start flowing. I rarely copy anything exactly from a picture....I use it for inspiration.

Loanne Hizo Ostlie: I have a drafting table that tilts. I also have a chair that is proportioned to the table so that I don't have to stand (although I do it anyway, LOL!). Also, I use the MULTI-USE EXPAND-A-SHELF tiers that I purchased from Wal-Mart®. These tiers allow me to line up all my paints at eye level so I can see what I've got right in front of me. I also stick unfinished heads on the tip of those glue bottles. There is an overhead drafting lamp that is great for evening work. I found these cheap, see-through jar stackers in which I put my beads. They stack on top of each other by screwing them together. All dolls that are waiting for their turn are stacked in a box beneath the drafting table. I velcroed a plain bedsheet to the side of the drafting table in order to hide the clutter below.

Lori Strawn: I find that newspaper, cardboard and other stuff to cover the work area very necessary. I've learned from a sad experience that nail polish remover and paint can ruin most tables, no matter how careful you think you'll be!

Amy Nardone: Each person has their own view of what their workshop should be, but I can tell you how I like mine. I have a big L-shaped desk for my sewing machine and serger. I also have a magnifying lamp as I paint there as well. I have a separate space for cutting materials with the table and cutting board. I have a rolling cart for all my paints and I keep all of my fabrics organized (as best as I can! LOL!) in those plastic 3 drawer ensembles in my closet. I have the dolls in separate 3 drawer ensembles. There is not a day that my room does not look "lived in". I constantly have fabric and dolls lying about getting ready for their "new look." The space is up to the artist, but it really helps to have some things organized.

Kelli "Jinx" Getchell: As I don't have a specific area of the house that I can use as a workspace, I have to keep things mobile. I work at the kitchen table most of the time so I have to be able to clean up quickly so the family can sit down to eat. I've tried to talk them into eating elsewhere, but they just won't go for it. :-) I keep all my supplies organized in small totes. When I work on a doll, I just take out the supplies I'm going to use and put them in small plastic baskets. I have one basket that I keep what I call the basics for painting. It has the basic colors of black, white, off white, red, blue, yellow, green, gold, silver, matte sealer, gloss sealer and modeling paste. In another basket are all my brushes, pens, pencils and similar supplies. This way, when I'm doing a repaint, all I have to do is grab those two baskets and I'm ready to go. All my supplies are kept this way. If I want to do some beading I just have to grab one or two small totes or baskets and I'm ready to go. Sewing basics in one box, fabrics in another, colored laces and trims, white laces and trims—everything has its own place. This way I can keep track of exactly what I have, find it quickly and clean up my work area just as rapidly. There is nothing worse then having to spend half an hour just finding the supplies you want.

Gael Singer Bailey: As far as my workspace is concerned, the area looks like a natural disaster just occured. Our Governor is visiting soon to see if I am entitled to federal aid to clean up my disaster! LOL!

J'Amy Pecheco: When creating your workspace, try to find a place that will allow you to walk away from your materials without having to put everything away each night. You'll be more likely to work on your creations if you don't have to get everything out to start only to put it away each time you work on them. I use a rolling cart with six small drawers for storing paints, brushes, perm rods and other materials. It can easily be rolled into the hall closet when company comes, and doesn't look too awful when left out. I also use small plastic boxes with divided compartments for storing small items such as shoes, beads and rhinestones. I keep a small section of one kitchen cupboard for storing my works-in-progress; they're handy, but can be hidden if I don't want visitors gaping at naked dolls. Your family will be more supportive of your "habit" if you try to avoid working in a space that is likely to cause them to have to shove dolls aside to make room, or to find arms or legs or strands of vinyl hair in their dinner. Keep in mind, too, that pets and small children may be very interested in your work, so find a way to protect it from little fingers and claws! I find a corner of the kitchen/family room area best; I can hide my work without too much trouble, but can also be part of the family while working.

Melinda Sprague: I like to have my stereo in my workroom. Music helps me to create and when I get stumped I can just sit back and listen to some tunes to get inspiration. I also have a few of those neat storage containers that have wheels on them for my fabric. They are clear or wired so I can see my fabric easily without having to search through it every time.

William Stewart Jones: A small electric fan heater is good to have for your workspace. I use a 10in (25cm) fan heater to force dry and speed up pieces on which I'm working. I set things in front of it and then work on something else. This allows me to work on several projects at once. An old-fashioned bonnet type hairdryer is great also. You can leave it on a gentle stream of warm air. I have a cutting/work table that is a piece of four by eight plywood. It's supported on four multi-drawer cabinets. I can have big plastic tubs filled with all the trims and fabrics I'm thinking about using on the dolls, and spread stuff out to see what works. I keep a file cabinet with folders of fashions and costume ideas that I cut from magazines.

J'Amy Pacheco: Fabrics and trims can be stored in plastic under-the-bed boxes; be sure to roll the fabric with tissue paper to avoid creases. I sort fabrics into boxes by type—glamour fabrics in one box, casual fabric in another. In addition, I try to keep similar colors together. When my creativity needs a boost, I just sort through my boxes; inspiration almost always follows!

Debbie Lima: I'm very lucky to have a craft room. I have a sewing machine and a drafting table (I sit up there to paint) with a magnifying light. I have my machine on a special craft table that has a hook up for my curling iron and hot glue gun. I bought some large heavy duty drawers for odds and ends such as paint, paint brushes, trims, doll shoes, hair and extra Barbie® dolls. I have a serger too that's on the other side of the room. Since this room has always been a sewing room I turned the closet into storage space. There are shelves from top to bottom. This is where I store my material, boxes for the dolls, photography equipment and other odds and ends. When I'm not working, I can walk out and shut the door and my three cats are completely off limits. This is my dream room.

Aurora Mathews: You never have as much space as you need!

Jim Faraone: Amen to that Aurora!

Shopping

Now who doesn't like to shop for goodies for creating your dolls? A whole day can be spent driving from one store to another gathering up delightful surprises to use. Looking, touching, feeling as you roam the aisles, the clerks stare at you in amazement at how focused we can be. Or they're probably thinking we're ready to shoplift! It's always fun going on a fashion doll makeover shopping frenzy!

Dorothy Fannin: I found that miniature shows are great for finding embellishments for hats and fashions.

Laura Fern Fanelli: Watch your local toy stores for sales on the low-end dolls. Good buys can be found if you check for sales.

Sheryl Majercin: Thrift stores and flea markets are great places to find unique and beautiful fabrics for your doll ensembles.

Jim Faraone: I totally agree with that Sheryl. You can get some great vintage fabrics sold in thrift shops and flea markets. Also, check out Goodwill® and the Salvation Army® for old outfits that you can use for the material. Old leather skirts are wonderful for making leather outfits for your dolls. The leather is nice and soft from wear and for a $5 skirt, you can get at least 6 outfits out of it. One of the biggest problems I had was finding odd colored sequins. I have not found a craft store or store with a craft section that sells anything but the typical blue, red, green, gold, silver and sometimes black (which is getting scarce now). I even checked with the store managers about this and they're remarks are, "Well, we don't get in other colors because no one buys them." I always respond, "Well, maybe

they don't buy them because you don't have them!" A lot of times, craft stores are not the way to go for truly creative people. Anyway, I discovered that all I have to do is go to a thrift shop and buy outfits that are already sequined with odd color sequins and cut them off to use. It may be a bit of a pain cutting off the sequins, but now I have wonderful sequins of all colors including a beautiful iridescent black. The outfits only cost me about $8 each, so that's not bad for a ton of sequins in odd colors. Thrift stores are also great for buying furs. I will usually pick out the coats there with the fur collars. I then bring them up to the cash register, and ask for a pair of scissors. I will cut the fur off the collars (under the fur is always a regular collar on the coat), pay the full price for the coat and then donate the coat back since it is still in great condition.

William Stewart Jones: Hey, Jim. Have you tried Cartwrights on the Internet for sequins? They have a wonderful selection of beads and sequins at http://www.ccartwright.com/.

Jim Faraone: I just checked them out, Bill, and you're absolutely right. I got some wonderful sequins from them. They have a very large assortment and seem to be adding new things every time I check them out. Great prices as well. They have my business now. LOL!

Kevin Kilmer: I also do the thrift shops. The best thrift stores are the ones that are the closest to a hospital. All the doctors bring their stuff to that one. One of the Goodwill® stores here is about a block from a hospital and there are always great dresses/shirts/etc. there and most look like they have never been worn. I've found a few things with the tags

still on, so needless to say, the fabric for the doll dresses is great there! I also work in a fabric store and always look for the clearance/manager's special stuff first, but buy all you'll want at that time, because when it's gone, it's gone. That is the stuff that they can't get back in stock.

Amy Nardone: I have found dresses from proms or weddings make great material.

Tricia Hill: While shopping for fabrics, I usually have a design/pattern in mind and color so I go through the aisles touching every fabric in site. I think about how it will drape, and how bulky or flimsy it is. I look at the weave—how badly will this fabric fray? If it's a print, is the print the right scale for 11-½in (29cm) doll? How easily will I be able to machine stitch this? Or will I need to hand stitch it? Will I need to sew through sequins? I basically look like a nutcase touching/feeling the fabrics, but I've found it better to really explore before purchasing, cutting and then saying to yourself, "Oops," and fighting with it. Or worse yet, having to start all over again.

Jim Faraone: I agree with you, Tricia. I also touch and feel all the fabrics when shopping. There are some wonderful sheer fabrics out there that are very eye catching and tempting to use, but they "run" like the devil. When I see a sheer fabric I would like to use, I pull the edges of it in two directions to see if it runs. I'm sure the owners of the fabric store are ready to kill me with runs in all their stock, but hey, I'm spending my money and I want to make sure the product is good enough to buy. LOL! Also, check on how badly a material will wrinkle. I usually grab the end of the fabric in

stores and clench it in my fist to see how it wrinkles. You really don't want to create an outfit that you have to iron every time you touch her. Sometimes for print size, I'll bring a nude doll with me to check things out. It may look silly, but it's better than wasting money. Once I wanted a flesh color material to do some "illusion" gowns and I must have bought 5 different beige color materials and none of them worked. I finally bought the doll with me and would you believe that a peach color fabric was the one that matched the doll's body perfectly. Never be embarrassed by bringing a doll with you into a fabric store. They think we're odd anyway! LOL!

Vonda Silliman: Check the Christmas ornament aisle in craft stores during the holidays for small-scale items. Sometimes they have miniature ornaments for the smaller trees that can be close to scale to what you may need. Also, check the wedding aisle in these stores. Pillars for cakes, metal rings, small flower accessories, etc. can all be used for the doll itself or used for props when taking photos.

Chrissy Stewart: When buying material, try to buy quality material. This always works better for the results you want. Make sure you buy the right material for the effect you want. For instance, stiff materials don't "drape" well and tend to look bulky when used for flowing dresses and such.

Jean Majercin: Cruise the thrift stores, rummage sales and garage sales for old jewelry. It is a much less expensive way to find rhinestones and other treasures for making doll accessories.

Jim Faraone: Good tip, Jean. I go to flea markets at times and buy the small strands of crystal necklaces from the 40's and 50's that one can get for around $10. I use the colorful crystals for necklaces and earrings on my dolls. If you go to a craft store, you can pay somewhere in the vicinity of $4 for three lousy crystal beads.

Cynthia Luna-Hennes: Look for bridesmaid dresses at thrift stores. Bridesmaids almost always look forward to getting rid of those dresses and they are usually pretty cheap. No matter how awful the design, they can have lots of goodies on them to use. They have nice fabrics, nice stiff netting with finished edges not to mention rhinestones, beading, bows and appliqués. Also, buy beaded necklaces and bracelets at the Dollar® store. There's a lot more beads for a buck and a more interesting assortment of beads than you can find at craft stores.

Jim Faraone: I use to check out the earrings at the Dollar® stores because some had great hanging charms on them that could be cut off and used as pendants on the dolls. They also had great cherub post earrings, **(see step 1)** and I bought a bunch to make pins on my dolls' outfits. All you have to do is **(see step 2)** cut the post tip at an angle with your needle nose pliers to make a sharp point and **(see step 3)** bend the post downward. **(see step 4)** Now you can insert it into the doll's lapel to make a nice pin. You can add a dab of Jewel-It® under the cherub or whatever post earring you decide to use to hold it securely in place.

Carolyn Marnon: I don't like to pay over $10 for a doll unless I am trying to create a very specific look. I find a lot of dolls at garage sales and thrift stores. I, personally, do not like to spend more than $1 for a rescue doll. There are many dolls out there waiting to be rescued, so I like to make my money stretch. Pay much more than a dollar and you could just as well go to the store and

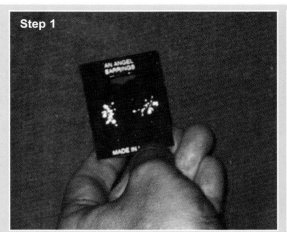

Step 1

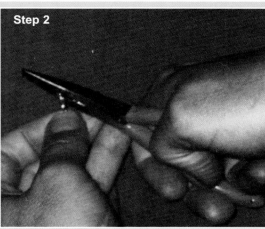

Step 2

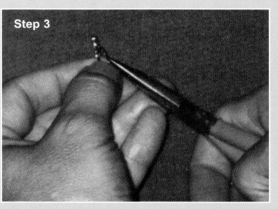

Step 3

Step 4

buy a cheap play doll that even comes with clothes. You can get really creative with garage sale dolls. If the hair is chopped or the doll is bald, you can reroot, flock, or try some funky new hairstyle on her. Shoes can hide toe and foot problems. Gloves can hide missing or chewed finger problems. There are ways to remove certain marks and spots from dolls or you could just cover them with your design. Keep an open mind when you see naked dolls for sale. They could become your next masterpiece.

Gael Singer Bailey: A beauty supply store is almost as good as an art store. They have miniature nail ornaments that make great jewelry.

Jim Faraone: I love rummaging through the beauty supply stores, Gael! I bet you can even use the tiny decals that go on acrylic nails for tattoos on your dolls.

William Stewart Jones: I'm always shopping for tiny trims, lace or prints. I stockpile them so they're available when inspiration strikes. I buy LOTS of stuff in white; it can be dyed or colored with felt pens.

Melinda Sprague: When buying material, try out some of the more expensive fabrics since a lot of fashion doll clothes don't really need an entire yard of fabric. Spoil yourself and get a smaller amount of a fancy expensive fabric.

Jim Faraone: That's true, Melinda. Once, while going through Bloomingdales®, I came across this beautiful black lace blouse with tiny red embroidered roses that was $123.00! I checked it out and figured I could get 5 outfits made out of this blouse, so picked it up in the largest size they had and bought it. I even told the salesladies what I was going to do with it, which horrified them a bit. LOL! I did get 5 outfits out of it, the dolls are all sold, and I actually still have the whole back of the blouse to play with on future

dolls. I certainly got my moneys worth.

J'Amy Pacheco: The best way to shop for materials for fashion doll makeovers is to be constantly on the lookout. Take advantage of sales to stock up on fabrics, trims and beads, whether or not you're ready to use them. Since dolls are small, you don't have to buy large quantities. Many fabric stores will allow you to buy as little as ¼yd (.23cm). Patterns often go on sale. If you maintain a diverse collection of patterns, you can afford to wait till new ones are discounted. If you frequently use a particular type of material, such as rhinestones, you can save money by finding a supplier that will sell to you in bulk.

Jim Faraone: J'Amy, you and Bill are right in stock piling materials for your dolls. Several times I wish I bought more of one item because the next time I needed it, it was nowhere to be found. If anyone finds something they really love, buy it all up now. It's not food so it won't spoil and it's better to have too much than too little when you really need it.

Gael Singer Bailey: As far as shopping goes, I purchased most of my dolls on-line from various places. Sometimes they have sales, plus I don't have to pay state tax. I am always on the lookout for vintage fabric. A JoAnns® near my home carries everything for painting, beads and ideas, but not all of their stores are as well stocked though.

Kelli "Jinx" Getchell: I keep a notebook to track everything I have for arts and crafts supplies. I even have swatches of the fabrics I have on hand so I could match threads and trims to them. I recommend this to any person starting out. You waste less money if you have that notebook with you when you go shopping. I still have the notebook, but I don't use it as much now as I can keep the information in my head. I tend to go shopping for one or two

items and end up with a bag full of stuff when I leave the store. I end up buying this and that to go with fabric that I already own, plus new fabrics. A stroll through a fabric or a craft store is a wonderful way to get inspiration. A new trim or type of bead can spark an idea for a whole new doll project On-line auctions such as eBay™ are also a nice way to shop for unusual fabrics, trims and jewelry findings. It's also a wonderful source for dolls. Many collectors buy dolls just for the outfits and then sell the dolls at auction where those of us who do fashion doll makeovers can pick them up at a bargain price. If you are going to buy from a dealer at an on-line auction, always remember to read the terms of payment and shipping carefully to make sure that even after your highest bid, you are still getting a good bargain. Also, check the seller's feedback as it will tell you a little about the seller.

Debbie Lima: I'm great with sales. At the end of the Christmas season I'll buy enough material to last me the rest of the year. Then all I have to do is shop for trims, ribbons and stuff. That doesn't mean that'll keep me out of the fabric stores. I still have an expensive bead and trim shop that I go to and a very expensive fabric shop that I can only afford to buy things on sale. I also hit this place after the holidays. This is the best way to increase your profits and make what you want.

Amy Nardone: Don't forget to check out the remnants! The best time to go is after New Years, Halloween and Prom time as much of the really fancy fabric is bought and the remainders are put in the remnants bin. Costume jewelry is also a great way to get beads. Furthermore, let everyone know what you do because people love getting rid of things like old clothes, fabric and costume jewelry.

Boxing and Packing Your Dolls

Once you've learned all you can learn (and we never stop learning) about creating your dolls, it's time to think about how you will box them and mail them out. Boxing and packing your dolls is just as important as your creations. Presenting them in a professional manner to perspective buyers is a big asset. Remember that when mailing out your dolls, the packing and box is the first impression the receiver gets.

Jim Faraone: When mailing out my dolls, I always send them registered mail with a signature required. This way you know for sure that the buyer did receive your doll. Or if the package is lost in the mail, you have a way to track it down.

Pamela Bachmayer: I use a long piece of flat metal or straight edge, large cutting mat and craft blade for liners in my custom boxes. I use poster board in various colors to enhance the doll and to hold her in the box. I cut rectangular sheets that will fit in the box and curve on each side up to the edge. To cut these sheets, I use my cutting mat (for measuring and cutting) and my craft blade. To give me a precise edge and protect my fingers from accidents, I use a wide piece of metal for a straight edge. I use metal for my straight edge as it does not get cut so I can count on a straight cut every time. Decorative twist ties and plastic wrap are used to keep my dolls in the box. I cut small slits in the liner (before inserting into the box) and insert my twist ties from the back so that the ends are to the front of the liner. I use a small piece of plastic wrap to wrap around the doll's costume to protect it before placing it in the box. The twist ties keep her firmly in

place but allows her to be easily removed. Mounting squares are used once I have added the twist ties to my liner. I use small pieces of mounting squares placed at the top and bottom of the box. I place the squares about a third of the way in so that the liner curves smoothly and forms a half cylinder shape within the box. I can move the liner a little bit to adjust it if I don't get it in quite straight but after a few minutes, the liner is there permanently. White card stock is good as I can fit several Certificates of Authenticity on each sheet.

Vonda Silliman: I find that perfect size boxes for dolls with big gowns and hair can be found at a cake supply store. They are inexpensive, some have windows and you can buy the cardboard (which is used to hold the cake) for the liner. Wallpaper can be used to decorate the liner and the outside of the box. Wallpaper books that are discontinued can be found at local wallpaper and paint stores, or if you're lucky, you may know a wallpaper sales rep.

Sharon Newman: I use cake boxes as well. I use ¼ sheet cake boxes. I cut the center out and glue in clear plastic that is used for overhead projection screens. I then hot glue the box together leaving the one side open so the doll can slide in and out of her liner. I then fold over the side and hole punch the 2 side flaps and the top flap. I use ribbon to tie the top so it stays closed. I then use rub off decals to decorate the outside of the box. The insert is made from white poster board. I cut and fold it to fit in the box. I punch holes in the liner and secure the doll with pipe cleaners.

Sharon A. Lawson: For decorating the front of clear cello lids on doll boxes just take

an 8in x 10in (20cm x 25cm) sheet of label sheet which you can find at most office supply stores. They are less expensive if purchased in a box of 100 through a labeling company. I download free graphics from the Internet such as flowers and ribbons that tie in with the doll I designed. On my photo program, I make an 8in x 10in (20cm x 25cm) collage. I make an outline on the 8in x 10in (20cm x 25cm) of the flowers in each corner and in the middle. At the bottom of the page, I put my logo. I then print this collage on the 8in x 10in (20cm x 25cm) label sheet. I only put a design in the four corners because 10in (25cm) is not long enough for most doll boxes. After printing the label, I cut out the two top pictures and then the bottom section including the logo. Then I just peel off the backing on the label and apply it to the front of the cello lid. Voila—a decorated window box! Now, to attach the doll to the liner, I keep the vinyl-coated wires from the original doll box. I poke holes in the liner with a small pointed scissors where I want to attach the doll to the liner usually for the arms, ankles and on each side of the waist of the doll. Insert the wire ties and twist on the backside of the liner. I make my liners wider than the width of the box and staple the liner from the inside of the box so that the prong ends of the staple are on the outside of the box (if you have a fuller gown it will not snag on the staple.) The doll will not come out of the box or come loose during shipping. Dolls tied in with ribbons sometimes come lose in the box during shipping. Now, for shipping dolls, try to find a box that is only a little bigger than the box the doll is in. Wrap the doll with cellophane wrap or put in a large resealable bag. Wrap bubblewrap around the doll

box and put it in the larger box so it fits in nice and tight. The doll won't get knocked around as much in shipping if it fits nice and tight into the shipper box. It will also help make the shipper box stronger so it won't crumple and damage the inner doll and box. The resealable bag or cellophane wrap will help protect the inner doll and box if the shipper box gets wet during shipping.

Jim Faraone: I get my boxes from one of those Mail-It type shops. They have white collapsible boxes (which I like to use since they fold up nicely to fit in a suitcase when traveling to do doll events) that are 6in x 6in x 12in (15cm x 15cm x 31cm) which are perfect for Barbie® dolls. **(see step 1)** I design a label for the box using my computer and print up 3 copies of it. Then I take photos of myself with my dolls and rubber cement them onto the 3 printed labels. **(see step 2)** I then take the 3 labels and rubber cement them to an 11in x 14in (28cm x 36cm) piece of heavy art paper and have the printers color copy the large sheet with the 3 labels on it. **(see step 3)** You cut the 3 labels from the color copy and they're ready to rubber cement to your boxes. To rubber cement the labels onto the box, just put a thin coat of rubber cement on the back of the label and on the box lid. Let them both dry a few seconds and then apply the label rubbing off the excess rubber cement on the box. **(see step 4)** This way I have nice boxes for my dolls that also display some of my other creations. Be sure to mention your creations in general and give some information about yourself on your box labels. And of course, include your website and email address.

J'Amy Pacheco: To protect customized shoes that are being

Step 1

Step 2

Step 3

Step 4

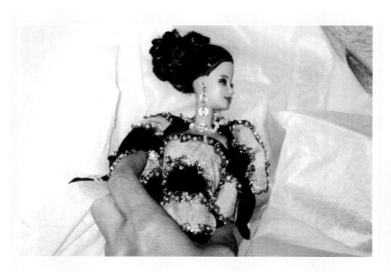

shipped on a doll, I cut small squares of tissue paper and place one under each shoe-clad foot. I pull the edges up around the doll's calf, and gently tie the tissue paper (not too tight!) with satin ribbon. It keeps the shoes from rubbing and the receiver gets to "unwrap" two little presents.

Jim Faraone: Here's tip for when I pack my dolls or wrap her to put in my suitcase for shows. If she has a fancy hairdo, say curls in the back of her head, I turn her head sideways as if she's looking over her shoulder. That way if things get crushed a bit, those curls are not the things being crushed.

Deborah Fagan: For transporting dolls to a show, I use some boxes that I get from a liquor store that held bottles of wine or champagne. They have compartments in which I place each doll with her stand. If some of them need more room, I can move the cardboard in a compartment and make it bigger.

Step 1

Step 2

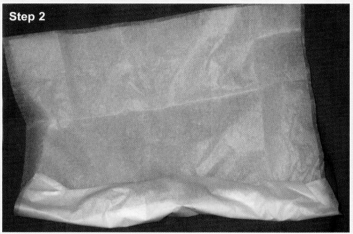

Step 3

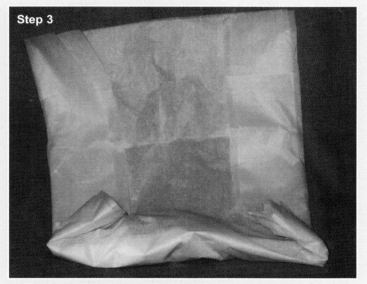

Step 4

Jim Faraone: When I pack for a show, I put all my dolls into one medium sized suitcase. To protect them, I line the bottom of my suitcase with clothing. Then I roll each doll in tissue paper. **(see step 1)** Using two sheets of tissue paper, lie the doll flat on the tissue paper. Keep the doll's arms down and if she's wearing a full gown, keep the gown down around the doll. **(see step 2)** Roll the doll twice in the tissue paper **(see step 3)** and then fold in each side, which will protect your doll's head and feet while traveling. **(see step 4)** Then continue rolling the doll in the tissue paper so she appears mummy-like. You can now start lining up the wrapped dolls in the suitcase. The bottom row is for dolls that have no problem being crushed and I put the more delicate dolls on the upper layer. I can usually get 3 layers of dolls in the suitcase. Then I line the top of the dolls with more clothing. The idea is to keep these dolls "snug" in the suitcase so that don't get jostled around with all the moving of loading and unloading suitcases at an airport.

J'Amy Pacheco: It's been said that "presentation is every-thing." It's certainly true in the packaging of a customized doll. Creative packaging can enhance the overall look of a doll and it doesn't have to be expensive. Buy plain boxes, and create your own liners. Cover the liner with coordinating wrapping paper, tissue paper, or fabric (for example, I once dressed a doll for a "road trip" and used a commercially-printed road map of California for the liner.) Just attach the doll to the liner with recycled twist-ties, or tie a length of ribbon around its waist. If you're shipping the doll, it's nice to fold tissue paper across the doll, similar to the way you would wrap a gift of clothing. It's fun for the recipient to unfold the tissue paper and "discover" what's underneath. If you are shipping a doll, prepare for the worst! Always use a doll box within your shipping container, and secure the doll as best you can. Attach the doll to the box liner in two places to prevent shifting during transit. Protect the doll's box by surrounding it with packing material. Make an extra effort to package your doll. You went to all that trouble to design it, don't send it out looking like a thrift store find! I once received a swap doll wrapped in a sheet of bubble wrap and squeezed into a too-small box. When I unwrapped the doll in the car, one of her broken earrings rolled out and under my seat, never to be seen again. The non-removable ball gown was crumpled from being squished in the paper and the doll's up-do was flat. It was a huge disappointment!

Katarina Sandberg: I like to make boxes to match my dolls' personalities and that is just as much fun as making the clothes. I use different kinds of boxes and for the liner, I am lucky to have access to an A-3 color-printer. I make my liner in MS PowerPoint™ by inserting clipart that I find on the Internet and printing it out on thicker half-glossy paper.

Jim Faraone: That's a good idea, Katarina, and maybe it would be fun to scan scenic photos and use those as the liner for the boxes. Nothing like a fairy doll with a forest scene liner or a high fashion creation with a photo of the Palace of Versailles behind her.

Miniatures, Props and Dioramas

It's always fun to add those little miniatures to your dolls to make them more realistic. It's also exciting to create an environment for your dolls, which can make an interesting display. I know that at the convention's competitions, the collectors go wild checking out all the diorama entries. Some are unbelievable with the tiny details not only put into each doll, but into the settings. Let's see what the group can come up with for props for their creations and dioramas. Discover how to put your dolls and props in to their own environment.

Ella Trumpfeller: Here's how to make a miniature vanity tray. You need the following supplies: a 2in x 3in (5cm x 8cm) oval picture frame, mirror, black material, pliers and glue. Just remove the glass from the picture frame and glue a piece of black fabric to one side of it. Then replace it back in the frame with the glass side up. Glue an oval mirror to the glass. Using pliers, break off the "stand" piece on the back of the frame. For mini flower vases, just take a 25mm cylinder bead (they come in lots of colors) and a miniature ceramic type flower. Put hot glue into the center of the bead and press the flower stem into the glue. Key chains, magnets and Christmas ornaments are excellent for finding miniatures. Buttons make great accessories for a hairpiece or clothing accent. You can also use different size beads and buttons to make perfume bottles and cosmetic compacts.

Pamela Bachmayer: Invest in some magazines and how-to pamphlets for miniaturists. They are often full of tips on do-it-yourself projects that can be easily adapted to the Barbie® doll or Gene® doll. Look outside your field of expertise such as craft or needlework magazines for ideas, do-it-yourself projects and new products.

Carolyn Marnon: This is perfect for me because my other main hobby besides fashion doll makeovers is making dollhouse miniatures. This interest has carried over into fashion doll scale. Anything I would make for a dollhouse, I would just double the size to make for a fashion doll. Fashion dolls are called playscale. If you do not want to make miniatures for your dolls, it is easy to find items at many stores. You just need to learn to see things in playscale. Sometimes you just have to see if it "looks" right with your dolls. Anything can be made in miniature. Things that are 12in (31cm) in our world translates to 2in (5cm) in the fashion doll world. It takes some getting use to in order to do the math easily. To make items, you can use basswood or balsa wood, which are easily available at the craft and hobby stores. The wood comes in several lengths and many different widths and thicknesses. You can also use mat board or foam core board. These are good to use in making furniture for your dolls. For softness, you can use quilt batting or thin foam.

Pamela Bachmayer: I have some tips on creating dioramas. Foam board is perfect for making the floors and walls for a diorama. It is very light weight and sturdy. It is easy to wallpaper and glue holds to it forever. You can glue your floors and walls together or tape them at the corners for folding. It can also be used to build steps, etc. Pieces of Styrofoam® can be used as a base to glue your foam board onto for support if you plan to build very high. To create marbleized floors: Paint the floor your base color. Use a feather to apply white, grays and black veins onto your floor. Use clear glossy varnish to seal your floor. A variation of the marbleized floor is marbleized tiles. Use a poster board or paint the base color. With a feather, apply white, gray and black veins. Use a paper cutter to cut out 1in (3cm) squares. Glue them to your floor in a random pattern and seal with a clear glossy varnish. The miniature department of your local craft store is a great source for miniature wallpaper and flooring. Most miniatures are not the correct scale though—many are too big for the 1:1 scale for which they are intended and are perfect for the Barbie® doll.

Jim Faraone: For wooden slat or parquet flooring you can buy those long flat strips of balsa wood. **(see step 1)** Take the strips and cut them the length you want and line them up side by side. **(see step 2)** For slat floors, just take a black ballpoint pen and ruler and draw on the slats. **(see step 3)** Turn your balsa wood and draw in your cross pieces on each slat. Then for that added effect, **(see step 4)** poke little nail holes on each side of the

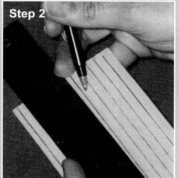

Step 5

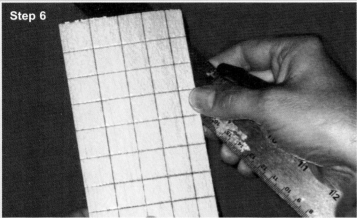

Step 6

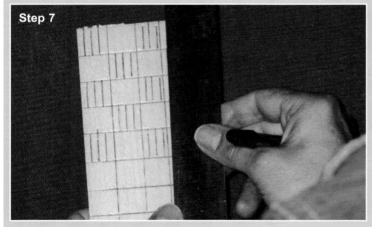

Step 7

Step 8

joining slats. **(see step 5)** The final step is to stain your floor covering and you're ready to glue it into your room setting. The indentation of the ballpoint pen in the balsa wood slats will stain a darker color than the rest of the wood, which gives a great effect. For parquet floors, **(see step 6)** measure off 1in (3cm) squares with the ballpoint pen and **(see step 7) (see step 8)** slat each square in an opposite direction.

Sharon Brendemuehl: I also make a few scenes and room boxes for my dolls. My favorite material is foam core. It is a very lightweight, but sturdy material that can be cut with an X-acto® or Stanley® blade. I use

it as a base for couches and chairs. One can use everyday stuff for their houses like upholstery material for carpeting. Stone shapes torn from paper egg cartons can be used on a floor or on a fireplace.

William Stewart Jones: A mirrored wall will increase the apparent size of the space. **(see photo 1)** For my prize winning millinery shoppe, I used three mirrored walls made of plexiglass mirror cut to size. **(see photo 2)** Cut out photocopied engravings were glued onto the mirrors to create the look of walls with framed mirrors. Mirrored surface cardboard can be used, but the reflection is less clear.

Photo 1

Photo 2

Step 1

Step 2

Step 3

Step 4

Carolyn Marnon: This is one of my favorite subjects. You can set up dioramas any number of ways. One of my favorite ways is by using an inexpensive bookcase. **(see photo 1)** I space the shelves so you have about 18in (46cm) of height with which to work. You want that extra space in case you want to hang chandeliers, other light fixtures or just to dangle things from the ceiling (like in a haunted house). Besides, your head doesn't hit the ceiling, does it? Therefore, your dolls' heads shouldn't bump the ceiling either. **(see photo 2)** I cover the walls with miniature print wallpaper and place rugs or flooring on the floor. **(see photo 3)** I then proceed to add furniture and accessories to my shelf unit room setting and **(see photo 4)** my dolls now have a place all to their own. I can create many different environments for them. You can also make a diorama inside a cardboard box, a wooden room box you have built (or had someone build for you), by using a science fair display board cut down to a more reasonable height, or by using a large glass dome. You could also fashion a diorama display using foam core board as mentioned before. If you have an old computer hardcase, you could take off the side and build a computer world for your doll. Perhaps she is working at her office computer in this scene or you could fashion that back wall as lots of computer functions like NASA might have. You could set up a diorama based on a painting you find that you like. Use the painting as the background and create the scene in front of it on top of your entertainment center, fireplace, or whatever space you have available. You could even put up a shelf, hang the painting over it and then construct your diorama on the shelf. Perhaps your doll could have a picnic with the Eiffel Tower in the background. She (or he) could be in a boat fishing with a scene of a lake or mountain in the background. Use your imagination and be open to ideas when browsing through the stores. You never know when something will catch your eye and you can make use of it for a diorama.

Jim Faraone: You're right Carolyn about using just about anything to create an exciting diorama. A large hatbox would be great to use as the casing for a hat shop for your dolls, or an old TV cabinet to make a diorama of one of your favorite TV shows. How about inside a ceramic pumpkin for a nice Halloween scene?

Gael Singer Bailey: I built ½ scale models. Houses, furniture and the doll house dolls. The ½ scale is 1ft (31cm) to 1in (3cm) so to convert things for my Gene® dolls, I sort of triple the sizes of things. I wish there was something that could give the exact scale. I am building several mock sets for taking pictures, just like the movie sets. I am building one out of foam core board. The window is a ½ scale French door with a picture of a sunset from a magazine. I also have a fireplace that I will cover with flat stone and miniature cement that can be purchased in miniature dollhouse stores.

William Stewart Jones: I photocopy ideas from magazines and books to doll size. It helps to see things actual size, so you can determine what kind of textures and patterns are necessary. I also adjust fashion pictures to doll size to determine button and fabric details.

Lori Strawn: As far as miniatures go, I tend to use "found" objects that can double as something else. For instance, my prescription allergy spray comes with a plastic safety ring around it that must be removed before use. The ring (it has a split in it so it can be clipped on and off) is the perfect size for a Barbie® doll choker or even a mini dog collar. Junk jewelry is another great source for miniatures. For example, I have jewelry from my childhood with tiny little dice and plastic fruit hanging from it. If you need inspiration, there are children's books (like the "I Spy" books) filled with pictures of small objects artfully displayed in unusual ways.

Jim Faraone: Check out the party supply stores for miniatures for your dolls. I have found wonderful miniature martini glasses at 3¢

each and some great champagne bottles in those stores. Just go up and down the aisles thinking miniature items for your dolls and not party supplies.

Carolyn Marnon: You can make different kinds of food boxes for your dolls by using advertisements in newspapers and magazines. Just cut them out and help give them the appearance of looking real. If it

is for a box of something, take an appropriate sized piece of wood and paint it a matching color then glue the cut out in place. Bags of chips, cat food, etc. cut out a piece of card stock a little larger than the ad, glue on a small piece of cotton, and then glue the ad on top. When the glue dries, cut around the edges, color the edges a matching color and use nail polish or other sealer to give the front of the bag a glossy shine.

Jim Faraone: Good one Carolyn. **(see step 1)** I also check out the ads in magazines and the Sunday papers that advertise books and records (CD's to the younger group. LOL!). I cut out the book cover or record album and **(see step 2)** take a thin piece of balsa wood, cut it the size of the book cover, and paint the edges white. I glue the covers onto the wood. **(see step 3)** They make great books and record albums for your dolls. It is best to find 2 copies of the book ads, so the front and back of your books match. If you want to go for more details, you can get very thin balsa wood and a cut piece for the front cover and one piece for the back cover. Paint both pieces white on the edges. When you glue the 2 pieces together, stick a little bookmark between the 2 pieces of balsa wood. If you'd like, you can then use a clear varnish to coat your books or record albums giving them a shiny appearance. Also, for small dinner plates for your smaller dolls, check out those little cups of cream that some restaurants give you for your coffee. If you look at the bottom of them, you will see that it's a dinner plate and just by cutting the bottom off the cup you are ready to fill it with food for your dolls.

Carolyn Marnon: You're getting me rolling Jim! LOL! I have also made a wireless microphone for my Madonna-doll by using black wire twisted into the proper shape and a tiny black pom-pom glued on the end for the voice piece. You can also buy tiny ribbon roses on stems in the bridal section of craft and fabric stores. These make nice bouquets of flowers when wrapped in tissue paper.

Jim Faraone: Over the years I have used bread dough for making miniatures. The ingredients are: 3 slices of white bread (no crust), 3 tablespoons of white glue and a teaspoon of glycerin. You just break up the bread into small pieces, mix in the glue and glycerin, and mush it together until it forms a dough. At first the bread and glue will stick all over your hands and become quite messy, but keep working it and you'll see it becomes a nice ball of dough. You can then break off pieces, mix some acrylic paint in it to get the color you want. You can make food or tiny props for your dolls. Bread dough air-dries so baking is not necessary. Just keep what you don't use in a zip lock bag to keep it from getting hard. There are some great books out there for making things such as fruits and vegetables, flowers and bakery items with bread dough.

Step 1

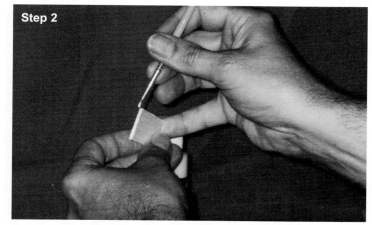

Step 2

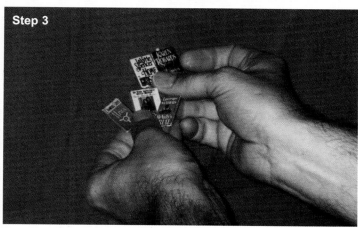

Step 3

Photographing Your Dolls

I bet you thought you were done now that you have learned many tips for creating your dolls. Believe me, there's a lot more to the fashion doll makeover world than just sitting there creating pretty dolls. The following topics will show you the other aspects of our special creative world. Each one is very important in its own way and should not be overlooked. We all, including myself, at times have a bit of a problem getting great photographs of our dolls. Photographing your dolls is very important since you use photographs for articles, websites, contests (which can definitely make or break you,) books and just plain showing off your creations.

Carol Jones: A digital camera is a wise investment for your dolls. Take several with a digital as well as with a 35mm camera. You can now get both a good digital and a good 35mm for under $400. Digital cameras allow you to quickly email your creations to the buyer for commissioned work, and a 35mm camera can give you an excellent quality print for your portfolio. The 35mm cameras range from point-and-shoots to SLR (single lens reflex). Point and shoot are fine for this, but the quality will be better with an SLR. SLR cameras are the type with the interchangeable lenses that allow you to get sharper photos. You can also get close-ups with the right lens. Going to a good camera store to inquire about these will give more insight.

Amy Nardone: Use natural lighting and don't be afraid to pose your doll other than an Army Sergeant. She needs to model her clothes to look good. Use a plain background and color that won't take away from the doll.

Michelle James: I agree that natural lighting is best. However, if using natural lighting, take the pictures on an overcast day or out of direct sunlight. Too much sun will wash out the colors much like using a flash. A simple backdrop can be created using two large sheets of foam board (one for the back wall and the other for the floor.) Then drape a solid-colored piece of satin over the "back wall." When using satin or other fabrics as a backdrop, make sure you iron out the creases prior to use. If using your scanner to capture images of your doll, know how to use your scanner to get the best pictures possible. All scanners have software that you can adjust the color, contrast, lightness, darkness and many other settings.

Joanna Bond: The backdrop color you use will not only affect the final appeal of the picture with respect to the way the doll appears next to it, but it also will affect your camera settings, lighting and color. You can't change the background and assume that everything else stays the same. Use a photo-processing lab that pays attention to color and cropping, and is willing to give you some good customer service. Take both front and back views, and side views too if necessary. And don't forget close-ups! For digital or scanned photos, learn some simple skills in a good photo-editing program. Learn to do color correction, sharpen and save the picture in the right format.

Jim Faraone: I photograph my dolls on my kitchen stove. (see step 1) I first take a flat cardboard box and place it over the burners to create a flat surface. (see step 2) I then hang a piece of fabric with masking tape to the back wall of the stove. You can drape the fabric or add another piece of sheer fabric to this to create different effects, but keep it simple. (see step 3) I then take a sheet of metallic oak tag (which can be found in craft sections of stores) and with masking tape, tape it to the material leaving the bottom curved which will give a nice "floating" effect to your dolls. Also, turn on the overhead light on your stove for a nice lighting effect on the metallic oak tag. (see step 4) Then I'm set to place my doll

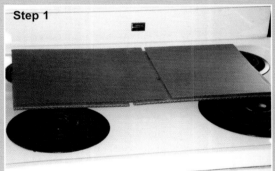

Step 1

Step 2

Step 3

Step 4

Step 5

Step 6

for photographing. **(see step 5)** I use my tripod with 4 flood lights. I lean against the refrigerator for steadiness and shoot. **(see step 6)** It gives my dolls a nice dramatic look with a touch of class.

Tess Barton: For me, the best results are generally achieved with a manual focus SLR camera or a good quality digital camera. Point and shoot cameras do not allow for good close ups and very frequently will focus on an object in the background. Natural light is by far the best lighting for photographing dolls. Flash bulbs will always overexpose colors and obliterate details in the photos. If you must use a flash, cover it with tissue or other relatively opaque white paper. If you have a detachable flash, swivel it to face at least 45 degrees away from the doll, rather than directly at the doll. The best light is outdoor light on a bright overcast day. Bright sunny days will give you a lot of shadows and contrast, and again, wash out details in the brightly lit areas. For indoor photo shoots, set up a miniature studio using screens or poster board and maybe a fabric background. To avoid using a flash, you should use spot light bulbs. General light bulbs give off a very yellow light which you will not appreciate until your photos are processed. "Full-spectrum" bulbs contain higher UV spectrum (more blue) and give a nice natural light effect. They are easily found in pet stores and places that sell reptile supplies. The best investment a doll artist can make is a set of screw-on close-up filters for a SLR camera. These are stackable magnifying lenses that allow you to take fabulous close-up photos. Without them, you cannot focus less than 6in or 8in (15cm or 20cm) from a doll, which gives you a photo of more than half of a doll. With these filters, you can focus as close as one eye on the doll. Avoid certain backgrounds. A busy background is distracting. A dark background will sometimes lead to washed out

photos because the cameras' light meter will average the light, and think it is darker than it is. A very light background will put the doll in silhouette. Light or medium blue usually works well, especially of you are taking pictures indoors, because it counteracts the yellow effect of light bulbs.

Carol Jones: A plain background with natural lighting works well. Using a piece of white poster board as a light reflector works very well for filling in shadows. Use only white or silver for this. Colored poster board will reflect that color over the doll. Sometimes you can get a windshield reflector from an auto parts store that is white on one side and silver on the other. They fold and shape the light well and are very inexpensive. White will look more natural, but silver adds a bit more sparkle to the sequinned and beaded dolls. Using a tripod will help steady you. Take several photos of the doll. Pose her as though she is a "real person." Get ideas from magazines. Posing her will make her seem more lifelike.

Jim Faraone: When photographing your dolls, keep their heads straight, side glancing or looking slightly down. **(see photo 1)** Try not to make your dolls look up because it will give the doll a heavy, jowly look. **(see photo 2)** Just see the difference a pose can make. Also, try to avoid shooting down at your dolls. This usually gives them a big head and tiny body, which is not a good look. Also, try to make your dolls look lady-like and keep their legs together. If you're working with a doll that has a wide stance and the feet cannot meet, try angling the doll so they appear together in the photograph, or make the doll pose in a walking motion which can help.

Carolyn Marnon: I don't take many pictures of my dolls, so I am not an expert on photographs. However, I do enjoy looking at the pictures others

92

Photo 1

Photo 2

have of their dolls. I like to see unique backgrounds, like a fabric that compliments the outfit the doll is wearing. I also like to see accessories added to the doll or flowers placed by a doll.

Debbie Jane Cates: To make an "invisible" crotch stand for your Gene® doll when taking photos, take a piece of poster board and put a hole in the middle that the raised hole on the base of the Gene® doll's stand will fit through. Place the base under the poster board and then the vertical piece of her stand into the hole. Then just place the Gene® doll on her stand. This also works with the Barbie® doll crotch stands also. Fabric can then be used over the stand's base.

Joan Champagne: I use a 35mm camera with a close-up lens. I've found that the best place for photographing dolls is outside or inside with a halogen lamp.

Juan Albuerne: I always use daylight for my pictures. My main tip is to take a piece of white cardboard or foam board and place it on the side of your scene (out of sight of course). Then set the doll. Look at the doll through the viewfinder, and move the white cardboard closer to the doll bit by bit. You will notice that the side of the doll's face becomes lighter when you approach it with the box. That's the effect that professional photographers get with that aluminum umbrella (you could use any box with aluminum too).

Linda Lynch Holman: Pose your dolls in life-like poses

using catalogue layouts, magazine ads and such for ideas.

Scott Shore: You're right, Linda, that getting the right pose is important. I try to have my dolls pose as if they are real models, either on a runway or in a private showing. I try not to have very much in the way of props and accessories though—maybe just a draped piece of fabric in the background.

Lim Shor-wei: If you don't have a tripod, put your camera on a stack of books or table. Then use the timer to take the photo to reduce shake and ensure a clearer picture. I use natural light and I find that 400 film is the best. I use the manual setting for the camera to slow speed, no flash, and check for correct exposure looking at the camera's aperture and shutter speed controls (camera manual will have more information). This will help to ensure clear pictures with no interference from artificial light, which can distort the colors. Also, a flash will "wash out" the colors of the items so that they don't look as "rich." Place the camera as far as possible from the object and use the zoom lens to get a close up. This will help to ensure some sense of depth for the photo.

Jim Faraone: Seeing photographs of everyone's creations is always fun, but it's more fun to see how those photographs were achieved. Like with all my "How-To" photos for my books, things are not always what they appear to be when the camera steps back. LOL!

Promoting Yourself

No matter how great your dolls look, people will not discover you unless you understand the few tricks of the trade in promoting yourself. Getting your name and work out there is very important because no one is going to come knocking on your door out of the blue. Promoting yourself is a delicate situation because you want to make yourself known, yet you don't want to come across as a "me, myself and I" type of person. I have seen many wonderful artists destroy themselves because of their egotistical way of promoting themselves. Your personality is a big factor in promoting yourself!

Ella Trumpfeller: Everyone should have a website. Frequently posting on message boards and auction sites is also a good way to get noticed. You may not sell from the auctions, but many times, I get referrals and sales because of the exposure there. Start a mailing list and send out pictures to the list whenever you have a new design. Advertise in doll magazines. Also, contact your local newspaper or set up at local craft malls/shows. Go to doll conventions. Exposure is the key!

Joan Champagne: To promote yourself, join web rings that relate to your work. Sign guest books and leave your URL; make an "about me" page on eBay™ and advertise your website providing a link so that when you are bidding, you will have that "ME" icon by your name—someone may click on it. Show pictures of your finished dolls on doll message boards to get people familiar with your work whether you are selling or just showing off your work. Learn how to make a website for displaying your dolls. There are lots of free website hosts who will offer you tips on how to get started.

Barb Wood: When a person purchases a doll from me on eBay™, I will usually ask that person if they would like to be on my "First to Know" list. I have been commissioned to do quite a few repaints and dolls that way.

Jennifer Urbaniak: Take advantage of free publicity on the Internet. There are sites you can maintain at no charge. Also, join web rings with other artists, utilized bulletin boars and show people what you can do.

Jim Faraone: Joining web rings is a good idea, but be careful of web rings and groups that form and become "gossip columns" and "sounding boards" for disgruntled and jealous people. You should find a group that works together well and not just a bunch of people getting together for a hen party or lynching. LOL!

Carol Jones: I keep a "portfolio" with me at all times. It is just a small photo album so that when someone says they would like to see my work, I can easily show them. I also keep a handful of business cards with me in case they are interested in ordering something. You never know when you might run into someone who collects! It is much easier than toting dolls wherever you go. The album shows the variety of work I do.

Jim Faraone: A "portfolio" is very important even if it's just for yourself. I have an album of all the dolls I have created from the beginning and it's fascinating to go through it at times to see how I have progressed through the years. Here is a sneak peek at the metamorphosis my dolls have gone through from the beginning.

Aurora Mathews: Brag! Show and Tell!

Jim Faraone: Getting your name and work out there is the main key. There are plenty of places to get FREE publicity. You should never have to pay for publicity! Send a portfolio of your work to various doll magazines since almost all will feature you for free if they like your work or story. Though magazines usually don't pay you for features about yourself and your creations, you should never have to pay a magazine to have yourself featured. Check out your local library since most libraries look for special displays each month. I have had my work displayed at several libraries in Virginia and I always leave my business cards with the librarian in case anyone is interested in learning more about my creations. Get out there and get your work out there because collectors want to see your dolls up close and personal. Many can take wonderful photos of their dolls, yet when collectors see the dolls, they can see the lack of quality and vice versa When the public gets to see your dolls firsthand, there is less hesitation to buy.

Vonda Silliman: Donate your dolls for various fund raising events. Schools, churches, nature centers, charitable organizations are all organizations to consider. Use them as gifts especially at highly visible events such as baby showers, birthday parties, wedding and holiday parties. The word will spread quickly and everyone will see firsthand what you have created.

Jim Faraone: Charity donations are nice, but do make sure you know all about the group holding a charity auction. Your donated doll is a tax write off, so make sure the group running the charity auction is equipped to give you the paper work to fill out for your donation. If they don't have the paper work, I would pass on it. Also, with donating to charitable organizations, try to donate to those events that YOU can attend to be seen with your doll. That way, those bidding on your doll can put a face and name with the creation. It's nice to be there to see that your donated doll is

getting the respect it deserves and not shoved into the background to promote a bigger named artist. Also, make sure you get the final bids on all the dolls in the auction. It's easy to say that something is a charity auction and yet you never know exactly where the money is going. Check out all the details before donating something into which you put your heart and soul.

LaDonna Moore: Ask your friends to attach your website link to theirs and vice versa.

Kert Hoogstraat: Show your work at a doll show at least once if possible. Even in this age of e-commerce, there will always be people who want to see firsthand what you do. It's also a great chance to really hear from collectors what they like and what they don't.

Jim Faraone: Check your personality! I have seen a few "cranky" artists out there who have snapped at a collector for touching or photographing their dolls. Getting cranky with one person may not seem like a big deal until that person tells 10 collectors what you did to them, and each of those 10 collectors, tells 10 more collectors what you did. Then it doesn't look good. Also, keep your egos in check. Believe me, you may fool some of the people some of the time, but you don't fool them all the time. People see through the facades and even those impressed with it at first, quickly become tired of it. Be proud of your creations, but keep yourself humble. Just be yourself, be cordial to everyone, and most of all, relax and have fun!

Karin Roberts: I agree with you, Jim. Reputation counts for everything. No amount of high dollar promotion will gain you fame and fortune if you have a reputation for inferior quality dolls or poor service. Every person you come into contact with is a potential customer. Always be friendly, appreciative of comments, and project a positive attitude. Work hard to consistently create the highest quality dolls that you can while

providing the best service. Don't be RUDE! There are times when people can be unreasonable. Smile and say thank you. If a customer complains about a doll and you are adamant that they are just being unnecessarily picky, keep your cool and address their concerns the best that you can. If a customer is beyond rude, cut all ties and vow silently never to deal with that person again. You don't have to lie down and let the world walk on top of you, but not every misunderstanding is a morale battle of who is right and who is wrong. Ultimately you will lose this battle because the customer is ALWAYS right.

Laura Fern Fanelli: If you go regularly into the local doll shops, ask them about displaying your dolls there for sale. Some will charge a 10% commission fee, but you'll get to know customers.

Scott Shore: I made friends with the store managers of some fabric and craft stores. Whenever I finish a doll, I take it in to show her off. I have gotten a few commissions for dolls by doing this.

Joan Champagne: As a last resort, you can do what I did the other day. I discovered that there were several computers that had been installed in the middle of the mall which were already connected to the Internet and were for public use (just in case you want to check your email while you're shopping!) I opened up my web page on a couple of them and walked away!! What a great way to advertise!!

Jim Faraone: ROTFLMBO!!! Great one, Joan! You're as bad as me. When I go into bookstores, I take my books off the shelf and face them forward in front of someone else's books. One time, no books were facing forward in the doll section, so I took my books out and found a space in the Antique section and faced my books forward there. They may have been out of place, but people sure could notice them when they walked by! LOL!

Doll Events and Selling Your Dolls

Selling your dolls doesn't have to be a scary adventure. All you have to do is jump in there with both feet. There are many collectors out there waiting to see your creations and you'll find that participating in most shows is a joyous experience. There are various techniques and tips to help make your dolls stand out in the crowd and attract more attention.

Jennifer Urbaniak: If there are doll shows in your area, think about attending and look for the tables with fashion doll makeovers. It is a great way to make a new friend and to see someone else's work close up and in person. It is quite different than seeing pictures.

Annie Muscatelli: Merchandising is a big part of the SELL. I feel that at a show you should make different levels to display your dolls. Make sure the table covering compliments your dolls and doesn't clash. If there is electricity available, take advantage to put a spotlight on one or more dolls that you want to feature.

Jim Faraone: Never lower the prices of your dolls. I know of someone who at the end of a show would lower the price of their dolls just to "get rid of them". Doing this makes buyers wait until the end of the show for when the prices are cut. This practice cut down on this artist's sales tremendously. Remember that shows are not flea markets, and you're not a flea market dealer. Have respect for the time and work that you put into your doll and get your fair price.

Kert Hoogstraat: Listen to collectors talking about what they like and dislike and try to work around what you hear. Also, keep your "dogs" and six months later revamp them. I've created lots of terrific dolls that had seen several shows without selling, but by simply reworking the facial paint, hairstyle, or accessories, they sold.

Charlie Dale: I have sewn in human scale for years and a very good friend who runs his own couture shop says the rule of thumb for pricing is the cost of all the materials times three and add cost of labor which then makes your retail price. I also write something about the doll on the back of the box like you would find on adult collector doll boxes. If this means research, so be it. I also describe what I have done to the doll (face painting, rerooting, original design, next doll in a series if it is a series doll) and, in small print, my contact information. I line all my boxes in tissue and use wrapping paper glued to the box insert to make it pretty and presentable. Each doll comes with a box, stand and certificate.

Sandy Cunningham: Since most of us end up with a table full, I use a "riser" on the back row of my table. This is made from plastic shelving that breaks apart for easy packing. I use two shelves about 18 in (46cm) high placed on the back of my table, draped with a fabric in my favorite color. Most of the time, I use gold lame or sometimes my signature lime color. Another good idea here is to display your most delicate creations on this back elevated shelf, out of reach of most of the "customer handling." I use extra decorations scattered among my dolls for attention getters. For example, doll size champagne glasses with mini champagne bottles. I also give these to customers with their purchase. Sometimes I use ropes of pearls draped around through the dolls on display (these are very reasonably priced after the holiday season.) I have a string of "plastic tube lights"—LIME of course—that I sometimes use to mix in with my dolls. Of course you have to be near an electrical outlet for this. If you have brides, display a doll size wedding cake on a glass top table (doll size,) the mini champagne bottles and glasses look neat here too. Doll size wooden furniture can be used with random dolls on display as well. Several things can be used to elevate and highlight the dolls. I use velvet and mirrored drums that are about 6in round x 4in tall (15cm x 10cm) on which to stand some of my girls. These were also purchased at discount after the holiday season. I also use a "mirrored battery operated" turntable, which is a real eye catcher. You do have to save up for these since they are rather expensive. Most of these items can be packed easily and compactly. Everyone loves "freebies" so I give away pens, notepads and other goodies to my customers with my logo on them. It does add to the costs, but I feel it pays off in the long run. Of the utmost importance, HAVE FUN MAKING AND SELLING YOUR DOLLS! Some shows may be great and you will sell several dolls. Others you may only sell one or two but make the most of it — make wonderful "doll world friends" and have a BLAST!!!! Meet and visit with the people who populate the doll world.

Kert Hoogstraat: Try to offer dolls in a wide range of prices.

Amy Nardone: Be pleasant and let people handle your dolls carefully. If they are serious about buying a doll, they need to know the quality of what they are buying.

Rose Rothhaar: To find information on shows, look in doll magazines, at doll shows you attend, at local doll clubs and doll shops, and on the Internet. You may want to check out a show before you actually participate. Fashion doll shows seem to attract more makeover collectors, but every area is different. Read the contract carefully; you may have to obtain state vending licenses. When working the show, arrive in plenty of time to set up so you do not feel rushed. It is also a great time to meet fellow dealers. Try to display your items at different eye levels. You can use boxes under a tablecloth, plastic risers or even invest in rotating display stands. Some people prefer to display in the box. Do what shows your dolls in the BEST light! Having a photo album of your creations helps a lot especially if you do custom work. The photos can demonstrate your versatility. Business cards are a must— some of your best sales can occur AFTER the show, so a business card will help them find you. A guest book is very helpful—you will meet a lot of friends (not just customers) and a book can help you remember them. Make sure your dolls are priced using tags or signs. This helps when your table gets crowded. Have a small emergency bag tucked away with have things like scissors, scotch tape, needle and thread, and hairbrush. Salesmanship is essential, but don't let it scare you. Engage in conversation with passersby. Give them a reason to browse your table. Ask them about their collections, where they are from, etc. Many times your dolls will sell themselves, other times you'll need to point out workmanship and/or quality of materials. Try not to just sit by your table and look bored; show enthusiasm. This is the art of your heart. The best tip is to have fun and share yourself with others. Doll shows can be a springboard for your talents. Try this avenue out and don't get discouraged if sales aren't booming. It can take time. Enjoy the experience and all the new people you meet who share your love.

Jim Faraone: Having a lot of dolls on one's sales table can cut down on sales believe it or not. When there are a lot of dolls on one's table it is hard at times for collectors to make a choice. If you don't get them to make a selection right away, they rarely come back to buy. Though I can't do this, I do know of one artist who brings a lot of dolls, yet only displays 10 dolls on his table at a time. With less dolls, many collectors think that that is all he has, so they buy fast so they don't miss out on one of his creations. When 5 dolls sell, he brings out another 5 and just keeps his table with 10 dolls. To me, this is fooling the public to buy and I'm sure a lot get upset when they come back later and see another doll that they would have wanted more than the one they bought. All ideas are great though and even I learned from his technique. I just do it differently. I usually put out a lot of dolls on my tables, but I divide them by categories. **(see photo below)** I will put all my eveningwear creations together, then my fantasy creations together and so on. This way, when a collector comes up to my table I already narrowed down their selections since they will go to the section they enjoy collecting. This way they can ignore the other dolls and not get confused seeing everything mixed together.

Karin Roberts: Be sure that your table is displayed in a manner that compliments and highlights your dolls. If you aren't able to have a sales table at the doll show, make up flyers and leave them in the lobby. Also, donating one of your creations for a door prize or raffle at a doll show is another great way to get noticed.

Jim Faraone: The main things you need at your sales table are: **(see photo 1)** business cards, which can be easily made on your own computer. In the beginning I had my business cards professionally printed. Then, my address changed and I had to buy new cards...then my zip code changed, then my area code changed. I found that now I can create business cards on my computer and just print them up, cut them out and they're ready to go. This way, any future changes can be easily fixed at no extra cost to me. Also, have flyers for future shows you'll be attending, sign up sheets of those with email addresses so you can contact them when you have new dolls, and neatly presented, clearly priced dolls. Also, if doll events let you have in-room sales, take advantage of that. Even if you don't sell anything in your room, it's a good way for the collectors to see what you will have in the salesroom. Some collectors like to comparison shop and this is a good way for them to make decisions before

hitting the salesroom. At larger conventions where they allow in-room sales, **(see photo 2)** make up a flyer to attach to the bulletin board so people know where your room is located. Make your flyer stand out, but don't make it too big because you will be sharing the bulletin board with many other dealers. The dolls you are selling are what is called "second market merchandise" which is legal to sell. What breaks a copyright law is when you advertise your dolls under the manufacturers copyrighted name of the doll. Though you have created these fashion doll makeovers, remember that they are not originally your doll and never, advertise them as a Barbie©

doll, Gene© doll or whatever doll you use. Using the doll's name in advertising is where you get yourself into trouble. Represent the sale of your work as coming from you the artist—never represent yourself as "Jim's Barbie© doll and outfits," Ginger's Gene© dolls," etc. Although you have created your own design for a fashion doll, that fashion doll was originally created by and the rights to the doll belong to someone else. On your sales table and in advertising, include a disclaimer, such as the following: _Doll Name is a trademark of Company Name. This (These) doll(s) are not sponsored by or affiliated with Company Name._

Photo 1

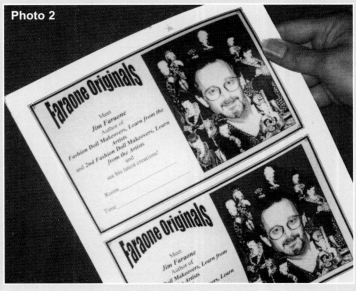

Photo 2

Websites, the Internet and On-line Auctions

Everyone has his or her own idea on how they want to set up their websites. Having a website is good so others on the Internet can see your latest creations which may or course bring in a sale. Once again, it is exposure for your work and if there's one thing you want, it's exposure. The Internet is also a great way to obtain information and even make some new friends.

Jim Faraone: Remember that the disclaimer goes on your website as well and never, ever use the name of a copyrighted doll in the title of your website. That breaks copyright laws and you'll be in big doo-doo!

Jean Birk: Learning to create your own website is like learning to do doll makeovers. Start with a simple design! Simple is the best even if you are an expert web designer. The object is to show off your dolls, not how much you know about coding and fancy graphics. There are plenty of websites that will give you "free" lessons on basic HTML coding. Basic design should include a "pleasant" background and fonts that compliment each other. Don't overdo using too many different font styles. Use 1-3 font styles for interest, but make sure they make the text easy to read. Keep the web page design organized, logical and easy to follow by using a main menu. The main menu should also be on each page so the viewer can easily maneuver to any web page on your site. Graphics should be small enough to fit on the screen without having to use the scroll bars and should load fairly quickly. Graphic files should be somewhere in the range of 10-20Kb in size. Also, crop your pictures so that the picture is mostly composed of the very thing on which you want to focus whether it is the doll or parts of the doll, accessories, etc.

Juan Albuerne: My own website? Is that possible? Isn't it hard to get one? Not at all! Today, with all the tools available on the Internet, getting a web page is within everyone's reach. It will take time of course, and you'll have to arm yourself with patience enough to create one, undo one, correct one, and replace one. You will need to choose a background, play with fonts, colors, setting texts and photographs. However, if you go step by step, it's easier than you think. I made my own web page through Yahoo!® with Geocities® and I'm very satisfied with the results. Could it have been better? Of course! But I wanted to get my own website where I could show my dolls and designs to the rest of the world. I would have thought it was a crazy idea a few years ago, but now I have my own web page and it was free. If a website was so difficult then why are there thousands and thousands of websites on the Internet that you can reach daily? You only have to go to any of the many offers on the Internet about free websites. If necessary, try more than one. Just go slowly and don't try to achieve it in a couple of hours.

Jim Faraone: Having a website to feature your creations is a great way of getting collectors to see your work. But once you create a website, stick with it. I have seen too many artists jumping ship from one site to another quite often. Moving your website around too often confuses the collectors who want to find your site. Find a good website source and stick with it. This goes for your email addresses as well. Find one and use that one for contact about your creations. Make it an easy email address to access without a ton of letters and numbers. Most collectors like an email address or website URL that is easy to remember.

Susan Yslas: Want to learn on the Internet? If so, go to a search engine and type in doll lists or Barbie® dolls and a whole new world is open to you. You can find information about anything.

Jim Faraone: You sure are right about that, Susan! I use the search engine many times even if just looking for ideas for a doll. It's also great to look up products that I want to buy and can't find anywhere else. When I did my series of "insect" dolls, I just plugged in "insects" on the search engine and it brought up hundreds of sites dealing with insects. Just looking at the photos gave me several ideas.

Susan Yslas: The computer and searches can be time consuming Jim, and you certainly can get completely lost in the cyber world. But I have also met so many new friends through the Internet. I met my best friend Beth Kinsley on the Internet five years ago. We discovered each other on a list and after several emails we became best friends. We talked and emailed daily and we finally started to do doll swaps. We then decided we just had to meet in person and I traveled 2600 miles to meet Beth at a mini convention in PA. I was wondering if we'd like each other in person. We finally met and I knew we were identical twins separated at birth. We are so much alike it's scary. We have been good friends for five years now and if we had our way, we would be living next door to each other with our own private connecting tunnel! LOL!

Joan Champagne: If you are creating your first website, it's a good idea to find someone who already has a website and who is willing to help you get started. I was fortunate to have an Internet friend who helped me with the basics through email. Although most website hosts give instructions on

getting started, some coaching may be necessary from someone who has already been through the experience. Fortunately, I had a very patient teacher. When I created my first website, I wanted all the bells and whistles. I had music, a scrolling marquis and all sorts of flashing lights. Guess I wanted everyone to know that I was capable of doing the extra HTML. As I became a more "sophisticated" web-mistress, I removed a lot of the glitz and glamour. I found out from others what I believe to be some important considerations. First of all, make it easy for people to navigate. Don't use a lot of java script and make sure that different browsers are able to view all of the content. Use either text or thumbnails on your opening page with links to your larger images. An opening page with lots of pictures or large images will take forever to download and some people may not wait around. If you prefer music, by all means use it—it's your site. Personally, I don't care for it and don't use it on any of my pages. I certainly don't mind if someone else uses it. I always have the option of turning it off! My goal is to add more content to my website such as miniature printouts, customizing tips and dolls from my personal collection. I think that this makes a website more interesting. It's a rewarding experience and a lot of fun!

Aurora Mathews: I personally like to see a first page with thumbnail pictures that load quickly so I can click to enlarge the ones I want to see close up.

Amy Nardone: Try to get yourself an image compressor program. Your pictures will show up a lot faster without sacrificing the quality.

William Stewart Jones: It's helpful to place "next" and "back" buttons at the bottom of each picture page so you don't have to go back to the main page each time.

Michele Frazee-Jackson: For those of us that are HTML illiterate such as myself, an "HTML converter" such as Microsoft Front Page® is a great blessing. It has easy ways to "dress up" a website such as backgrounds, buttons and counters.

Elizabeth Anne Dean: In the fashion doll makeover business, it is almost essential to have your own website. It's the perfect way to promote yourself and showcase your dolls. With a website, you can market your dolls worldwide. But most people think you have to be a computer whiz or commission someone to create a website. The truth is, you can build a website completely free of charge and with minimal computer skills. It's as easy as point and click to create text, background, graphics, links, and other features. You can upload and manage your own files without having to use a file transfer protocol. These websites also come with free email. Although these page builders don't require you to know HTML to build your page, I recommend learning basic HTML—it's fun and easy. When I first began customizing, I was so computer illiterate, I barely knew how to log onto the Internet. Since then, I have taught myself HTML and built several websites. A great book to help you learn how to create your own website and basic HTML is, "The Complete Idiots Guide to Creating an HTML 4 Web Page, Third Edition".

Joanna Bond: If you hire someone else to build the bulk of your site, have them teach you how to make updates. That way, you don't have to go running to them whenever there is a new doll that you'd like to get up on the site. Include a "what's new" section and learn to code it yourself. Remember that some people have old, slow computers, and site add-ons like music and trailing cursors are only going to take away from the dolls. Some people may actually go elsewhere as soon as they see that they'll have to wait for bells and whistles to load. Some people also have small monitors, so don't design a huge screen for your site that will require any scrolling. Include an obvious section on the artist, who you are, how to contact you and how to order dolls from you.

Rachel Steinberger: When I'm surfing websites, there are three things that just drive me up a wall: broken scripts (so that a little grey box is continually popping up in front of my face), squished pictures (where they've been squashed more in one direction than another), and broken links to pictures (c'mon people, it's your own site, can't you make them work?) And ya wanna know why these annoy me so much? Because they're really all easily preventable by just double-checking that your site is working! There's one thing that sets a good website apart from a bad one and it's not a sound effect, great graphics, or pretty fonts. It's organization. An intelligent menu of choices, like Salesroom, Gallery, Bio, Links, that is easily read and leads me to exactly what I want to see. It's much easier and more rewarding to navigate than an infinite string of pictures linked together.

On-line Auctions

Many of the artists sell their dolls on on-line auctions. Usually their dolls are listed as "OOAK" (One-of-a-kind) and there are always good tips on selling your dolls on these on-line auctions. It can be a wonderful, yet vicious place to sell dolls, but with tips maybe we can make things go more smoothly.

Aurora Mathews: With on-line auctions, make sure your pictures are clear and large enough to see the detail of your work. Look at the dolls that are selling and really study the techniques that the artist uses (pictures, description, layout, etc.).

Laura Fern Fanelli: I list more than one auction at a time. EBay™ asks when you list if you want it to be a featured auction. This is more expensive, but I've noticed that if it is a featured auction, it usually closes higher. So my idea is to list one as a featured auction and then in the auction under "description" I mention to check my other auctions. Those are not featured auctions, so they are among a large group that could be overlooked. Therefore, the one featured auction is the hook. A good clear picture is a definite plus on the featured auction. The buyers need to like and want the doll and then they will check out the other auctions. It is easy to check the other auctions as there is a place to click on the auction itself to see the other auctions of the seller.

Jenny Hughey: Always make sure your auctions are pretty and eye-catching. Use a software package to make a colored background and pretty fonts to accentuate your auction. Remember less, is more though. Don't use too many fancy add-ons like animated cursors, etc., because the longer an auction takes to load, the more chance a potential buyer will get discouraged and move on. Also, like everyone has been saying, and it can't be said enough, make sure your pictures are clear and detailed. The more detail you can show of your creation, the better.

LaDonna Moore: I've noticed a lot of viewers don't have a lot of time, so try to keep it short and sweet and right to the point and keep that download to a quick view.

Amy Nardone: Be prepared for the good, bad and ugly. Most people I have dealt with have been fast with payment or at least provided me with an explanation if they were running late. There are some who retract bids. I had one and it really messed up the rest of the auction. I also had some not pay at all. Don't be afraid to find out from other people if they have dealt with a particular person. Look at FEEDBACK. Very Important!!!!

Jim Faraone: Yes, there sure is the good, bad and ugly on on-line auctions, Amy. There has even been one person who bid on artists' dolls under several false names and then retract bids to mess with the artists. Another would go into chat rooms and ask people what their on-line auction "names" were and then they'd track down the auctions these people were bidding on and outbid them purposely. Then they would refuse to pay for the winning bid to the dealer. That's why I feel that these on-line auctions should be set up so at least they can track down who an individual is in case things like this happen. Of course, some people who do this are well known because they are so "thrilled" with their antics they can't keep their mouths shut about it, and you know how fast news travels in the fashion doll makeover world. LOL!

Juan Albuerne: A few years ago, it would be unimaginable to think about getting practically anything through an on-line auction. Yet today, it's a very common practice among Internet users. Since I live in Spain, I was forced to participate in those auctions if I wanted to get collectible dolls for a reasonable price. When I started my collection, many of these dolls were not available in retail stores. So I had to try the on-line auctions to get an interesting collection that wasn't possible before. Of course, on-line auctions are a different way of purchasing, and many people can be afraid of the hazards like sending money but the doll never comes, bad packaging, etc., yet it never happened to me. I've bought many things through on-line auctions and I've never felt swindled. All that I purchased came to me in perfect condition and within a reasonable time even though I live in Spain. I've never had any problems with sending money (though with the shipping cost that I've paid by now I could have made another wonderful collection of dolls). I'm completely satisfied with my dealers (the same way I hope they are with me). You have to follow the basic good manners on both sides and you'll have no problem. Don't forget to set a rating feedback for your seller or buyer because that will be the very best way for the rest of the world to know that you are a good dealer/buyer.

Anke Scharfenberg: As I am from Germany, it's sometimes very sad when it says on an on-line auction that they only ship to the US. Because of that, I want to tell you what you can do, like when I sell overseas. The price for shipping depends on the way you ship. Airmail Express is usually very high, Airmail is the fastest alternative and surface takes months. Let the buyer know that shipping is higher than usual. For the shipping itself, you have to fill in a declaration form, which depends on whether you send a small parcel or an insured parcel. In either case you help the buyer if you declare them as a gift. If you send them insured, let the buyer know that beforehand as this sometimes gets into gray areas because in Germany we don't have these specials codes anymore. In Germany, the big parcels are always insured for a certain

amount. So you see, shipping overseas isn't that hard if you put the doll in a big enough box and secure it very well. I have done a lot of these transactions on eBay™ and I always found new friends.

Laura Fern Fanelli: The advantage of eBay™ is the feedback system they have established. Buyers are leery of purchasing from sellers with no feedback, so if you are new to eBay™, first establish yourself with purchases of several small inexpensive items and leave feedback to your seller and they in return should leave a positive feedback for you. Then with the positive feedback you can begin. When listing your doll/item for sale, remember to state somewhere in the description, "I reserve the right not to sell to those with hidden or multiple negative feedbacks." This is to leave yourself an out if your doll catches the eye of a deadbeat bidder. Use a reserve for your doll. You have spent time creating this lovely doll and you should make sure you get what you want. Most on-line auctions want to make the most money possible so they don't like reserves. If you are not using a reserve your item will sell, regardless of the price, and of course the on-line auctions will get a percentage of the sale. Use the reserve, because your time and energy have gone into your creation and you want to be sure to sell her for what she is worth. One other suggestion on selling—if you donn't want to list a reserve, start your bidding at the lowest price you are willing to take for your doll. Then watch the action. When you are listing your doll, if she is a one-of-a-kind, put OOAK auctions for buyers. That way, if they put in a search of OOAK, they will find your doll in the listing. Research ahead of time how much your doll will cost to ship to its new home. In the auction description, remember to tell any prospective buyers the amount of shipping (and if you need extra for insurance). Buyers tend to be leery of open-ended costs.

Jim Faraone: I know that just about everyone lists their dolls in the doll category list. Have you ever thought about listing your dolls on another category? Our doll creations are also known as "Cross-over Collectibles." A cross-over collectible is any collectible that could sell in various places. For instance, if you do a doll as a celebrity, you could also list that doll in a Celebrity Memorabilia category. Fantasy dolls could be listed in Sci-fi categories and dolls created in the historical period could be put in a category of Historical Memorabilia. Don't think of the obvious, but go for something that is a bit different.

Amy Nardone: DO NOT get discouraged. The more you sell, the more people will recognize your work. Include clear and detailed pictures with a PLAIN background, which is important. Don't add all the extra foo-fah, it slows the page down and may cause impatience on behalf of the prospective buyer (although some people like it, this is my opinion). Be willing to answer any questions prospective buyers may have.

Michelle James: Don't use images that haven't been reduced in size. The bigger they are, the longer they will take to load and your potential bidder may get tired of waiting and move on to the next auction. Always put a disclaimer on your auction that you are not affiliated with the doll's manufacturer in any way. Include a link back to your website (if you have one) to generate more traffic for your site and stir more interest in your dolls.

Katarina Sandberg: Before editing any photos for your auction, save a copy of the photo so you always have the original intact in case something should go wrong during the process. Try to crop the scans/digital pictures, at the scanning moment so only the necessary item shows in the photo. Try to keep the background "calm" by putting a piece of fabric behind the doll

or by using a wooden/stone/painted wall. Do not take shots in front of the computer screen or at the working area or any other place that will distract the buyer from looking at your doll. Keep file size small because the bigger the file the more a person will have to wait for loading, which means people might tire and leave. Make thumbnails instead. And I mean THUMB nails—don't just "resize" pictures by clicking on a corner and drawing it towards the middle, as the picture file is still the same size as the original. Rather, make a copy of the big picture by changing the size and RESOLUTION, which can be found under the Photo/Image/Edit-menu depending on which program you use. And be sure that the program keeps the ratio of width or height so it resizes them equally by percentage. Rename the new smaller picture by adding for instance "_sm" after the name. Then you can make a link to the bigger, original photo instead. This makes surfing faster and easier for visitors to your auction/site..

Jim Faraone: Never get discouraged with on-line auctions if your dolls don't get any bids or never reach your reserves. On-line auctions have their "hot" seasons and their "cool" seasons. Plus you can never second guess what the public wants. Remember that during the summer time, many collectors are getting ready to attend national conventions, so they are saving their money. You may get some sales during the Christmas season, but the majority of collectors are spending their money on others for gifts. Now January may be a good time because a lot get money for the holidays and are ticked that they didn't get what they wanted for the holidays, so they may be looking to spend their money to get themselves a nice gift to add to their collection. No sales is not a reflection of your work, so never let it get you down. There is a home for every doll!

Contests and Competitions

Contests and competitions can be a lot of fun if you can handle it. I usually don't like competitions because I don't enjoy seeing artists competing with one another, but at times a competition or contest can be exhilarating. It keeps your creative juices flowing and it makes you strive to do the best you can. Of course, there are those few that can't handle competitions and contests because either their competitiveness is dangerously strong or some actually cheat in order to make themselves come out ahead. You would think that these contests and competitions come with million dollar prizes. LOL! I always say that if you can't stand the heat, stay out of the kitchen. If you can take the heat, then by all means enter and have a blast with it. Also, be happy for your fellow artists.

Lynn K. Johnson: After the thrill of seeing my doll win a blue ribbon and on display for all and sundry to view, the beautiful doll was lovingly packaged for the return journey home. Carefully ensconced in a conspicuous location, the judge's tag still dangled from her arm. The tight wad of paper containing the judge's score and comments revealed an interesting result. The top score of 100 was crossed out with a single line and a score of 98 was penned. What the....! On one of the many elements, a 2-point change was made after the initial score was decided. The top score would automatically qualify the doll for a sweepstakes ribbon, but the judge altered the ballot! No handwritten explanation was offered on the paper slip.

Jim Faraone: When entering competitions make sure you READ all the rules and regulations. I do find that some artists like to look for loop holes or change the rules to suit their own purposes. The rules and regulations are very important and if not followed, they could disqualify you in a competition. I do find that many contestants don't read the regulations and wind up missing out on a lot of things. Rules are rules and should be followed to a T! It is up to the artist to get their entries in on time and not for the contest administrator to wheedle around deadlines just to suit your purpose. I believe that the deadline for contests should be set in stone and not changed no matter how good an artist's creation is. It is not fair that those late comers to have had the extra time to work on their creations in comparison to those who followed the deadline. With judging, I don't think that every category should have a 1st, 2nd and 3rd place winner. What if one category features 3 poorly made creations—does that mean that the least offensive doll should be a 1st place winner? Then the winner of that 1st place ribbon goes around promoting themselves and collectors begin to wonder what is wrong with those creating fashion doll makeovers? At times, it actually begins to pull down the reputations of all the artists when collectors see these "winners" and start to back off or not checking out other artists' creations..

Barb Rausch: I'll say up front that I've been fairly lucky the times I've entered competitions; the times I've won blue ribbons in my category at the National Barbie® doll Conventions, my work really did deserve them. I was just lucky the judge or judges thought so! On the other hand, public mail-ins/email voting makeover contests are basically a "popularity contest" with no qualified judges. Since they are NOT professionally judged, it behooves anyone who enters to take the results with a LARGE grain of salt and NOT be crushed if they haven't placed in their categories! And even PROFESSIONAL judges are only human. You can't let one judge's decision affect your work negatively! On the other hand, even a win doesn't mean everything either! What counts in the long run is if your work sells for what you charge for it, and continues to sell.

Jim Faraone: Well put, Barb! Some artists take these competitions way too seriously and think that they are set for life after winning. Especially with "popularity contests" it is well known that a few have had friends vote for their dolls just so they can say they're a "winner." Can they actually feel deep down that they truly are winners? How can one be a winner when they only won because they conned half the world into voting for them? I always encourage people to vote for what they like...not for what a friend did. One contest on the Internet had been cancelled due to "stuffing the ballot" and then the so-called "winner" who was caught having friends stuff the ballot whined that they had been cheated because they "won" and the contest was cancelled! I say everyone who gets involved and enters a competition is a winner. Those who cheat in competitions or are overly competitive are the true losers. Get involved, but don't let it all go to your head.

Linda Lynch Holman: I don't feel there is any better advice than to enter what you feel is your very best work, and enter because you want to have fun with your work. One can't take any type of contest personally because there are too many behind the scenes factors. I have found quite a few contests to already have winners in mind before they are finished. These have been mostly small competitions. Then there are the ones where everyone lobbies for votes from everyone and anyone with whom they come into contact. The lobbyists don't always win or place, but they do make it hard for artists depending only on their style and creativity. However, over all, I feel if your work is "THE BEST" in your eyes, eventually it will find a market, or place in a competition. It's all about timing...being in the right place at the right time.

Karin Roberts: With contests and competitions, start early. Projects that are rushed to meet the deadline will show the signs. Create for the "theme." If the contest has a theme or category, make sure your entry is appropriate. This is not the proper time to make a statement or get yourself noticed. Submit accurate and complete information when you enter. Don't forget to put your name on your entry. Forgetting to label your entry with your name can have disastrous results! Make sure that you permanently affix your name to the back of the photographs in permanent marker that can't fall off like sticky notes always do. Double check that you have followed the rules to the letter. No need to get yourself disqualified by not following the rules. Use a critical eye or enlist the aid of a friend or family member to critique your entry and/or pictures BEFORE you send them off. Make any changes or improvements as needed.

Jim Faraone: Your right, Karin, about starting early with creating your entries for a contest or competition. At times artists get lazy and instead of creating something special, they just go through their old stock. The fun part is creating something special and unique. Challenge yourself to create something the world will love, but mostly, what you love.

Scott Shore: I always have some of my more critical and opinionated friends look at my entry either in person or in a photo. They have definite ideas about balance and color, so I am always open for a critique.

Tour Dolls

Some of you may have never heard of tour dolls, but they are an exciting and fun way to "play" with your makeover or regular dolls. The adventures of your dolls can be hilarious and even educational and you'll soon be envious of your doll's travels.

J'Amy Pacheco: Hey Jim. I'm really into these tour dolls so can I give the group an explanation of them?

Jim Faraone: You sure can J'Amy. Even I can't wait to hear all about them. I know it's a fun adventure for those involved.

J'Amy Pacheco: A doll tour can be a wonderful way to "play Barbie® dolls" with your far-away friends. Here's how it works. A group of people form a tour group, and each person sends a doll "on the road" for a designated amount of time. (see photos 1-2) The three groups in which I participated each chose a one-year period. Each person on the tour hosts a traveling doll for a designated period of time (we chose one month), taking pictures of it in their locale and recording its travels in a journal that ac companies the doll. Each host provides the visiting doll with a new outfit and some regional souvenirs, and then sends it on to the next person on the list. By the end of the tour, the doll has visited each tour participant, and arrives home with a new wardrobe, an interesting travel journal and photos. One person should serve as the tour organizer and should try to make sure the dolls keep moving on schedule. A schedule should be prepared before any dolls are mailed and a copy should be provided to each tour participant. Remember to allow for travel time! A tour website is an excellent way to keep track of the doll's progress, as well as to show off pictures taken during the doll's travels. Before any dolls are mailed, each person should commit to finishing the tour. It's difficult to revise the schedule mid-term and it's not fair to the people who have already hosted the drop-out's doll. The group should agree about what is expected of each host. Some, of course, will have more fun with the tour and will go above and beyond the call of duty. Here's some advice. Be creative in selecting your tour doll. Poseable dolls are the most fun; you can photograph them in some REALLY creative situations. If you're in love with a doll that isn't poseable, pop the head, and put it on a poseable body. Try to make sure there are no doll duplications on the tour. It can be confusing if several people send the same doll. Give your doll a name and personality. Write the doll's "story" in the front of the journal. If possible, make it justify the doll's spending time traveling. Is your doll on the run from the law? Running away from an arranged marriage? On a quest of some sort? My 2000 tour doll was named "Jill B." and was a newly-unemployed executive from a major corporation traveling the country in search of gainful employment. Use your imagination! Come up with a theme for the tour if possible. One group in which I participated did a "Barbie® doll 40th Birthday" tour in 1999, and then a "Millennium Tour" during the year 2000. Send the dolls out with as little as possible: a journal or diary, in which her host can record the details of her travels; a photo album; a disposable camera and a light-weight bag to hold her clothes and souvenirs. Hosts can use the album to store any pictures they take and develop or they can opt to use the disposable camera, which goes with the doll to its next destination and is ultimately developed by the doll's owner. Keep it light to save on postage.

Photo 1

Photo 2

Photo 3

Photo 4

Photo 5

Arrange the mailing schedule to shorten the distance between hosts to save on postage. Don't mail dolls all the way across the country and back if they can be mailed shorter distances. Consider a special tour or an alternate schedule for international participants. For example, ship several dolls at once to an out-of-the-country participant, and let that host keep the group for several months. Integrate the dolls into your daily life. Snap photos of the doll trick-or-treating with your children, wrapping Christmas gifts or coloring Easter eggs. Photograph the doll "playing" in new-fallen snow or on vacation at Disneyland® with your family. **(see photos 3-5)** The more you "play" with your tour doll, the more fun YOU

will have with the tour! Use accessories like doll-sized cars, luggage and furniture in your photographs. Also use human-sized accessories. Pictures of dolls trying to do "human" things like pushing a lawn mower or making margaritas with a real blender can be pretty funny! If the doll has a limited number of outfits at the beginning of its tour, there won't be much variety in its pictures. Consider using your own doll clothes for pictures of your visitors. If you use your own, there is more variety, AND you won't have to try to remember what goes back in the doll's box when mailing time rolls around. If someone on the tour attends a "big" event, like the National Barbie® doll Convention, consider making

arrangements for the whole group to attend. As a group, our tour dolls attended the 1999 and 2000 conventions in Pittsburgh and Tulsa wearing matching outfits and specially made badges. Be creative and have fun! I've photographed dolls on the Walk of Fame in Hollywood, **(see photos 6-7)** and "shopping" on Rodeo Drive in Beverly Hills. I've taken them to work, to concerts, to the taping of a television show, to the movies, Las Vegas and to the beach. After a significant earthquake in 1999, I put my visiting doll in the Barbie® doll house and photographed her surrounded by toppled furniture. With her souvenirs, I included the front page of my local newspaper from "Earthquake Day." On the 4th of July, I treated my tour doll and her buddy tour dolls to a relaxing afternoon in the pool. **(Photo 8)** I once persuaded an officer of the L.A.P.D. to pose with a group of dolls on Hollywood Blvd., and talked a western celebrity into taking one on stage. You'll be surprised at the reception the Pink Princess and her friends will get out in the "real world." Stay in touch! When a doll arrives at a new destination, the host should email the doll's owner with a copy sent to the rest of the group. If the doll does something interesting, send an email. The advantages are twofold: the entire group gets to stay on top of what the dolls are doing and may get inspired to be more creative and lazy hosts can print and paste emails in the doll's diary! Have your visitors mail a postcard home now and then. It's fun for the doll's owner and makes a great souvenir at the end of the tour. Keep it funny! Funny pictures and emails add spice to the tour. If the tour participants have children, consider having a "Junior Tour." Appoint an adult to serve as the tour coordinator, and have the children duplicate the adult's tour activities—well, maybe substitute chocolate milk for the margaritas... If some of the participants cann't yet write, use scrapbooks instead of journals. Make sure each

participating child is under the supervision of a responsible adult!

Jim Faraone: Great write up J'Amy and it's even gotten me excited about doing one. It could be fun as a Christmas gift for those on the tour. If the dolls are sent out each Christmas, the following Christmas would be like one big present opening up your returned doll and seeing all the new goodies.

Carolyn Marnon: I did my own tour doll as part of a swap. The first swap I did had a "vacation in my hometown" theme. Since my husband was in the Navy at the time, I redressed the Barbie® doll in an anchor-print dress and gave her tennis shoes for climbing all the hills of San Francisco. I then took the Barbie® doll and we went sightseeing around San Francisco. I took pictures of her on her towel at the beach, standing next to a sign at Pier 39, having a ride on a pedicab, on the Treasure Island pier with the San Francisco skyline in the background, and a few other locations. I put all the photos along with some postcards of the city in a small photo album and sent the Barbie® doll off to her new home with her "vacation" photos.

Elizabeth "Beth" Kinsley: Tour dolls can be a lot of fun especially if your family isn't afraid to help out. This past summer I took a Barbie® doll to several NASCAR races. My hubby, being a very good sport, carried her all over the racetracks in a back pack with her upper body sticking out and her hand waving. One of the race cars was on display (#17 of Matt Kenseth) and no one was allowed to touch it. I asked the man guarding it if I could get a picture of the Barbie® doll on the car and he got so tickled he even put the Barbie® doll inside on the steering wheel. He said that she was the first Barbie® doll to be in the car and would be the only one!!! :-) He was such a great sport!!!

Photo 6

Photo 7

Photo 8

Doll Swaps

Doll swaps can be a lot of fun and they can also be frustrating as heck. The most important thing is to make sure the swap moderator is on the level and being fair to everyone. Stay clear of moderators who choose the best artists for themselves, or is just out to get free dolls for their collections.

Jim Faraone: Yes, even I do swaps on rare occasions with friends especially during the holiday season. Swaps can be enjoyable if you choose the right groups.

Susan Yslas: Jim, I run a lot of doll swaps so can I talk about what doll swaps are?

Jim Faraone: You sure can Swapmama....I mean Susan! :-)

Susan Yslas: A swap can be done between a big group of people or as small a group as two people. A swap is the agreement of at least 2 people who are interested in customizing a doll for the other person with the intent to swap the newly customized dolls. A swap usually contains a theme (ie: Christmas, Halloween or Millennium), and it always has a spending limit or an amount to be spent. It also has a date to be mailed or a date to be sent. It is up to the Swap Coordinator or whoever is in charge of the swap if this is a secret swap (not telling your partner who you are) or it can be a swap where everyone knows who his or partner. The Swap Coordinator will set up the rules to this swap. The Swap Coordinator will decide the name of the theme, amount to be spent and the date to be mailed. After you are assigned your partner, it's time to make a new friend or many new friends. I email my partner if this is not a secret swap, as I like to talk to and tease my new partner. I like to ask questions to find out what is her favorite hair color, eye color and favorite dress color. I tend to try and customize a doll to my partner's likes. I love to ask questions and give hints, which helps as we go along during the swap. I sometimes ask to swap with a newbie swapper so I can give them confidence in doing a swap like giving them help with the hair, painting, jewelry and sewing tips. I have organized and been the Swap Coordinator to numerous swaps and can say there is nothing like the built up excitement of sending off your swap doll or being on the receiving end of your swap. I like to synchronize our mailing dates so we can receive our swaps near or close to the same date. I also like to be on-line with my swap partner so we can open our swaps together. After receiving your swap, you post to your group about what you got and how thrilled you are, so the Coordinator can mark you off the list as having sent your swap. There is nothing like making a swap doll according to someone else's preferences. I know I have done a good job when I do not want to send it. That is the first clue that I have done a good job on this swap. Join a swap on an email list and make a friend. You will never regret it.

Kim Burie: Doll swaps can be a wonderful way to build your doll collection, make new friends and get to see other people's work. The swaps in which I have participated that were most successful were ones where both sides communicated what they did and did not like. This way, the person receiving the doll wasn't disappointed, and the person making the doll didn't have to make something he/she didn't like. It also alleviates some worry that your hard work ended up in the garbage because your partner didn't like her.

Barb Wood: I have done many list swaps and private swaps, and I have been very pleased with them. One thing that I make sure to do is to include a doll stand with the name of the doll, my signature and date on the bottom of the stand.

J'Amy Pacheco: Don't put any less effort into a swap than you would into a commissioned work. Consider your swap to be one of your professional peers, and ask yourself, "Is this how I want my work to be viewed in the fashion doll makeover world?" There is nothing more disappointing than putting effort into a doll made especially for one person, and feeling like the other person didn't reciprocate. This doesn't mean you have to be as good as the best artists to swap; it means simply that you should give the project your best effort! Before swapping, ask your swap partner questions about themselves. What's their favorite color? Do they like foofy ballgowns, or mod styles? Do they prefer holiday-themed dolls, or would they rather have something more generic? What hair colors do they like? Which face molds? What kind of music do they like? What historical periods interest them? Asking questions might spark your creativity, and you might end up finding out you have enough in common to become friends. If you're not going to make your swap mailing date, be sure to let your swap partner know. Most people will understand a delay, and will appreciate being kept informed.

Joanna Bond: I agree that you don't save your worst dolls for swaps because they are free. Do your best stuff just like you would if you were trying to sell it. Always be proud of what you send out because you never know who'll see it or where it will end up.

Carolyn Marnon: I love participating in swaps. There has only been one time when I have sent a doll and not received in return. I was very disappointed at first, but as time goes by, you realize it is just a learning experience in life. The dolls I have received have been fantastic. They all stand together on one of my doll shelves. They bring me such joy to look at and remember friends I have made through the doll swaps. Swapping fashion doll makeovers is a great way to get to know new people and add a wonderful doll to your collection that is like no other.

Elizabeth "Beth" Kinsley: I also LOVE swap dolls. I have sent as far away as Australia and New Zealand. It is such a thrill when you receive one. You never know what treasure you will find! I have had very good luck with my swaps and have only had one that didn't send. This is a good way to experiment with different techniques.

Melinda Sprague: Count me in on loving swaps as well and you can do all kinds of swaps. It's up to the two swappers. A color swap is fun, where both people do a doll around a specific color or colors. Or a holiday swap, that works with ANY holiday out there. A theme swap is fun also.

Jim Faraone: When swapping dolls at a party, a fair way to do it is that each person that brings their wrapped doll to swap should get a number and that same number is put in a paper bag or bowl. Then when the time comes to swap, a wrapped doll is selected, a number is drawn and the holder of that number gets that doll. This way everyone has a fair chance at swapping with all the artists involved instead of some just picking the best artists for themselves. If it's an on-line swap, instead of the moderator choosing the best for themselves and everyone else getting the "leftovers," there should be an honest system. For instance, those wanting to swap could email the moderator just the numbers of their address. Then the addresses could be put in numerical order and 1 trades with 2, 2 trades with 3 and so on. You could use birth dates or anything in order to give everyone a fair chance at swapping with others.

Rachel Steinberger: Once I participated in a Valentine's Day swap. I was initially very hesitant to do so since I'm not the flowers and lace and frou-frou type and that's a lot of what Valentine's Day is. But I liked the people in the group and wanted to encourage the makeovers, so I did join and just let my swap partner know that I wasn't really into fluff. She sent me back the most wonderful doll. A Kelly® doll dressed as a Hershey's® Hug, with arms outstretched to hug and no lace or flowers in sight! My swap partner was so amazingly creative as to capture the theme despite a big handicap! Since then, I have never hesitated to enter a swap!

Charlie Dale: Here's an unusual swap story. I had found a wonderful woman through the Internet and we had agreed to a Victorian theme Barbie® doll swap. Everything was going rather well and neither of us had seen the other's work. The doll I sent was Queen Elizabeth I, but the other person was still working on mine. When she had my girl done, she gave it to a very good friend to take to the post office for delivery. Well, on the way to the post office, this gentleman was in a horrific accident. The truck was totaled and he had broken his back. The artist had no idea where the truck went, if the doll survived, or if she would ever see it again let alone give it to me. Well, she finished another doll and for some odd reason waited to send it. Low and behold, one morning she opened the door and there was a destroyed box on her front door. There was a note attached saying that is was being returned to the owner from a stranger as they found it near where the accident happened in a ditch and they wanted the recipient to receive its contents. She asked if I wanted the original doll or the other she had made. I chose the one that survived the trauma. I wanted her because of this great story of the Barbie® doll surviving great peril to bring joy to a collector and she is one of my most prized dolls in a collection of over 120 dolls.

Stress and BURNOUT!!!!!

Yes, we all get that burned out feeling at times when we're tired or just have an artist's block. It's normal and one shouldn't worry about it. It's just a way of telling you to step back, smell the roses and take a break. Working too long on a doll or getting your brain too filled up with ideas can slow down the creative process for you.

Laura Fern Fanelli: Excellence only comes with break-through....eventually we all hit a wall. Set the doll away for a few hours and take a walk outside and clear your mind. Then return with a new eye and new determination. It can be done and you will succeed! It is also extremely important to have a network of others whose work and ideas you value. Brainstorming with other artists in person or via an email list can be a valuable way to achieve growth or breakthrough or overcome burnout. Lastly, there is such a thing as not wanting to let go of a project and working it to death. Being a happy doll artist also entails knowing when you have finished your doll rather than nitpick changes.

Aurora Mathews: Just take a break and do something else. Go to a convention and look and study other artists' work for inspiration. I never work on a doll (especially a client's doll or a "portrait" doll) unless I really feel like it.

Rachel Steinberger: I agree that looking at other artist's dolls can really inspire your doll-work. Just be careful that you still put your own creative touch in and don't just copy their doll. One fun way to stimulate a doll concept is to start out with a title and then create a doll to fit it. It's more fun if you can get someone else to create 3 or 4 titles for you, so here's a first list of suggestions: *A Touch of Spice*, *Marina*, *Childhood Revisited*, *Essence of Silk* and *Wait Till Your Mother Gets Home*. I find beautiful illustrations in anime really inspiring. Especially in the fantasy series, the combination of foreign outrageous outfits with an artist skilled at drawing very flowing robes make for gorgeous costumes. Ideas evolve, so if you have a doll idea that seems neat, but just doesn't seem quite finished yet, draw and write down everything you can think of about that idea right now. Either you'll hammer out enough detail that the idea seems ready to make or you can file it away against an idea-lesson-progress ideas. When a picture inspires you or strikes you as beautiful, put it in a scrapbook for later inspiration. When making a doll that's a representation of a doll or character, try looking at a picture of the character/person for a while. Then walk away for 10 or 15 minutes (or more). Next, sit down and just think (or write down) what it is about that picture/person/character that sticks out in your mind. The characteristics that come to mind are the ones that are most important to capture since these are the person/character's defining characteristics. This helps me focus on capturing the best likeness I can. Gee, did I get off the topic? LOL!

Lori Strawn: My favorite way to re-energize and get new ideas is to read. Yes, read! When you read, you picture the characters in your head. Use these "mind-pictures" to inspire new dolls. You can even focus on a particular genre of literature. For ideas on fairies, centaurs and other magical creatures, try reading science fiction. Dig into a biography to get "under the skin" of a famous person, past or present. If you're not up to an entire novel, a beauty magazine can inspire with photos of avant-garde makeup techniques or hairstyles.

Michelle Candace: Alter the customizing tasks that you work on to avoid burnout. For instance, if you have been doing a lot of sewing, try painting one day instead. Be sure to take time off each week for yourself and your family. Working like a mad scientist will cause burnout too.

LaDonna Moore: Try something new and different, like a different doll or style.

Laura Fern Fanelli: Try to finish your current project before adding 15 more. It is an easy trap to get into to have 20 dolls that become ongoing projects with none being finished at all!!!!

Tricia Hill: Because I draft almost all of my own patterns, I go into each project with it being an experiment. If the end result comes out looking great, then that is wonderful too! I've learned to take breaks "away" from the project when I feel frustration levels getting out of hand. We ALL experience frustration when we try something new and it doesn't come out perfectly. My best and only advice is to take a breather. Come back when you're more relaxed and it WILL come to you. The light bulb will always come on when you are in a more relaxed creative state of mind. :-)

Joanna Bond: Do what you love; otherwise your output will never be more than half-hearted. Study, experiment, dabble. Set new standards. Make new rules. Try new things. Solve problems creatively. Give yourself plenty of room, time and love. Watch what others are doing; not so you can try to be like them, but so that you can let them inspire you. Note what works and what doesn't work for you. Don't confuse being inspired with copying. Let your own style emerge as you work. Close your eyes and imagine. Listen to music. Open a window. Go for a walk. Talk to your dolls. When you're blocked, let go. Do something entirely different for a while, and believe that your ideas will start to flow again eventually. Most importantly, don't force anything and be proud of what you accomplish. Go into a craft, fabric or art store that you've never been in before. The little out-of-the-way stores can be gold mines! Develop an appreciation for other arts and incorporate aspects of them into your art.

Kim Burie: I tend to obsess over things until I burn out. Luckily for me, I have several hobbies that I enjoy, so when I feel like I just can't do "x" any more, I move on to "y." As long as I don't pressure myself, I eventually get back to "x." Forcing myself to do that thing that I am burned out over usually makes me very stressed out, and then I get a complete block, so that is the one thing I never do. This is supposed to be fun, isn't it? Deadlines are also very stressful for me. If I receive an order for a doll, I always pad the time frame by at least a couple of weeks. This allows me time in case I run into a problem, have a family emergency, or run into any

other obstacle. The vast majority of the time, I finish before the set deadline and a customer is always a lot happier to get an order early rather than late!

Carolyn Marnon: If you want to do swaps, don't overload yourself with too many at one time. Those deadlines will often come much faster than you thought they would. There is nothing like feeling the pressure of getting a nice doll done before that deadline is up let alone the pressure of getting more than one done in time. My advice is to take it slow to start with (unless you are one of those lucky people who seem to whip out a doll at least once a day that looks absolutely gorgeous.)

Kert Hoogstraat: Try doing a series of five or so dolls using just one pattern, but making every doll unique and one-of-a-kind in the details. This is a great way to bust "designer's block"!

Jim Faraone: The first thing to do is make sure you take breaks. I take a 10-minute breaks at least every hour when I'm working on my creations. Just watch TV for 10 minutes or look out the window or do some stretches. Another thing is not to overload yourself with projects. You can't do everything, so you have to set priorities. If you're trying to make dolls to sell for a big upcoming event, then you'll have to stop selling your dolls on an on-line auction if you don't have the time for both. If you want to enter a big contest, then some time will have to be taken away from other things so you can create your entry. To say "yes" to every charity auction, every commissioned

piece, everyone who wants a free donation is suicidal! Learn to say "no" — after you do it once, it's a lot easier to do it again. Work at your own pace and don't overload yourself. And NEVER let anyone make you feel guilty for doing so.

Lori Velazquez: I try to do my projects in steps. Most of the dolls are around the same size and their outfits are related in theme. Due to this, I can adjust a pattern altering it slightly for different uniforms. Sometimes I'll wait a couple of days and just try to sew it all in the car or while watching TV. This way I don't overload myself and it is more enjoyable.

Respecting Your Fellow Artists

It's always nice when a group of people who are interested in the same thing can get together and work well in cooperation. One reason I started my Yahoogroups™ list was because I have seen and heard about other groups that love to criticize and tear down other artists. This is sad because I feel there is room for everyone. Talking down about another artist or their work only reflects on those doing the backbiting. Maybe they think it makes them seem important, but it only shows their true personalities. As I always say, if everyone paid more attention to what they are doing and not looking to see what others are doing, their own work would improve greatly. As Charlie Brown once said, "Individually these fingers are nothing, but when they band together they become a fighting force." Yes, a fighting force to all come together and share, learn and grow.

Rachel Steinberger: Give credit where credit is due. Many doll artists are very, very nice people who will happily share with you any of their techniques. However, the technique is still theirs, so it's common courtesy to let people know who taught you a technique. In a sentence, don't steal credit for someone else's idea of creating a method and the hard work of perfecting it. I'd like to offer up the Art of Constructive Criticism. Simple as it sounds, just a few simple points remembered by both the giver and the receiver make it much more constructive and less, well, critical. For the giver, start with something positive such as a compliment. It helps the receiver feel better about the later criticisms if you let them know there's something about their work that you like. If worst comes to worst and there's absolutely nothing you like about their doll, try something general like "How creative" or "I would never have thought of making this!" with a smile on your face. However, if there's something specific you do like, point it out—"Great eyes, so expressive" or "You did a fantastic job fitting the dress." Have some tact when commenting. "That dress is so ugly I wouldn't give it to my dog as a chew-toy" can easily be replaced by "The design/fabric of the dress just doesn't work for me." Same idea, but far less harsh. This is one case where humor can only be applied very, very gently. Try to make criticism with suggestions for improvement. "The dress doesn't fit correctly" isn't nearly as helpful as "The dress could be greatly improved by using a commercial pattern to fit the bust line." Stick to your guns. The receiver, unless they have a lot of self-control, is almost sure to object to your criticisms...it's human nature.

110

So be firm about your honest feelings. Don't back off just because the other person is upset. When you make your comments, think how you'd feel as the receiver. In other words, follow the Golden Rule—treat others as you would have them treat you. It's quite likely that you will be the receiver at some point! For the receiver, remember, you asked for this. Most reasonable adults will keep their mouth shut until you ask for their honest opinion, and then they will give you ALL of it. So if you don't want their honest opinion or constructive criticism, don't ask for it. Actually listen. The instinctual reaction of anyone receiving criticism, whether friendly or not, is to defend themselves and their work with excuses, alternate explanations, etc. You don't have to agree with what you hear, but at least listen to what the other person has to say and think about it. Otherwise, you might as well not ask. Your consolation, the people you ask may very well be wrong. Especially in something subjective like fashion doll makeovers. People's opinions differ.

Jim Faraone: I believe in respecting one's fellow artists as well. It's unfortunate that there are some grammar school antics in the fashion doll makeover world (as in all aspects of life) and the best way to deal with those types is to just totally ignore them. Never stoop to their level and stand as an individual and not someone's puppet. With some, fighting adds fuel to their energy! They thrive on it! It's their life, which must be a pretty sad life. If you find someone who loves to bash other artists, the best thing to do is stay away from him or her. If you are an individualist and not a follower, you'd be wise to stand by yourself. The fashion doll makeover world (as well as any collecting world) is a small world and news travels quickly. Never be associated with juvenile troublemakers because they will only pull you down with them. Respect your fellow artists because there truly is room for everyone. Help one another, share with one another, and enjoy each other's company. Many of the long time artists have a blast together at conventions and many are surprised at how well we all get along. I guess they think we are competitive with one another and nothing could be furthest from the truth. One wannabee "artist" made the comment that they wanted to "get rid of all the long time artists and bring in their new regime"! ROTFLMBO! I had to laugh at that remark because it showed that this wannabee didn't care to be a part of a group—they wanted to *be* the group! Show respect to the other artists and if you don't have anything nice to say, keep quiet! One should never stoop to the level of those who love to viciously criticize. The best thing is to ignore them. It's not the idea of "demanding" respect, but "commanding" respect. There's a big difference.

Kathleen Forsythe: I think all artists should be respected and we should remember that each of us is an individual. We are different in a lot of ways and we should be able to see some good in everything. Remember that although we mostly communicate through the Internet, we are people behind these emails and we have feelings.

Rachel Steinberger: The keyword is "fellow" here. "Fellow" is defined as "member of a common group or society." So everybody is in the same boat. True, some people are up on deck enjoying the sweet smell of success and many are down below in the cramped bowels of the ship (yes, we all saw Titanic) but everybody has (or should have) the same goal in mind—to create the best dolls they can and have fun doing it.

Jim Faraone: That is so true Rachel! Some don't realize that their actions reflect on a group as a whole at times. Even when someone doesn't have the patience to improve the quality of their work and starts promoting their work all over the place, it can pull down the group as a whole. Or when an individual who is not quite ready yet, wants to start teaching techniques and writing about their techniques, it pulls down a whole group. One must tone their craftsmanship to the best of their ability and have that inner respect to do the best that they can. If you don't have that inner respect, you can't expect others to have respect for you and your work.

Karin Roberts: As in everyday life, no two individuals like or appreciate the same things. This is true with makeover artists. I would never be so presumptuous as to think that everyone will love my creations as much as I do. Neither should you. It is acceptable to dislike some things that are created; it's even expected. It's what you do or say as an expression of your dislike that can hurt us ALL as a doll community. It won't hurt YOU to keep your mouth shut when all you really want to say is, "It's hideous!" Constructive criticism should be HELPFUL, not hurtful.

Why Create?

I thought that since more than half of this book has given you our tips on how we create and how we go through the experiences of fashion doll makeovers, it would be nice to end this section with "Why we create our dolls?" Each individual has their own special reasons and feelings about creating their dolls. I always joke and say I create mine because I have a lousy social life!

Jim Faraone: For me, creating keeps me off the streets and makes the neighborhood safer! LOL!

Laura Fern Fanelli: Creating takes me out of the every day world and into a world of fantasy. It's a fun world to be in and it also distracts me from day to day stuff. I also use it as a pain relief. It gives me pleasure.

Barbara Fowler: When I saw your first book, Jim, I thought, "That looks like fun," and it is! I guess it's just the satisfaction of creating and changing something to reflect myself— my feelings and my style. I love it!

Juan Albuerne: Personally, I like beauty and enjoy seeing beautiful things. Since I am a painter, I discovered that I could mix two different things that I liked very much—dolls and painting. Add this to my love for the movies, and what more could I do? You can create something that is completely unique to your own talents. It's like you had a daughter, a new daughter every time that you finish a doll. You look at her and many times you ask, "How could I create that?" The fact is that your new daughter is there before you, looking at you, thanking you for giving birth to her. You created her from your heart,

which makes you happy and a filled with a peace.

Sarah Worley: In creating my dolls, I get a feeling of fulfillment and a smile— first MY OWN, and then from someone else who thinks she's beautiful! I can "lose" the days' frustrations by immersing myself in a doll project, and feel a sense of accomplishment when she's finished! I get something we all need occasionally— an upper/warm fuzzy/emotional high! They're good therapy! Wish I had time to do more!

Joanna Bond: Being an artist and toy collector, doll making brings these two facets of my personality together. Why does any artist do what they do? It's some internal driving force, and they need it like they need oxygen. I'm only happy with my life when there's a lot of creativity in it. It's really difficult to explain why, other than just that I have to. It's what I do. Being creative makes me healthy. I love working until bedtime and then having a hard time turning the light out because I want to continue to gaze at my work. This may also explain why so many of my dolls incorporate glow-in-the-dark elements. I also love the personality aspect of this art form. I'm not just making something to view; I'm making something with a face, a name, and a story. There's an added imaginative element there. Sometimes I think my dolls come out of a great story that I have yet to write. Doll customizing is inherently light-hearted. It's a toy after all.

Tricia Hill: For me, my greatest satisfaction is watching someone's facial expression when they first see one of my creations. It's a thrill knowing that I can create something that transpired from my own imagination and then can

tangibly be put into a doll that someone else can also enjoy! The excitement from the first design drawings to what unfolds throughout and then sewing on that last bead! Oh wow! With each new doll I do comes more ideas and better techniques. Designing my own creations has additionally given me the opportunity to not only share what's in my own imagination, but also presents me with a creative outlet that I've always needed but never before focused on any one thing.

Debbie Lima: When I create a doll I think that each one is just beautiful. Of course, as my talent has grown, I've gone back to some of the first ones and I don't like them as much as I did at the time. Although, there are some early ones that I still love. I look at them with pride and can hardly believe that I made them. I love making the patterns, painting the doll, doing the hair, making the costume and looking at the final product with pride.

Kevin Allen: I get a very special feeling when I show my mom a new creation or tell her that I sold one. Then I see the pride on HER face! The joy of creating and the money it brings in is nice, but nothing can beat my mom! Her being proud of me for something she helped me learn to do is priceless!

Linda Lynch Holman: I guess the biggest thrill is to take a doll everyone has deemed unmarketable, and down right ugly, and then turn her into a Beauty Queen. I create for a number of reasons. Usually it is because I have this burning idea in my head that won't stop until it becomes a reality. It's sort of like a "Vision Quest" type of thing. The most enjoyment is when I create a doll for someone's birthday, wedding, etc. They are always so thrilled

with their doll. So I guess the enjoyment it gives me is having a talent to share with others. It has made me grow in different areas of artistic design with my dolls. It has shown me there is always something new to be learned and shared with others. Becoming a Fashion Doll Makeover Artist has enlightened me to myself, and what I am capable of achieving artistically.

Lim Shor-wei: I get satisfaction from the process of learning and trying new things. That's why I never do a repeat of anything. Sewing for my dolls is also an outlet for my fashion ideas. I like ensembles—color coordinated outfits with accessories, suits, fitted day dresses—but won't get to wear these for myself, so I allow my fashion fantasies to come alive on my dolls.

Lori Strawn: Like most folks on the list, I have an innate need to create. Ideas for dolls appear in my brain, and I simply must get them out! The satisfaction of seeing these ideas come to life...well, few things could be more rewarding. I also treasure taking a "well-loved" doll and turning her into a beauty. It's like giving her a second life. Best of all, of course, is just seeing the looks on people's faces when they see my finished creations. "You made that?" "Make me one, too!" It's darned hard to get a better high than that!

Lori Velazquez: I create for two reasons. One is to learn enough so that I can finally make my two dolls that are to be modeled after the story I wrote, "I Love Fantasy." The second reason is to be able to create those dolls and fashions that would go with the rest of my Sailor Moon® doll collection.

Tess Barton: I always loved working with my hands and designing and creating. I'm a doctor, and over the last several years have been devoted to medicine and study. I began to feel like I was lacking something really important. Doing fashion doll makeovers gives me an artistic outlet. It's not just a hobby; it's an obsession. When I'm really frazzled or stressed about work, I work on dolls. I feel like I'm really creating something special. For me, the dolls really become tiny people, and they each have a personality and a style of their own. Working on dolls gives me such satisfaction; so much I can't begin to describe it.

Melissa A. Klein: When I sit down and pick up a doll I am working on, I get to go to a different place. In this place, there are no kids yelling, "Mommy he did...." "Mommy I can't....." "Mom! Can I...." There are no bills, no dull 9 to 5 job. In this beautiful place there is just complete peace. I start working on my doll and I can almost physically feel the tension and stress lift like a cloud. If you looked really hard, you could probably see it float away. In this place, I get to let the creativity flow, especially when painting. The colors just seem to mix of their own accord and give each doll her own special personality. This is a wonderful place from which I have to return unfortunately. But I know that it will always be there and I can get there anytime I want and it is all mine.

Aurora Mathews: It is really fun! Yes, I do some dolls for clients for extra money, but at the same time, when the client is pleased and the doll turns out great, I feel good inside about what I have done and sometimes just about making someone else feel happy with their new doll. I love art. I love to paint. I love beautiful things and creating what I feel is beautiful makes me feel good. If I got no money out of this, I would probably do less of it, but I would not stop creating or being artistic. I am having the happiest time of my life being able to express myself in different types of artwork, which includes my dolls.

Jean MaDan: Life is stressful these days—more than ever. Working on dolls gives me a chance to ignore the ugly parts for a while, and concentrate on the peace and beauty life offers.

Scott Shore: What I get from re-doing a doll is the pure satisfaction of creating something that is both beautiful to the eye and is also an artistic outlet for me. I love doing this. It is more than a hobby for me. It is a great way to escape, and let out the artist/sculptor in me. I strive for perfection in all I do. I love it when company comes over and catches a glimpse of a new doll or even one that I have moved to a new spot. It evokes conversation and, I hate to admit it, it feeds my ego.

Gael Singer Bailey: I always see something I want to change—eyes, hair, nails, lips. Fortunately beauty is in the eye of the beholder, and everyone has different eyesight. I love taking fabric and holding it and trying to see what that particular fabric should become. Then I try to make a pattern or combine patterns to get the desired look.

Dorothy Fannin: I get a lot of pleasure from taking a fashion doll that has been mass-produced and giving her a new and distinct personality. In creating molded hairstyles, I never know how they will turn out. Seeing the finished work always has the element of surprise for me. I guess that's why I enjoy creating molded hair. The greatest pleasure I've received since working with dolls has been the exchange of new ideas, swapping dolls with people around the world, and most of all, the wonderful friendships I've made on-line with other doll designers.

Stefanie Baumler: I think what I get most out of my dolls is simply an outlet for my creative energies. I have a desire to be creative and to make beautiful things. I've gotten into many different crafts since I was a child, driven by this desire, which I believe runs in my family as my mother and grandmother also create(d) beautiful things. It's also "my" time, when I can be alone and quiet with my thoughts, which isn't easy to do with a toddler!

Natalie Tetzlaff: I have an outlet for my creativity. I can take this doll and turn her into something no one else has. She is a creation made by me. I can turn an idea in my head into a three dimensional, tangible object. I value the uniqueness of each doll I make.

Barb Wood: I like creating my fairy dolls because it is my "escape" from the real world. I have always enjoyed seeing the final outcome of a project even though I usually change things about a hundred times before I am satisfied. It really does relax me!

Shirley Amador: I get pleasure from creating something beautiful and unique. I also enjoy having someone appreciate and enjoy my dolls. I think I enjoy giving that pleasure to someone else more than creating a doll for myself, although I love collecting dolls and do have a couple that I find I can't part with. LOL! I have worked for several years as a criminal paralegal and have seen so much pain and suffering that when working on a doll I find that I am very relaxed and enjoy it so much. I love all parts of it from the repaints to sewing the costumes to watching for a bid on eBay™. I know it is just a little bit to add to someone's life, but when I get feedback that someone really loves my creations, I am happy that I can add that little bit of beauty and enjoyment. Doing these makeovers have added a whole new dimension to my life.

Amy Nardone: One reason I create is because I was lucky enough to have inherited my artistic talent. Fashion dolls are a great way to create expression without limiting yourself to paper and canvas. If I see a vision of a gown, or a particular look I like, I know that down the hall I can re-create what I like. I don't do it for the money (yes, that is an added fringe benefit.) I do it as an outlet for my creativity. And the best added benefit is meeting fellow doll artists and forming lasting relationships, different as they may be, and having a special bond.

Jenny Sutherland: Creating for me is an outlet, a freedom to express myself when I see things that inspires me. It takes me away from every day life, and lets me create my own world so to speak. Although frustrating at times, it's still one of the most enjoyable things I do.

Kathleen Forsythe: I create because I love to create with fashion dolls. It is productive to makeover a doll and know you can do it. I get something in my mind and love to see it come to be on a doll or the gown that I am working on. I create because I have lupus and a few other of its ugly sisters. When I work on a doll or bead a dress, I can crawl into my own little world and relax and stop myself from being VERY sick. I have done this for 30 years and it seems that whenever there is a crises going on, my dolls get very detailed!!!

Jill "Kitty" Racop: I know some of those on the list gain financial satisfaction (yeah, must be nice!) or recognition, and some just follow the impulse a doll or fabric brings. But for me, it's mainly for the satisfaction of seeing something that I want, and no one else provides, taking shape. My personal fashion doll makeovers have ranged from a character ("Highlander" Amanda-nobody made dolls/figures from the series) or a revision (recently gave the GenGirl® Tori® doll and Mari® doll short haircuts that suit them much better than the yards of ponytails Mattel™ gave them) to an addition to an existing line (a redhead, and a white-haired Holiday Totally Hair® doll some years ago). Most of my creations has simply been to satisfy that "nobody makes it, but I want one!" feeling.

Kelli "Jinx" Getchell: It's my outlet. I have to be creative in some manner; otherwise I don't function correctly. I draw, write, make teddy bears and rag dolls, paint and now I do fashion doll makeovers. Each finished doll is an accomplishment. It starts with just an idea in my head of how I want to remake a doll and slowly I bring the idea to completion. This for me, selfish as it sounds, it's all for me.

Rachel Steinberger: I create for a variety of reasons. One is just because I love the mythical creatures and fantasy heroines that I create. Another is that it gives me a chance to rip-up and torture dolls, which I'm not sure why I enjoy so much, but it is very satisfying. And also just to see (and prove) that I can do it. One of the nice things about doing fashion doll makeovers is that each project has a clear beginning and a clear ending. My daily job is very wishy-washy. There are so many things going on at once and so many things that keep coming back to you to redo. My fashion doll makeovers give me that final sense of accomplishment much more frequently than I get at work. Plus, the finished product is more easily enjoyed by more people!

Stephanie Brown: Stress relief! There's nothing more soothing than the hum of the sewing machine. The quiet time that I get to spend on the dolls is also quite nice. Also, making someone happy. It is nice

knowing that something that I have created can make someone very happy. It's nice to hear that someone received the doll as a gift and was absolutely thrilled with it. I guess it gives you the "warm-fuzzies" and if my dolls can do that, it's well worth the time and energy put into the whole creating process.

Jennifer L. Brown: I would have to say that first and foremost I get the extreme pleasure of seeing a work of imagination come to life before my eyes. I like knowing that my first attempts at restyling hair by cutting it on dolls as a child can be repaired and I can give new life to my dolls. I have only done a few dolls, but I see improvement in my skills and I am challenged to try new things. I usually find working on my dolls relaxing and I enjoy making a doll that is especially for someone, like in a swap.

Elizabeth "Beth" Kinsley: I love giving and receiving fashion doll makeover dolls. When I redo a doll, I try to design her to the taste of the person for whom I am making her. It brings me a lot of joy to know that the person receiving my creation will enjoy her and cherish her for years. When I receive a fashion doll makeover doll creation, it immediately becomes the pride of my collection and is cherished. It gives my heart a full feeling knowing someone worked so creatively for me. The fashion doll makeover dolls I have are the most important part of my collection and loved immensely!

Michelle Candace: Dolls are truly magical! They have this wonderful power of touching our hearts and leaving us in awe. Creating fashion doll makeovers and fashions allows me to be a part of this magic!

Jillian Manning: Because it's fun! Is there a better reason? I think that, secretly, I must have been yearning to play with dolls

for years, and it took me this long to find an excuse. Creating is very satisfying. It's always good to look at something you've produced yourself and think, "I did that."

Karin Roberts: Sometimes I create just for a challenge to see if I can make a certain idea come to life. Other times I create with the hopes of pleasing a particular audience. Mostly, I create because I enjoy the creative process as much as the finished project.

Sharon Marquiss-Morris: Sewing and creating is like reading a good book. You can get lost at times. I forget about drinks that I made for myself. Food goes cold and I find stuff in the microwave that I forgot! I always loved to get lost in a storybook as a child, and now I like to get lost in "creation land." I find it relaxing, plus I get something beautiful at the end (notwithstanding mistakes!)

Charlie Dale: What do I get out of creating my dolls? Well, it is many things and I would say that the first thing I get is the satisfaction of creating something very special for my own collection that the mass market doesn't have or giving something to someone else's collection. It brings me so much joy and really is part of my playtime with my dolls.

Debbi Sherart: I create because it seems to be in my blood. I get lost in each creation. The enjoyment comes from seeing what the finished product will be, because he/she never seems to turn out the way I picture him or her. They almost seem to talk to me and tell me what it is that they want. As far as enlightening my life, all I can really say is that I have made some wonderful friends once I discovered the on-line world of makeovers—friends that I never would have "met" if not for the Internet—friendships that will last.

Jim Faraone: Creating can be a highlight in anyone's life. I create because I enjoy it and that is the most important part. It's not how many dolls you can make in a day or how many dolls you can sell, but it's a craft that makes you feel good about yourself and your work. There is nothing like seeing your idea come to life before you. What a confidence builder that is. It gives you self-pride that you have created something that you only dreamed of previously. I want to take this time to thank all those artists on my list who have contributed their tips, bios and photos to this exciting book. Without your help, this book most likely could never have been done. It was a pleasure working with all of you and this book shows that we can all work together to help build the fashion doll makeover world. It proves that the artists can all work well together without the backbiting and competitiveness. It shows that we are a family, caring and sharing with one another. I also want to thank those who have supported me and my books. The only mistake with this book is that I told you in the introduction to "lurk" on this Internet chat page in book form. One should never lurk, but get out there and get involved. Lurking gets you nowhere, but getting involved opens many doors for each and every one of you. Come on and join in on the fun. Dolls are no longer just toys for little girls!

Jim Faraone
19109 Silcott Springs Rd.
Purcellville, VA. 20132
(540) 338-3621
Email: jimfaraone@erols.com
Website:
http://www.erols.com/
jimfaraone/
Yahoogroups List:
FashionDollMakeovers-
subscribe@yahoogroups.com
or contact Jim Faraone

Featured Artists

Lynn K. Johnson

I am a contributing writer to many international and national dolls and crafts magazines, a doll artist, and a doll costume designer. My fashion doll clothing patterns, doll collecting, and cloth doll how-to articles are featured in and on the covers of *The Cloth Doll, International Doll Designs, Doll Castle News, Crafts, Crafts 'n Things, Dollmaking Crafts & Designs, Doll Collectors' Price Guide,* and *Nutshell News.* My original, historically garbed, sculpted fashion dolls have won many blue ribbons and sweepstakes ribbons in doll competitions. A "Favorite Gene

Designer Award" winner, I have over two decades experience in designing and creating fashion dolls and fashion doll clothing. As a fashion doll consultant to

Cathy Meredig, founder of the "Happy To Be Me Doll," I designed the outfits for the doll and book line. Inspiration for designs comes from an extensive background in fashion history, art and multi-disciplinary field of arts and crafts. My expertise with fashion dolls and their couture reflect that "passion for fashion dolls" with spectacular results!

Email: stars@highstream.net com - Website: http://members.fortunecity.com/dolls9/

Jean MaDan

I started customizing dolls in 1999. My wonderful husband John supports the family, and

makes it possible for me to do this work full time. I've always loved crafts and sewing, so it seemed very natural to me to try fashion doll makeovers. I saw my first customized doll in June of 1999, and thought, "WOW! I can DO that!" I picked up a couple of books that taught the techniques I needed to do successful Barbie® doll makeovers, and was soon involved in the process of creating my own dolls. I've branched out to include the Gene® dolls, which I really love, as well as some of the other larger dolls like the Elle® doll.
Email: madan49@aol.com - Website: www.madandolls.com

Scott Shore

Originally from Philadelphia, Pennsylvania, I graduated from the Philadelphia College of Art with a degree in Interior Design, and also studied fashion design. About one year ago, I started collecting Bob Mackie Barbie® dolls. I was fascinated to say the least. I also knew that I could make gowns for the Barbie® doll. I have developed my own unique style, and today I have a website devoted entirely to fashion doll makeovers.

I was lucky enough to find Jim Faraone's books and join his doll web ring. Jim's books have shown me how to do makeovers

correctly, and the people in our group are always sharing ideas.

I love searching for fabrics and accessories. I am passionate in creating gowns and different hairstyles. I have been commissioned a number of times to

make custom dolls for people that purchased my dolls from internet auctions.
Email: slshore@adelphia.net - Website: http://www.geocities.com/sl_shore

Joelle Cerfoglia

I am 33 years old and live in a small town called Ladispoli near Rome. I have a 7-year-old little boy that tries to understand why his old mom still plays with dolls! Maybe I never really grew up. I have always been a lover of everything that is art and lately I have discovered the great joy of Barbie® doll customizing. I started by collecting Barbie® dolls, but then I have discovered the world of OOAK's and this

has turned on a light that won't be dimmed. Here in Italy, customizing is not very widespread. Some Italian friends and I are the pioneers of this new world of Barbie® doll collecting and I infinitely hope that it explodes in all its beauty! I love creating something that is completely mine and give something really unique!
Email: jcerfoglia@libero.it - Website: www.geocities.com/joelle670

Barb Alexander

I have been crocheting for over 28 years. I like to crochet because one can be so expressive with it. When one crochets, it reflects one's inner being. I am 65 years old and married to Don who is 66. We have been married for 47 years. We have six children, ten grandchildren and one great grandchild. I have been designing for the 11-½in (29cm) fashion dolls for about 4-½ years now in crochet. But I have just discovered the wonderful world of fashion doll makeovers. Since becoming involved in this, I

spend almost all my time at it. There is so much to learn and I love every minute of it. I especially like the combining of crochet and fabric in design—the look and feel of the two mediums adds texture to the outfits and is uniquely different.
Email: fisnhook@infohiwy.net - Website:
http://www.crosswinds.net/~dollectables/index.HTML
or
http://www.geocities.com/Heartland/Prairie/7016/barbs_nook.HTML

Vicki Young

I love to crochet! I am grateful to my grandmother who patiently taught me this beautiful art which has now become my passion! For four years now, through my business, "Victoria's Treasures," I have been creating and crocheting doll clothes. Initially, I used patterns, but I have now begun creating my own line of designer gowns, as seen here.

I can spend up to 20 hours crocheting a doll gown! With experience, I have learned to redo hair and makeup (including

rerooting) as well. I am always trying new techniques such as crocheting with pearls, beads, pom-poms, buttons and sequins and am always on the lookout for new crochet threads for unusual effects! Most recently, I have begun combining crochet with fabric to create some unique and beautiful gowns! I must admit though, seeing others enjoy my doll designs has been my greatest satisfaction!
Email: Vtreasure@aol.com - Website:
http://www.victoriastreasures.org

Linda Lynch Holman

I was born and raised in a small rural town near Branson, Missouri. After graduating high school, I moved to Kansas City, Missouri where I was employed by Hallmark® cards for fifteen years. Later, I moved to the Chicago area with my husband and son. I attended college in the Chicago area studying Physical Therapy with a minor in French Language. I am an active member of the Alliance Francaise de Chicago.

Five years ago, I became involved in doll collecting. I started creating one-of-a-kind fashion dolls after reading Jim's book. I have been creating OOAK's for about two years now. Two of my first makeover dolls were in the 1999 BMA Awards competition.

I enjoy using doll finds from garage sales, flea markets and thrift stores most. These dolls are sometimes a real challenge to the makeover artist. I use any fashion doll when creating my OOAK. One of my childhood dreams was to always be published, and see my work in print. These things are becoming fulfilled thanks to some really great people I call friends.
Email: Rouge@ibm.net

Elizabeth Anne Dean

As a child in the early 60's, I spent many long hours absorbed in play with my Barbie® dolls. Not much has changed since except that now I enjoy creating Barbie® dolls unlike any others. This hobby has allowed me to put my background in landscape oil painting and tailored sewing to good use. I try to bring my OOAK dolls to life by using color, contrast, and unpredictability. I have also created a unique line of finely tailored couture for fashion dolls. My dresses are exquisitely detailed—delicate buttons, small satin bows. I enjoy re-creating the charm and style of the vintage Barbie® doll. Accessories add to the nostalgic mood of my ensembles with impossibly petite hand gloves, purses, stockings and more. I find my best creative inspiration comes from nature—a walk on the beach or an afternoon in the garden.
Email: myenglishgarden@yahoo.com -
Website: http://www.geocities.com/myenglishgarden/index.HTML

Fran Czosnek

I always loved growing up with the Barbie® doll. About five years ago, I started collecting Barbie® dolls. On my quest for vintage dolls, I found some lovely OOAK's at a local doll show. I was immediately drawn to these works of art. At every show I would search out the talented artists to admire their work. Until one day I decided that, I too, wanted to be a fashion doll makeover artist. So, here I am! I owe it all to my mother, who is always encouraging me to express my creativity. Customizing fashion dolls is a fun and exciting hobby, and a wonderful creative outlet. Currently, I am a registered nurse working in the emergency department in Tucson, Arizona. I devote my spare time to creating one-of-a-kind "Frantastic Creations." This is definitely one pastime that I hope to enjoy for a long, long time.
Email: FCzosnek@aol.com -
Website: www.geocities.com/frantasticdolls

Dorothy Fannin

In collecting fashion dolls, my interest has varied from year to year. I started out with play dolls, then changed to NRFB dolls, and then later to Designer Collector dolls. At present, the most prized dolls in my collection are the fashion doll makeovers dolls I have swapped dolls that I have customized for other artists' dolls. My main focus in customizing has been with molded hair dolls. I first became interested in the process after seeing Kayandem's work in Jim Faraone's first book, "Fashion

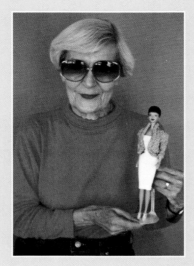

Doll Makeovers." Since then, I have created several new original molded hairstyles. For the past two years, I have been making hats for fashion dolls. Most of my hats are made from felt and other fabrics, although I have also used recycled emails and dryer lint. I'd like to invite you to visit my hat boutique, "Chic by Dorothy," as well as my doll site, "Living Dolls."
Email:
dfannin2@mindspring.com -
Website:
www.mindspring.com/~dfannin2

Becky Kelly

Ever since I can remember, I've been involved in the creative process. As a child, I enjoyed giving my dolls hair cuts, as well as performing operations...ok...I admit it, I was one of those children who destroyed her dolls! So it was only natural that as I began to replace my childhood dolls, I gravitated to those that needed some repair.

I enjoy creating dolls in many styles. My favorite type is the fantasy doll. I enjoy making mermaids, seahorses, fairies and centaurs. These creations are quite labor intensive and involve

some "minor" operating skills. The dolls I tend to gravitate toward are the Gene® doll, the Skipper® doll and the Kelly® doll and all her friends. I find the Kelly® doll creations enchanting.

I have worked in many mediums including painting and fiber arts such as quilting, knitting, crochet and tatting. These skills have been invaluable in the process of creating my designs.
Email: frivolite@yahoo.com -
Website:
http://www.angelfire.com/ca4/
FrivolitesDolls

Rachel Steinberger

By sewing, painting, beading and occasionally sculpting, I make a variety of imaginative doll creations. My ideas are drawn from many sources including period fashions, famous fairytales, comic books, children's cartoons and oriental culture. My favorite doll to work with is the Kelly® doll, because her adorable little face guarantees a darling result. Under my Frankensteinian guidance, the Kelly® doll transforms into comic book heroines, sci-fi stars, anime characters and even the occasional fairy. I also enjoy working with the Barbie® doll whose larger scale allows me to add more detail and try things impossible on the Kelly® doll. In

my "lab," the Barbie® doll metamorphoses into creatures of the imagination including princesses, genies, mermaids and aliens with unusual skin-tones. Why are all my creations fantasy-based? Because doing fashion doll makeover dolls is my escape from the everyday, normal and boring. Inside my workroom, I can make the impossibilities of the outside world become reality for a few small plastic dolls.
Email:
rsteinberger@bren.ucsb.edu -
Website:
http://members.nbci.com/artemi
x/main.HTML
or
http://www.geocities.com/wings
nthingsdolls/

Tricia Hill

Beyond creating fashion doll makeover dolls, I'm also a collector of modern and vintage fashion dolls. I relish collecting and restoring vintage and mod Barbie® dolls! Besides being a junior clothing designer for the Barbie® doll in my early years, my interest in designing fashion doll makeovers seriously took off just this last year, and has since sky rocketed with enthusiasm! Having over twenty years in the sewing industry has played a major role in designing. With all of the commercial patterns available, I still prefer to draft my own. I'm particularly fascinated with designing 1930's and 1940's era costumes. The ideas are endless, and I am at present venturing into creating celebrity dolls.

My friends know me as Trish, and I was raised in Littleton, Colorado, where I've since returned to my roots to raise my own family! I receive wonderful encouragement from my husband and 2 beautiful sons! Email: Sptfyre@cs.com - Website: http://www.bytricia.com

Sharon A. Lawson

My infatuation of dolls did not start in my childhood. At the age of 49, after purchasing my first Barbie® doll (Billions of Dreams), I decided to try and make my own gowns in the styles I loved—colonial style and ball gowns with big full skirts. The Internet has had a big impact on my hobby. Not only in helping my dolls get recognized, the group at FashionDollMakeovers@yahoo groups.com helped me to expand on my creations, learning new techniques and

letting my imagination come to life. Most of my dolls are commissioned by other collectors that have seen my creations on my website. I love designing a doll for the sheer pleasure of knowing that it is admired and loved by other people. Thanks to Jim for creating his books and the Fashion Doll Makeovers list for the artists to learn from and to enjoy other artists' creations.
Email: mslawson@sisna.com - Website: http://mslawson.tripod.com/

Juan Albuerne

I am 44 years old and was born in Gijón, a town in the North of Spain, Europe, where I still live. My three passions are painting, movies and dolls. When I realized that transforming dolls into movie stars could feed my three hobbies equally, I began to work willingly. Though my first love is the Barbie® doll, it was a Charice® doll, a beautiful American doll impossible to get in Spain, that I found the ideal for the features that I needed—mature in appearance and the right face to create different personalities. What more could I ask for? My first transformed doll is dated from 2000, the magical year. She was Joan Crawford and

I have been working without a break since then, trying to reach the impossible—perfection. Perhaps some day...from now on, the future has the floor.

Email:jualbu@asturvia.cajastur.es
Website:
http://www.juanalbuerne.com

Kim Burie

I started doing fashion doll makeovers in the spring of 2000, and while I enjoy many types of materials and techniques, I specialize in crocheted costumes. I mostly use 11-½in (29cm) dolls (the Candi® doll and the Charice® doll along with the Barbie® doll and friends), and my favorite parts of the customizing process are doing total facial repaints and rerooting hair. While I use a lot of new dolls in my creations, I live for those great garage sale finds of older abused dolls that I can transform into new beauties! I live on a pretty little river in northwestern Wisconsin with my wonderful husband, Matt, and our menagerie of assorted pets. I work full-time for my family's third generation machine manufacturing corporation doing mostly computer design and publishing work. I have learned so much and met so many nice people since joining FashionDollMakeovers@yahoogroups.com. I am very thankful to have found this list.
Email: kimb@softhome.net -
Website:
http://northernbelledolls.
homestead.com

Jennifer Hughey

I am 31, and have always been a "doll nut." Starting when I was a kid, I had what I called my "bucket o' dollies" (a large plastic hamper just chock full of them!!) I collected on and off through the years, but the kind of dolls in which I was interested just weren't made. I wanted some fantasy creations, medieval maidens, sorceresses, fairies, etc. I saw Jim Faraone's first book, *Fashion Doll Makeovers* at a bookstore, and I was hooked! I didn't realize people customized dolls!! Now I was able to make the dolls I always wanted to see. I have been doing fashion doll makeovers since late 1998, and I have learned (and am still learning) so much. Thanks to FashionDollMakeovers@yahoogroups.com, I am able to talk with other fashion doll makeover artists and share tips. In fact, I met a fellow artist who lives right here in my own town!! Small world!!
Email: jennysmi@earthlink.net -
Website: www.pandorasattic.com

Jillian Manning

I'm interested in the history of fashion and clothing. I also do some sewing and lots of embroidery. It occurred to me about eighteen months ago that I could combine these two interests by dressing fashion dolls in period clothing. I have a reservoir of fabrics and threads, so I just needed some dolls. I started collecting well-loved 11in (29cm) dolls at fetes here in Australia and became fascinated by the variety available—hollow bodied, solid bodied, fully articulated, full heads of hair, hardly any hair...hmmmm, that's a problem. That's when I discovered Jim Faraone's Fashion Doll Makeover series. What a mine of information! But I needed to know more!! I contacted Jim and he kindly invited me to join his Yahoogroup™. That was a revelation. The wealth of information available from this creative group of people has been invaluable. So far I've completed just two dolls, but I'm thoroughly enjoying my new hobby.
Email: majillian@hotmail.com

Kevin Allen

Four years ago, my interest in collecting the Barbie® doll returned from my childhood after seeing the great new lines market. I had Internet access, so a whole world of dolls was opened. I joined a mailing list about the Barbie® doll. There were doll artists on the list, and when I saw their work, I was amazed! I had to try fashion doll makeovers myself! I learned the basic techniques—painting, rerooting, and lashes. I became frustrated because I would make a doll that would look good and then I would be forced to put her in a store bought fashion. That wasn't good enough for me, so in December of 1999, I asked my mom to teach me how to sew. On Super Bowl Sunday 2000, we pulled out the sewing machine, fabric, a basic pattern and began. I never realized how much was involved in sewing until then. She had her work cut out for her, but succeeded!
Email: mimmit@msn.com -
Website:
http://www.angelfire.com/ky2/kevinnbg/originals.HTML
or
http://www.angelfire.com/ky2/kevinnbg/male.HTML

Sharon Marquiss-Morris

As a child, I loved to watch mom turning out wonderful garments for me and my sisters from a cranky old Singer® sewing machine. It was very heavy and it worked by turning a wheel on one side, by hand! My first attempts at sewing were made on this machine. Later, as a married woman with four children, I re-kindled my sewing interest by making summer frocks and doll clothes for my daughters. There was a long break, until I discovered fashion doll makeovers, which a new friend introduced me to. This opened up a whole new world for me that I never knew existed. Although I have only been customizing for a few months, I have enjoyed it immensely. My 13-year-old daughter has even set up a home page for me to display my work. I am also selling on eBay™ under the name of Sharon Marquiss. All in all, I have to say that being a part of the doll world is very rewarding, not the least of which includes the wonderful world of fashion doll people, who are in my opinion, the best there is!
Email: Chiablis@aol.com -
Website:
http://hometown.aol.com/chiablis/index.HTML

Deborah Cates

I've loved dolls for as long as I can remember, and I've been making fashion doll clothes since before I could sew. I even did some of my first makeovers before I was ten. Unfortunately, those attempts ended up ruining the doll! I started seriously making over fashion dolls in 1996. I make my own patterns, shoes, hats, jewelry, repaints, hairdos, and I've even hand-painted material to get the effect I want. A background of briefly making dollhouse dolls helped my sense of scale. However, I can look at and see something else that can be approved upon on every doll I've ever made over. It still amazes me to discover something else I don't know about doll makeovers. I don't have time for my dolls to be a full-time hobby, but there is such a thrill when an idea cumulates into something that I can say "Wow!" about.
Email: anniecates@ionet.net -
Website: http://www.ionet.net/~anniecates

Joan Champagne

After graduating from high school, I attended drama school in New York City and worked in the professional theater for many years as actress/singer/dancer. Eventually, I left the City but always had some kind of creative outlet. Little did I know when I got a computer in 1998 that it would open up a new world for me. Although I had already started collecting dolls, I never dreamed that I would end up customizing them and creating a website to showcase my work. My tastes run from the sophisticated styles in day and evening wear to styles representing the 1940's and 1950's. My advice to new fashion doll makeover artists? Create what YOU like and don't be afraid to learn all you can. Have fun, have patience with yourself and don't give up!! Email: theater23@yahoo.com - Website: www. angelfire.com/biz3/ny2/index. HTML

Joanna Bond

I am a writer, mother, toy collector and doll transformer. I'm one of those incessantly creative people that infuses art into everything. I use decoupage, found objects, clay, plastic, and anything else out of the proverbial box, to make fashion dolls into something a toy company would never produce. I love to break the rules of what constitutes doll hair, clothing, or accessories; the shock of metal wings, for example, or iridescent hair. Irony, spirituality, music and the human mind inspire me. Conceptual warriors and mythical creatures pepper my universe. A fashion doll is not a mannequin, but a canvas! The Internet provides a huge opportunity for an artist. You can get instant feedback from people around the world, buy and sell, and find supportive camaraderie from like-minded artists. It's incredibly inspiring. Email: mojo@freakydeakydolls.com - Website: http://www.freakydeakydolls. com

Sandy Mahan

I am a 59-year-old government worker that has lived in Columbus, Ohio, all my life. An inherited 1966 twist and turn Barbie® doll started this fashion doll hobby about three years ago. I have been in one art show and advertised in a doll magazine. I have a website sorely in need of updating and my co-workers think I am talented, (Wow!! What more could you ask for?) I am my biggest critic, so I don't always see what others see in my work. I prefer hand-sewing and leather and fur (faux or real) are my specialties. I do some machine sewing, but most of the intricate pieces are done by hand. The fact that I like tailored clothing is reflected in my pieces. I try very hard to make things that a person can easily envision a real person wearing. My satisfaction is the key to why I do this. Email: sans41@aol.com - Website: http://sudfds.tripod.com/index. HTML

Kathy J. McLeod

I lived in Florida all of my life except for 9 years ago when we moved to a small town in North West Arkansas. First off, I want to give all the credit to my father, the LORD almighty, for the talent I have is His and not mine. I have always worked with my hands and loved to sew. I use to sketch long gowns, which was for my own entertainment, but nothing became of it. I started sewing just about everything my children and I wore. I guess you could say we were a OOAK family and I really enjoyed it. My daughter got me interested in doing OOAK dolls. I am so glad for I have the best time of my life doing them. This has brought us closer together.
Email: sunshine791@alltel.net

Elizabeth "Beth" Kinsley

I am a mother of two grown sons and have been married 27 years to my wonderful husband. He understands my obsession! I always loved crafts, so when I heard of the fashion doll makeovers, I knew I had to give it a try. For the last several years, Fashion Doll Makeovers has become a big part of my life. It has put me in touch with so many great people over the Net. One of them is now my very best friend. I have been lucky enough to win a few contests with my creations. I started out by sewing the outfits. I then progressed to boiled perms, and did a little face painting. Now I am doing eyelashes and more advanced face painting. I have been listening to a lot of the professionals on this list and have been getting some good tips for making my ladies' makeovers. To me this is really a work of love!
Email: Beth55@charter.net -
Website:
http://bhotn.homestead.com/

Aurora Mathews

I do repaints of the Gene® doll, the Tyler® doll and other 15in (38cm) and 16in (41cm) fashion dolls. I have also worked on a few 11-½in (29cm) dolls. My background in art includes the following skills: I am a seamstress, pattern maker, beadwork designer, beadweaver, lampwork bead maker, and an artist, painting in oils, acrylics, and water colors. I wrote, illustrated, designed and published, "The BeadAholic Quarterly," a publication for beaders from March 1994 to March 2000. A friend I had met in the bead world introduced me to the beautiful, collectible fashion doll, Gene Marshall® and I was hooked immediately. I now spread my time doing repaints, beading and a little sewing, in that order.

I found Jim Faraone's "Fashion Doll Makeover" group on-line and am now forever lost in a world of dolls. What makes it so much fun for me is that I am able to use any and all of the skills on my dolls! I love doing OOAK fashion doll repaints and celebrity doll repaints. I love art in any form!
Email: auroram@cybertrails.com
- Website:
http://server34.hypermart.net/auroram/

Laura Nelson

Dolls have always been a part of my life. I loved my Malibu Francie® doll to death as a kid. I remember my mom and I sewing for her; I still have all the patterns we used. I still have the same love for my dolls, only on a larger scale. I learned porcelain doll making during a 6-year stay in Germany and I moved to fashion dolls 3 years ago. I reroot hair, create and sew for dolls from the Gene® doll to vintage to mod Barbie® dolls to the Barbie® doll's little sister the Kelly® doll. My favorite outfits are my vintage and mod Barbie® doll recreations I make using the computer. I recreate the classic patterns and then print and sew copies of the vintage clothes. Since I have the patterns on the computer, I am able to resize them for other sizes of fashion dolls. I also love to make Kimonos for my dolls. I have created patterns for fashion dolls ranging in sizes from the Kelly® doll to the 36in (91cm) My Size Barbie® doll. Creating for dolls has allowed me to meet so many new and wonderful friends from all over the world. I can't imagine my life without creating for dolls!
Email: Laura3966@aol.com - Website: www.auntie.com/laura

Joyce Marie LaFave

I was a born doll artist! As a little girl I would cut and curl hair and do makeup with colored pencils and crayons. From scraps, I sewed special outfits for my Barbie® dolls and played dress up. I was the designer and they were my runway models! With my little Brownie® camera in hand, I lined the girls up for fashion shots! I still love to take pictures of them! In the 40 plus years that I have been doing makeovers, I've gotten bigger, and so have the fashion dolls! But the LOVE of doing makeovers has stayed the same. I have met so many wonderful people that share my passion! I love to talk about, and share the tips that I have learned from Jim Faraone's books and his FDM Yahoogroup! Let's share our passion and do what brings us a "look of joy!"

Email: lookofjoy@webtv.net - Website:
http://community.webtv.net/ LOOKOFJOY/LOOKOFJOY

Jennifer Urbaniak

A childhood passion was rekindled during a trip to Barnes and Noble® bookstore. I picked up a Sarah Eame's book and became fascinated with all the vintage fashions pictured. I left with the book and headed straight to my parent's attic to find my childhood treasures. Sadly, nothing survived my younger sisters. I then went into a frenzy buying Barbie® dolls. I went back to the bookstore and came across the *Barbie Bazaar®* magazine and picked it up. When I first saw the fashion doll makeovers contest, I was aghast. I couldn't believe anyone would remove a doll's paint or restyle their hair! I thought they were ruining the Barbie® doll. Months later, I came across an article on Dan Goh's dolls. I was in love. I then went back and looked at old contests and articles. They were beautiful! How did I not see it before? They were art, and I couldn't wait to be a part of it.
Email: Emailjensgems@cs.com - Website: jensgems.homepage.com

Donna Felton

It all began a few years ago while reading the Nov/Dec issue of *Barbie Bazaar®* magazine. There was an article about an artist who did fashion doll makeovers using regular issued play-line dolls. I was in absolute awe! They were exquisite! My first Barbie® doll show soon followed where I had the opportunity to see even more beautiful creations up close and personal. Soon, fascination gave way to inspiration and I mustered up the courage to tackle my first makeover project. Then came my second and so forth. I soon found

that I had a preference for doing high fashion daywear. One day, on a visit to a local downtown gallery, I saw the most amazing old Baroque music box depicting velvet clad performers dancing around an elaborate stage. It enchanted me (and so did its $5,000.00 price tag). It was then that I decided to take my doll customizing in a whole new direction, and so, "Theatrical Dreamworks" was born.
Email: DONNAKINS@webtv.net - Website: www.TheatricalDreamworks.com

Shirley Amador

I started collecting dolls when I was four years old. My mother taught me to make doll clothes at a young age. As a teenager I still loved dolls, but would not share my creations because I thought I was too old to play with dolls. As an adult and mother of five daughters, I had many dolls around and became a serious collector and discovered that dolls are for adults, too. My daughter, Carol, is part of the group and had been doing makeovers for some time. I have worked in a very stressful job as a criminal paralegal for the past few years and needed an outlet. This whole idea became irresistible to me. Soon, I was

doing my own makeovers and was a part of this wonderful group. I am now working in the law field part-time and spending a lot of time doing makeovers

and repaints.
Email: gracedolls@earthlink.net - Website: http://www.touchofgracedolls.com

Barb Rausch

I am a lifetime Katy Keene fan, a commercial artist who has worked in animation (JEM®- Truly Outrageous!) and drawn licensed Barbie® doll coloring and paper doll books for Western Publishing, and BARBIE® doll and BARBIE® doll FASHION comics for Marvel®. My makeover dolls have won first place awards in their categories at the national Barbie® doll conventions in Albuquerque and San Diego, and the 1998 Southern California regional. At the 2000 national convention in Tulsa, both of my entries in the

Barbie Bazaar® magazine Makeover Competition won awards.

My specialties are male dolls and period costume of the 17th and 18th centuries. I have an extensive library of books on the history of costume, and I draft my own patterns from scratch. My favorite modern fashion era is the 1980's, especially the designs of Karl Lagerfeld and Christian Lacroix. I find the hardest part of doll costuming is finding patterned fabrics and trims of the right scale for the dolls.

Lori Strawn

Hmmm...my life story. Simply put, it's "little girl who loves the Barbie® doll grows up into big girl who loves the Barbie® doll." I'm really an amateur when it comes to doing fashion doll makeovers. I don't feel nearly as talented as the other folks in this group, but I enjoy it. It gives me yet another creative outlet. In my "non-doll" life, I am a writer of children's books, as yet unpublished, but I'm still hopeful. I spent 12 years in advertising, and love the freedom of my new career. So far, all of my dolls have been gifts for my nieces only. I do all of the painting, jewelry and hairstyling/rooting. However, I can't sew a single stitch! The outfits you see on my dolls are store-bought, except for the little punk girl. I cobbled together her outfit myself!

Email: loristrawn@yahoo.com

Kristina Ammons

I am married with 3 children and live in Vancouver, WA. I have had a love dolls for as long as I can remember. Once, I even turned down the chance for a brand new bike, and begged for a Barbie® doll instead. My mother taught me to sew at a very young age, and I started making all my Barbie® doll clothes myself. It was a hobby I truly enjoyed. I was in my late teens before I really got my doll collection going and I collected all types of dolls. Now, I am only collecting high fashion dolls. I started doing fashion doll makeovers two years ago and my first victim was the Tiffany Taylor® doll. Shortly after that, I was introduced to the Gene® doll, and then came the Tyler Wentworth® doll. The larger fashion dolls are my favorites. I would say my favorite theme would be fantasy and I enjoy making fairies the most. So far, all my creations have been sold on eBay™.

Email Kriss366@aol.com -
Website:
http://www.geocities.com/kristinas_kreations

Carol Jones

I have always loved dolls, but started seriously collecting five years ago. Last year, I was looking for dolls on the Internet and came across a website devoted to fashion doll makeovers. I thought, "I could do that!" and set to work on my first doll, a recreation of my wedding day. Then I discovered the Fashion Doll Makeovers Message Board, which gives me great tips and techniques and allows me to talk to others in the field. Since then I have designed more than 20 dolls, including Gene® doll repaints and commissioned work. My mother, Shirley, started designing soon after I did. Although we are 400 miles away, she and I talk just about every night about our new dolls. I enjoy the creative outlet designing gives me. I have done bridals, mermaids, and celebrity recreations. I never thought my love for dolls would lead to a great business.

Email: CJJones99@msn.com -
Website: www.CJCollectible.com

Sharon Brendemuehl

In view of most people, I am a mother of three teenagers, soul mate to a gentleman who is not sure what to think of me sometimes, owner of two dogs, and a seamstress by trade. To an elite group of friends, they know a collector of many things, packrat extraordinaire, a kit and art supply accumulator and a fashion doll makeover artist. My only credentials are wanting something different. My favorite theme to work with is fantasy. I love castles, wizards, sorceresses and fairies. With fantasy, it is all

imagination and one can do what they think it should look like.

I love doing many different hobbies, such as cross stitch, home decorating, painting, dollhouse miniatures, cooking, reading and sewing. Everything I do has helped in one way or another with my work in fashion doll makeovers and my 1/6- scale houses. Creating something unusual from the ordinary is a great feeling.
Email: ladandlass@excite.com - Website:
http://members.tripod.com/ladsandlassies

Ella Trumpfeller

In 1996, upon connecting to the Internet, I became the co-president of the US Chapter of Dolls International Prestige Collectors Club, founded in Italy. PurrFashion Designs began in 1998 by accident when I made a cat doll from a scarred vintage Francie® doll. Cats have always had a special appeal because of my dance background. I have been the owner/director/teacher of the Dance Centre School of Dance and Body Designs Dancewear (retail store) since 1982.

In addition to cats, I also make fairies, fashion dolls, trailer trash and drag queens. I have donated to conventions, charities and participated in swaps. My greatest joy, in addition to dance, is working with dolls and communicating and helping others on the Internet with similar passions. I also enjoy website designing and management. The makeover industry is growing so fast these days and I am very happy to be a part of it.
Email: Ella@purrfashiondesigns.com - Website:
http://www.PurrFashionDesigns.com

Laura George

Georgee Girl Designs began in May 1999 when I discovered that I could combine my love of dolls with my desire to be creative! I enjoy designing a variety of creations that range from celebrities and couples to historical dolls and everything in between. With fashion dolls as the perfect model, I get to be a hairstylist, makeup artist, fashion designer and photographer rolled into one! I find inspiration everywhere including fashion magazines, movies, fellow artists and history books. I have sold my dolls to collectors all over the

world and I get satisfaction from knowing someone is enjoying something I have made. I thank all my customers for their continuing support and motivation. Thanks also to my biggest fans, my mother and grandmother for their encouragement and guidance and to my husband who always s upports my dreams. I hope collectors enjoy viewing my dolls as much as I enjoyed designing them.
Email: Laurgeo@hotmail.com -
Website:
http://www.georgeegirl.com

Kevin Kilmer

I am 40 years old and I have been exposed to the doll world for almost all of my life. My folks owned and operated a reproduction doll making and repair business for many years, which is where I caught the bug for doll making. I learned to sew from both of my folks and I think my dad, who has since passed away, would be extremely proud of my work so far! I started out just following along with the pre-painted doll paint to get used to doing the doll work on such a small scale and have now graduated to completely redoing the facial painting and making dolls into high fashion dolls and

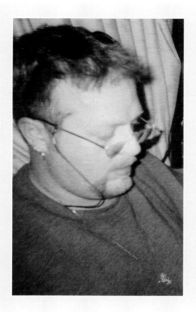

celebrity look-a-likes! Having even performed some plastic surgery on some of the more recent dolls that I have been making! I find it very therapeutic and a lot of fun to see the progression of the doll from start to finish. Hopefully one day I will become a great doll artist! I think the one person that was most influential for me has to be my dad. THANKS DAD! I LOVE YOU!!!!
Email: Dollman26lee60@webtv.net - Website: http://community.webtv.net/Dollman26lee60/CLICKDesigns byKevin

Melissa Klein

I am the artist behind "MyssiKay Designs". I am relatively new to this wonderful art of fashion doll makeover dolls. I started collecting the Barbie® collectable dolls again about two years ago. About ten months ago, I got a computer and found an on-line auction for the first OOAK doll that I had ever seen. I was hooked! I have always loved painting and crafts, so customizing dolls was a natural progression. I have been doing fashion doll makeovers for about 6

months now and have recently started selling my creations to other doll collectors through my website and on-line auctions. I still have quite a ways to go in the learning process of this art and have gotten TONS of help from many other wonderful doll artists, many of whom are also members of this fabulous group.
Email: myssikay@aol.com - Website: http://www.angelfire.com/art/myssikaydesigns/index.HTML

Amy Nardone

I have been a doll artist for 5 years, thanks to Jim Faraone's first *Fashion Doll Makeovers* book! What more could a person ask for than to use a fashion doll for a canvas? I currently have worked on the Barbie® doll, Gene® doll, Charice® doll and Willow® and Daisy® dolls. I remove all traces of that factory paint on every doll. I then meticulously repaint the face using high quality acrylics and sealers. Each doll gets her eyelashes rooted to give her a more lifelike and glamorous look. I feel the facial aspect of

the doll is very important. All of the ensembles on my dolls are original. I only do one-of-a-kind creations to make the doll more unique. All the embellishments are sewn by hand. My machine does the basics. This is more than just a "hobby" for me. This is a creative outlet, plus a great way to meet fellow artists, beginners or professionals and most importantly, friends! I couldn't be any happier.
Email: anardone@toad.net - Website: http://www.toad.net/~anardone

Vonda Silliman

I became a makeover artist in February of 2000 after discovering my childhood Barbie® dolls in a trunk in my mother's attic. They needed to be restored and when I looked for information on the Internet, the world of makeovers unfolded before my eyes. After successfully restoring my older dolls, I purchased several newer dolls on the secondary market. With these dolls, Jim Faraone's books, and the fashion doll makeovers list, I soon found myself repainting faces, rerooting hair and eyelashes, designing fashions, creating tiny jewelry and enjoying it immensely. Each of these finished dolls is truly one-of-a-kind with a unique look and "personality". My favorites to create are fantasy and glamour dolls. However, I look forward to exploring other areas. Each doll is numbered, comes with a Certificate of Authenticity and is also uniquely painted with the artist's signature—a miniature sunflower.
Email:
TheWonderofDolls@cs.com -
Website:
http://www.thewonderofdolls.
homestead.com

Loanne Hizo Ostlie

I've been doing fashion doll makeover dolls of all sizes for about a year and a half now. I began Tabloach Productions (a combination of my name and my husband and daughter's names) way before I discovered customizing dolls. My brother had given me a customized Ninja Barbie® doll that came in a customized display box. This creation inspired me to try my hand at customizing the most available doll worldwide...the Barbie® doll. I also discovered customizing Kelly®-sized dolls

were just as intriguing. I especially like working with different kinds of medium, fabric paint, wire, molding paste, clay, foam, etc. Because I get bored easily, I always try to venture into what other artists are more likely to stay away from. If there is a medium or technique that hasn't been discovered, you can surely bet that I'll be the first one digging my hands into it and experimenting.
Email: Tabloach@Yahoo.com or
Loanne@Tabloach.com -
Website:
http://www.Tabloach.com

Michele Frazee-Jackson

I began fashion doll makeovers in the spring of 2000, and have found it to be a great outlet for my creative energy. My mother, a renowned woodcarver and painter, inspired me with a love of the arts since I was a young child. I still have a folder of clothing design sketches that I made as a youngster. Since then, I have had the wonderful opportunity to take my childhood dream and turn it into reality. It is amazing how an average doll can be transformed into a special work of art with paint, fabric, body repositioning and so forth. I get ideas for my creations from unique pieces of fabric, special beads, or the way a facial paint comes through on the doll. The possibilities are endless with fashion doll makeovers and I look forward to further expanding my skill and talents in the future.
Email: michelefj@aol.com -
Website:
www.designsbymichele.net

Rose Rothhaar

When I started collecting fashion dolls, I never realized what a wonderful subculture I would discover. Meeting fellow collectors and attending doll shows and conventions brought a new joy to my life. SPECIAL ADDITIONS started with makeovers of 11-½ in (29cm) fashion dolls and now include 15in to 16in (38cm to 41cm) dolls. I strive to have my dolls show a complete look; from the styled hair to linings, finished seams and hand-sewn detail

work. Photos of my dolls have appeared in *Barbie Bazaar®* magazine, Doll Reader® and Miller's®. I was honored to receive awards in the BMAA contest for two years. I was a featured artist in Jim Faraone's book, *Second Fashion Doll Makeovers*. One of my goals is achieved when I see a collector fall in love with a doll. I can see the doll will be a "Special Addition" to a loving home.
Email: Roseinct@aol.com - Website: www.special-additions.com

Sharon Newman

Dollsbysharon was created in January 1999. We create glamorous and fantasy creations that are one-of-a-kind dolls which include facial makeovers, beautiful gowns and hairstyles. I originally started designing fashion doll makeovers to help pay for my fashion doll makeover purchases. This has since changed, I have developed an obsession for creating dolls and before I finish one I am working on, I am planning the next one. I usually work on about 4 dolls at a time to keep from getting bored.

This way I can switch off between dolls. It takes me a minimum of 16 hours to complete each doll because I will not rush them just to finish them. I spend most of my free time working on my dolls. I have made so many great friends through Barbie® dolls from both selling and buying. This is one hobby I hope lasts for a very long time.
Email: coolrider@mindspring.com - Website: http://www.pages.about.com/dollsbysharon/main.HTML

Kelli "Jinx" Getchell

I started collecting Barbie® dolls as an adult. Even at flea markets and tag sales I'd be searching out Barbie® dolls and other fashion dolls. I'd take those beaten up beauties and restore them so they looked like new dolls. Then I ran across a copy of *Fashion Doll Makeovers* by Jim Faraone. What an eye opener. I didn't just have to dab paint here and there to restore a doll to her former glory. I could repaint and restyle a doll to be whatever my imagination could envision. It

took until his third book for me to work up the courage to actually give it a try.

My formal art training amounts to a few art classes in high school and the skills my grandmother taught me as a child. Makeovers are a wonderful way for me to combine my hobby of collecting dolls and my artistic talents.
Email: JinxKJ1@aol.com - Website: http://www.geocities.com/jinxkloe/whimzees.htm

Sarah J. Worley

When my daughter went to college, she gave me permission to sell some of her toys and dolls. I discovered the realm of eBay™ and the amazing world of fashion dolls including OOAK dolls, the extent of which I didn't realize existed! I then attended my first doll show in Raleigh, NC. Since that time I have enjoyed escaping into an enthralling world of fantasy and glamour that has become a hobby of tremendous enjoyment! My family is very supportive. My son told me he

was very proud of my hobby - that was one of the dearest compliments I've gotten! My regular bill-paying job is as a child protective services social worker. The departure into designing dresses, redoing hair and makeup on lovely dolls has given me not only a wonderful creative outlet, but a way to meet some of the nicest people I've ever had the pleasure of getting to know!
Email: sworley@intrstar.net -
Website:
http://sarahstyle.terrashare.com

Christie Unger

Until recently, my life was consumed by all the "grown-up" distractions in life. The last thing on my mind was my beloved childhood friend the Barbie® doll. It was not until I logged onto the Internet, and landed on a doll makeover site, that my interest was renewed. As I clicked on each stunning doll, my mind raced and the spark of creativity began to flicker. "I can do this!" As I researched my new hobby, I came across the "list". It is a

great resource for a beginner like me. Not only do people share their work, but are generous enough to offer helpful tips and suggestions. To me, the atmosphere feels like an on-line brainstorming session that inspires creativity without promoting uniformity. Although I have only been dabbing in my hobby for a year, I have enjoyed every minute of it. It provides a certain amount of freedom and release.
Email: girlmonk@yahoo.com

Carolyn Marnon

C's Craftique, my doll and miniatures business, was inspired by my love of fashion doll makeovers and creating dioramas. I started collecting the Barbie® doll and her friends in 1994. The first swap I participated in during 1996 brought me into the customizing field. I do not have a certain style; I design whatever my imagination has conjured up. I am not an expert seamstress, so I like to use unusual materials in designing my dolls. I have made tops of stretch sequins, skirts of

tulle strips, bodies covered with flocking, and have embellished store-bought outfits to fit my creative vision.

The doll that has given me the most pleasure to make is a portrait doll of my sister-in-law, Stefanie, in her wedding dress, with a background of the area where she was married. It is important to bring personal items into my dolls; they have a story that can carry on with the doll and perhaps become an heirloom one day.
Email: marnon@ameritech.net

Anita Healy

I have been doing fashion doll makeovers for nearly 2 years. I started out customizing 11-½in (29cm) dolls and have recently gone into customizing 15in (38cm), 15-½in (39cm) and 16in (41cm) dolls. My fashion ideas/inspiration come from watching runway shows, reading high fashion magazines and of course some of my own style blended in. When creating a doll, I make it a point to always pay attention to detailing, scaling, accessorizing and packaging. I also take extra care and time when choosing new fabrics for the dolls. My husband Jim creates all of my boxes to match each doll's theme by airbrushing and using different cut-aways for windows. Many of my customers do not de-box so they are very pleased when they see the detailed display boxes.
Email: AHealy9011@aol.com - Website: http:// anitahealydolls.50megs.com/

Melinda Sprague

After attending Cosmetology school, I knew the basics about human hair and makeup applications. When I could no longer work in that field and wanted a creative outlet similar to my field of studies, I chose to make over fashion dolls. With the help of a friend I found an email group that was all about Fashion Doll Makeovers. I started slowly. First concentrating on hair, I then moved on to repaints and rerooting. I learned about adding eyelashes, separating the fingers and reshaping the arms and hands. There were so many people who were more than willing to share their information.

I then took a sewing class and tied it all together to make a complete OOAK doll. Since then I've sold a few, and I keep quite a few too, some I just can't let go of. But still my favorite part of fashion doll makeovers is repaints.
Email: mydragonmoon@yahoo.com - Website: http://www.geocities.com/ SouthBeach/Shores/5241

Michelle Candace

While growing up I had artistic abilities, but never had an outlet for these abilities that I was passionate about until I rediscovered dolls. I started doing fashion doll makeovers about 1-½ years ago. My first attempt at sewing proved to be quite challenging, as I had not sewn much before. I then became interested in painting and hair rerooting because I wanted to restore my vintage Barbie® doll from childhood. I found information about fashion doll makeovers on the Internet and in magazines and tried some techniques. Through trial and error I have learned the most. Now I am totally hooked and love designing. My favorite dolls to design for are the precious Topper Dawn® dolls and vintage Barbie® dolls. It's very satisfying taking a sad vintage doll and breathing new life into her. In the future I plan on creating more fantasy themed dolls. I believe this will allow me to be fully creative with my abilities.
Email: michellecandacecustomdolls@ hotmail.com - Website: www.geocities.com/Heartland/ Creek/9482/customdollshome. HTML

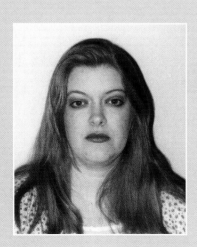

Pamela Bachmayer

I designed needlecraft projects for craft publishers, kit manufacturers and pamphlet publishers for 10 years before I retired a few years ago. I designed under the name Pamela Noel (I'm remarried now). My specialty was crocheted garments for all ages and I was a regular designer in magazines such as Crochet Fantasy®, Home Crochet® and many others. I've also designed and written instruction pamphlets for Leisure Arts® and Design Originals® and kits for Bernat® yarns.

I started collecting dolls again a few years ago when my

oldest daughter moved out and took all hers with her! When I discovered the world of OOAK's, I was very excited. What could be more fun then combining what I love most (creating) with my favorite doll, the Barbie® doll! I'm also a newlywed, a mom and grandmother! Everyone in my family is involved with the Barbie® doll, from helping with shows to playing dolls with Grandma!
Email: pbundy@juno.com - Website: http://users2.ev1.net/ ~harlanba/pbdesigns/index.htm

Kathy Van Camp

I live on a 120-acre farm in Osseo, Michigan with my husband who is a retired policeman. I have two sons (Brad and Brian) who grew up sharing their space with all my dolls. I have made and collected dolls my entire life. I guess, I simply never outgrew them! I've made dolls out of cloth, fimo, cernit and porcelain. I even sculpted my own dolls and learned how to make my own molds.

With the coming of on-line auctions, I discovered the dolls of my youth and began collecting vinyl dolls from the 50's and 60's. Many of these came with years of grime, missing hair and paint and broken parts. That is when I got

into the restoring of dolls.

It was over the Internet that I came upon Jim's book. I bought the first one and immediately sent for the other two. It was so exciting to see the many fascinating interpretations of fashion dolls from the artists in the books.

I guess it was contagious, because I knew I had to customize my own Barbie® doll. So with the help of Jim's books, I just finished my very first Barbie® doll makeover. There is something fulfilling about creating your own fashion doll makeover! I have rediscovered the Barbie® doll and can't wait to begin my next makeover.
Email: trinity@frontiernet.net

Doris Griswold

I have loved dolls all my life, but seriously began collecting in 1988 when my husband bought me a porcelain doll in a grocery store as a fun or gag gift. (Bet he wished he had passed on this purchase!) I'm a Home Health Nurse and an elderly patient gave me a castoff doll that belonged to her granddaughter in 1990, a 1976 Ballerina Barbie® doll. This doll was dirty and naked, so I cleaned her up and bought her an

outfit. This began my love of fashion dolls. I now have many dolls in my collection and most of them live in my late mother-in-law's mobile home that is located in the rear of my home. I had a knee replacement three years ago and began doing fashion doll makeovers at this time to have something to do while recuperating from surgery. I especially like to customize little Kelly® type dolls.
Email: Grandl@aol.com

Jamie Wiley

I have been involved with designing OOAK dolls for about a year now. I became interested in making my own OOAK dolls after seeing an article on the amazing Renee Coughlan in the *Barbie Bazaar®* magazine. Having always been a huge fan of magic and fantasy, I was immediately drawn to those lovely centaurs and fairies. Thanks to the Internet, I was able to find out how to change a boring old pink box Barbie® doll into an imaginative work of art. Through various email lists, publications and fellow artists, I have learned to do so much, from sewing and beading to face painting and hair styling. This is truly an amazing form of expression allowing the use of various mediums to achieve a unique work of art. The artists in this book are exceptionally gifted and I am honored to be included with them.
Email: kryshen@aol.com - Website: http://members.xoom.com/drrahl/wyntir.htm

Matthew Shain Flinchem

I am the creator behind Designs by Shain. I have only been creating OOAK dolls since the early part of 2000. It all started when I came across some dolls who needed some repairs and new hair and I gave it a try. From that point on I was hooked. I was born and raised in Baltimore, Maryland and I am now 27 years old. I do not create makeovers as a career—it's a hobby. If I made it a career it would then become work. I use only top quality fabrics and paints for my dolls. All costumes and clothing are my own designs and I do not use patterns. In the beginning I used patterns but feel now that I create a much better look and my own personal style without them.
Email: designsbyshain@cs.com - Website: http://designsbyshain.tripod.com

Lim Shor-wei

I live in sunny Singapore with my son and husband. I've been involved in sewing crafts for more than 10 years, but my interest in dolls started in 1997, when I was surfing the net for ideas for my wedding. There, I stumbled upon fashion doll sites and now I have the Barbie® doll, Jenny® doll, Gene® doll, Tyler® doll, Willow® doll and others. I sew for all of them and will also buy other dolls to sew for.

My sewing scale is varied, but I love recreating the fashions and life-style of the 1930's-60's. I sew a range of day and night ensembles plus basic mix and match pieces. I also like to make romantic clothes and clothes that reflect my Asian culture using traditional Asian fabrics such as batik, Thai silks and Chinese brocades.

More fashions can be viewed on my web page. I look forward to hearing your feedback.
Email: Shorwei@yahoo.com - Website: http://www.geocities.com/shorwei

Stephanie J. Brown

I live in the small town of New Castle, IN. I have a beautiful 10-year-old daughter and am currently expecting my second child in Feb./Mar. 2001. I began doing fashion doll makeovers in June of 1999. I really enjoy the whole aspect of redesigning a doll and giving it my own sense of style. I took basic art classes in school and am currently expanding my sewing skills with a dressmaking/design class. I get a lot of inspiration from bridal magazines and some fantasy books. I think my favorite fashion designers have to be Bob Mackie and Vera Wang. I hope to continue doing doll makeovers for a long time. Nothing is more satisfying to me than seeing a bare doll turned into a beautiful work of art.
Email: stephb64@yahoo.com - Website: http://members.nbci.com/captivations

Tracy Lake

I grew up in a four-bedroom home. My family occupied three of those bedrooms. The fourth bedroom was known as "The Barbie® Doll Room." We owned every doll, accessory, vehicle and house that room could hold (thanks mom). I wish that I had that treasure now. Unfortunately, I lost interest in fashion dolls as a teenager. I rediscovered the Barbie® doll when the Gone With The Wind® series was offered. The combination of that tempting doll and timeless movie was too hard to resist. I have since discovered the joy of finding a doll's unique personality with fashion doll makeovers. I enjoy creating one-of-a-kind beauties using my imagination and any fashion doll that I can obtain. It's been interesting learning about painting, hairstyles and all the other necessary skills. It's also put me in touch with so many wonderful doll people. There's nothing more rewarding than new friends.
Email: Tracy@tracystreasure - Website: http://Tracystreasure.com

Charlie Dale

I have been a Barbie® doll admirer since I was little but have been a serious collector for six years. With a background in Visual Display/Merchandising and an education in Fashion Design, my dolls are known for impeccable fit, Haute Couture hand sewing techniques as well as creative packaging. My dolls come with accessories, artist box, doll stand, doll biography, and Certificate of Authenticity. I love creating glamorous gowns as well as doing "theme dolls" such as famous people, historically accurate costumes and research into historic people. I bring class and style to my dolls considering that I have been doll designing for two years. I am a member of several on-line clubs including Jim Faraone's list. My work has appeared in the 2001 *Barbie Bazaar*® magazine National Makeover Contest.
Email: CharlieDale9966@aol.com

Shirley R. Heater

My passion for designing and sewing for dolls began with childhood hand-sewing and crocheting. By age 11, I was creating my own clothes on my grandmother's treadle. Being short required alterations and I enjoyed mixing patterns and deviating from instructions. Later I sewed for others (wedding, prom, men's suits, custom draperies).

My focus returned to dolls in the 60's and 70's, selling custom fashions in my "Mini-Mods Fashion Catalog" and publishing my original patterns and newsletter. After an archaeology degree and years of research and writing, my interest in dolls rekindled in 1997. Since acquiring Aileen's Petite Fashions, I now publish "The Fashion Plate" for dolls, a newsletter/catalogue featuring "On the Runway...: exclusive new patterns" and "From the Archives" reprints of my earlier patterns.

Favorites range from vintage/retro fashions for the Barbie® doll, Ken® doll, Skipper® doll, Francie® doll and the Tutti® doll to the G.I. Joe® doll, Crissy® doll, Velvet® doll, Dawn® doll, Newborn Thumbelina® doll and the Gene® doll. Selective custom makeovers enhance the look! Email: srheater@home.com - Website: www.mini-fashionboutique.com

Barb Wood

Greetings from the "Jerzy" shore!! Although I am originally from Trenton, N.J., I now reside in South Jersey with my husband, George and my daughter, Jessica. I am currently working in a Pathology Laboratory in a South Jersey Hospital.

I started collecting Barbie® dolls for my daughter in 1988 but didn't start doing fashion doll makeovers until 1997. I have always loved drawing and painting. Customizing a doll gives me a 3-dimensional canvas. During my childhood, I was always fascinated with the fantasy realm so my dolls usually have a magical appearance—lots of glitter and wings! My daughter usually has some creative ideas and will occasionally sketch them for me, but most of my work is just sheer imagination! My creations include fairies, mermaids, butterflies and any other kind of fantasy doll! The more glitter and glitz the better! Email: Jerzygyrl98@yahoo.com - Website: http://dollsbyjerzy.homestead.com/index.HTML

Andrea Densley

What I loved most about my first Barbie® doll was her miniscule wardrobe. At the age of 8, armed with a child's toy sewing machine and a stash of fabric scraps, my designing career began. I spent my youth sketching, sewing and studying fashion designers.

During college at Brigham Young University, I gleaned the knowledge of experts like Professor Anna Demos, a meticulous European couturier, and theatrical designer Jan Polanich, a vibrantly creative artist. I was an award-winning student designer in the theatre department, eventually graduating with a BA degree in fashion design.

Now I own a costume consulting business, and design historically costumed dolls that are styled on original costume sources and period art. I'm a reference librarian, and I sing with a 19-piece big band, "Swing Forever." I live in the lush Pacific Northwest with my husband and six children and a very noisy dog. Email: adens@juno.com - Domain name: costumehelp.com

Patti Tompkins

I create and customize small vanity items, sunglasses and other small treasures for the Barbie®

doll. I also design and create display cases and armoires for the Barbie® doll, which are still in the designing mode. I express one-of-a-kind items only and will not take orders for duplications. I wish to keep everyone feeling special, so my clients will have something completely unique. I use some of the finest materials such as gold leafing, 22K gold charms, gold and silver filled chains, 100% Swarovski crystals in various shades, beveled and straight cut mirrors, etc. I am currently in the midst of building a website for you to browse and just email me for its availability. I list all of my items on Ebay.com under the name of rupato. I have named my business Crystal

Creations and I pay strict attention to detail and perfection in all that I create.

A big thank you and tons of hugs to my absolute best encouragement team on earth, Karen, Marie, Jan, Chris, Rose,

Debbie, Mom and Dad, I love you all so very much. I love doing what I do and hope to bring some joy of my creations to you!!!
Email: rupato@aol.com

Sheryl Majercin

I've always loved to draw, paint and sculpt...anything creative. I learned to sew gowns for the Barbie® doll by age ten. Years later I still LOVE designing them and have expanded my designs to include ensembles for the Gene® doll. Once I stumbled into the world of fashion doll makeovers, I was instantly hooked. Painting, sewing, designing all rolled up into one! The Barbie® doll and Gene® doll were the perfect canvas for endless fashion doll makeover possibilities. I strive to cover a wide variety of custom dolls,

from fairies to bombshells. I enjoy creating new looks through facial repaints and try to give life to each doll through expression. I take great care with my designs and focus on detail. In doing so, I have developed my talents as a cobbler and milliner for both the Barbie® doll and the Gene® doll. Creating unique looks for Fashion Dolls has not only become my passion but an endless learning experience.
Email:
dndolldreams@yahoo.com -
Website:
http://www.designsand
dolldreams.homestead.com

Linda R. Lehmann

The art of fashion design always spoke to my heart. Beautiful clothes worn by "movie stars" initiated my fashion interests. As a child, I wanted someday to capture the essence of apparel and express my own ideas of lines and patterns in doll designs and products I would make. Taking what I saw and eventually turning that into crocheted wardrobe items for my Barbie® dolls, I also developed interest in customizing and repairing the Barbie® dolls. Now I've begun participating in Internet

commerce which makes my varied products and creations available to the world! Such technology also fueled my husband's interest in helping me create doll fashions and patterns. I'm grateful for the opportunities to display my handiwork, which I hope will be of inspiration to you. We desire to further this charmingly traditional art form with the excitement of our advanced technological age for your benefit!
Email: lindarae@jackpine.com -
Website: www.geocities.com/
lindaraeleh/index.HTML

Patriciann Palka

Rumpled brown grocery bags...what treasures they can hold! Born into a family of garment workers, I fondly remember the eager anticipation, the delight of opening them, spilling out their contents... fanciful scraps of flocked nylon and tiny floral, remains of a day's work, tokens of affection my grandmother and aunts brought home from the factory to challenge my creativity. My earliest attempts at competing for Coco Chanel's chapeau were full-skirted, avant-garde drapings of 1940's silhouettes I viewed on our (black and white) TV. My dolls displayed the height of continental chic, and should someone question the reasoning behind the pins and scotch tape, I simple replied, "An artiste explains nothing!" Designing a degree in Switzerland, I packed my sketchbook and journal and fashioned a global merchandising career. The advent of computers brings me full circle, experimenting with digital designs for today's contemporary fashion dolls.
Email: couture8@yahoo.com

Lisa Howell

I started collecting Barbie® dolls about 7 years ago and have about 200 dolls in my collection. I began buying played-with dolls and began repainting rescued dolls in the Spring of 2000. I have tried several reroots and have been pleased with most of the gals I've rerooted. My first attempts at face painting were terrible, but over time I think I have improved. I have only just begun to sew for my makeovers, so most of my dolls have Fashion Avenue® outfits on for the time being.

I thoroughly enjoy being a member of the fashion doll makeover group (even though I'm mostly a "lurker") and have applied many of the tips from the list to my own style of makeovers. However, once I hone my sewing skills, I hope to become a more "active" member of the FDM list!
Email: LHOWELL@WK.NET

Laura Fern Fanelli

I was born in San Francisco before Barbie® dolls existed. I wanted to own a doll with high heels and earrings but alas all dolls then were baby dolls. I was also interested in drawing as far back as I can remember. If I couldn't own a fashion doll I could at least draw one! In elementary school and through high school I was usually the one doing the decorations and artwork. After high school I went on to what I thought was a noble calling....and became a nurse. I've enjoyed public service but missed the joy that I found when drawing and painting. I recently returned to Mission College where my major is Fine Art. I also discovered Jim Faraone's wonderful *Fashion Doll Makeover* series and am now happily combining my very favorite things....Art and Fashion Dolls! I love fantasy and contemporary design and enjoy being a Makeover Artist.
Email: fernice@earthlink.net

Debbie Lima

Let me start by saying that this is the most rewarding hobby I have ever had. When I had to retire early, I had no idea of what I was going to do with all my extra time. I was watching a TV show on hobbies and there was a makeover artist. Immediately I realized that this would be perfect for me. I knew how to sew and do hair already so I had a start. I had no idea how much more I had to learn. With the help of the Internet, I found the fashion doll makeovers and Jim Faraone and his very helpful books. With the help of all the Internet members and their advice I have improved my skills enough to sell a couple of dolls. That was over a year ago, I love what I'm doing and can't ever see myself without my dolls.
Email: dlima@gte.net - Website: http://www.members.tripod.com /daldesignerdolls

Colleen Malmquist

I was born and raised mostly in San Diego. I attended three years of Jr. College working on my Illustration major. I didn't get into fashion doll makeovers until two years ago when I saw an article in a fashion doll magazine on rerooting the Gene® doll to be a redhead. It looked like fun to me, and I immediately went out and bought myself a Barbie® doll and some doll hair to do my first reroot. I have been hooked ever since. I like doing medieval garb and fantasy type characters. Although I have only done 11in (28cm) dolls so far, I hope to do my first 15in (38cm) doll soon. Fashion doll makeovers help me combine other hobbies I enjoy, such as sewing, beading and painting. I hope to do it for a long time.
Email: rusulka@cox.net

Jean Majercin

The Barbie® doll is the ultimate fantasy figure to every little girl. I rediscovered the Barbie® doll of my childhood when I began making furniture for my daughter's dolls. I noticed that the Barbie® doll's décor options were limited to pink plastic and...pink plastic. I decided a revolution was in order!

I create custom furniture for the Barbie® doll and Gene® doll collectors. I strive to make each piece unique and realistic. I love experimenting with new furniture designs with an array of fabrics,

textures and colors. The Barbie® doll and Gene® doll can now have a sofa in black velvet, a chair in red satin, or even a chaise lounge in a wild animal print. I often include little extras like wooden tables, miniature magazines and fur rugs for fun. Whether I am designing furniture or creating a new OOAK Barbie® doll, this is a hobby I have grown to enjoy and love sharing with others.
Email: ohbusymom@pacbell.net - Website: http://www.geocities.com/ ohbusymom

Debra Jo Van Dyke

I have always collected and made dolls, miniatures and paper dolls. The nucleus of my Barbie® doll collection is my childhood bubblecut Barbie® doll with several incomplete outfits. My aunt taught me many needle arts and crafts and I learned to make clothes for my dolls. As an independent History study at Calvin College in Grand Rapids, MI., I researched, furnished and created inhabitants for a 1/2th scale ca. 1776 Colonial saltbox home. I have also developed a

series of 1in (3cm) dolls, which are a doll house doll's fashion doll collection. As a member of the Original Paper Doll Artists Guild®, I draw high fashion, animal and fantasy themed paper dolls. Seriously collecting the Barbie® doll since the late 70's, I like to change hairstyles and outfits, adding my own accessories. Since I work in smaller scale, it wasn't until 1999 I made my first OOAK Barbie® doll fairy. I intend to make more! Email: Neferkiti@aol.com

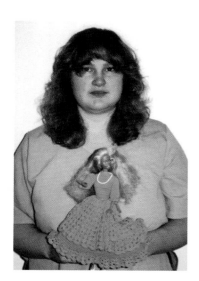

Stephani Knutson

I am 32 years old, married and live in Duvall, Washington, with my husband and 6-month-old son. My first dream as a child was to be a zookeeper and over the last 15 years been involved with several zoos as zookeeper, volunteer and educator. Currently, I am a veterinary assistant and receptionist at the Exotic Pet and Bird Clinic. Where do fashion doll makeovers fit in? Well, my second dream as a child was to be an artist. This dream became a real endeavor on

my part in 1994 when I started my own business—Wildlyfe Images and Fantasy Art - which includes pursuits in illustration, textile and fiber art, fashion doll makeovers and doll clothes, graphic art, miniatures and more. I particularly enjoy crocheting doll fashions, but also knit and sew them. I use commercial patterns, but I like to make adjustments or design my own. Email: wildlyfe@telisphere.com - Website: www.wildlyfeimages.com

Katarina Sandberg

I am from Sweden and have been collecting dolls since 1994 when the 35th Anniversary doll was released. At the same time I

started making clothes for my kid's dolls and thought it was lots of fun. Since then my collecting has become more pointed to the l'il world of the Kelly® doll and her friends and so has my clothes making. There is so much fun in making these tiny outfits and it is a big challenge as they are so small. Lately, I have done some swaps including these l'il rascals and an example is a l'il Snow White. I am too afraid to make any repaints yet, but I have bent an arm and permed some hair.

I have done a Halloween diorama, Trick or Treating Leopard Leile and Wizard Willie, which was easy. Leile is dressed in a cat suit made from a pajama pattern and Willie's robe is just

cut out from a jersey with a hole for the neck. For 11in (28cm) dolls I usually make gowns and capes, but I have also made some casual wears, although finding the right fabric for it is a bit difficult.
Email: kattisdolls@crosswinds.net or kattisdolls@hotmail.com - Website: http://www.crosswinds.net/ ~kattisdolls/

LaDonna Moore

I live in Ohio and I have been collecting dolls for six years. It all started by finding a Barbie® doll at an antique store that needed to be rescued and it has

carried on since then. My favorite doll is the Barbie® doll. I have been designing dolls for over a year and I started by joining a Barbie® doll club and the members introduced me to designing and it caught my attention right away. The thoughts of new designs are constantly in my mind.

My favorite one-of-a-kind design to make is brides. In the designer world I'm considered a newbie, but I experiment and gather all the information I can. I have a husband, Martie, and a son, Matt, who encourages me with my designs.
Email: mmoore@greenapple.com
Website:
http://mooredolls.CJB.net

Gael Singer Bailey

I started repainting Barbie® dolls as a child. I was never happy with the way all the dolls looked alike. I then started repainting her eyes, lips and nails. I also designed and made all types of beautiful and unusual outfits for my dolls.

Last November 1999, I discovered the Gene Marshall® doll. I loved everything about her except her eyes, lips and nails. I went about repainting the Gene® doll's face, then bought another Gene® doll and did the same thing. I didn't know at the time that other people did the same

thing. I have now discovered a whole new world.

I prefer working with green eyed redheads. I completely repaint her face and design original gowns and accessories using vintage fabrics and furs. I make all my own accessories, hats, handbags and jewelry including rings.

I also collect dolls from the Franklin Mint® like the Diana, Marilyn, Liz Taylor and the Kennedys.
Email: Kipperwitz@msn.com -
Website:
http://communities.msn.com/
BAILEYSORIGINALS

Cynthia Luna Hennes

I must have received the "doll gene" from my grandmother. She absolutely loved dolls but I don't think she ever had a doll as a child, coming from a poor pioneering family raised in the wild woods of Washington state. I received my "artistic/sewing gene" from my mother who is a wonderful artist and seamstress, so it's no surprise that I'm now involved with fashion doll makeovers. Customizing dolls combines my love for dolls and lets me express my artistic side.

I have many dolls in my personal collection, a lot of them inherited from my grandmother. I have at least 600 Barbie® dolls. I have always been involved with dolls in some way, from learning to sew and design clothes on my Barbie® doll in 1959 to researching and creating antique reproduction doll clothes for porcelain dolls in the 1970's, and I'm still designing today!
Email: luna@tstonramp.com
- Website:
http://www.barrysdolls.com
/bellaluna/index.htm

Leslie Hampton

Did you ever wonder what happens to a swinging twenty-something bartender living up in Daytona Beach after last call? Well, here I am! Fifty-five, married with two children and three wonderful grandchildren. When the bright lights got too bright, I opened a ceramic shop, added a family, and settled in for the duration, but the smoke-filled rooms caught up to me in 1995 and I retired due to a heart and lung condition.

My cousin, Paula Spencer, introduced me interested to Barbie® dolls and fashion doll makeovers. Even though we have never met, we have collaborated on a few dolls, mailing them back and forth until we have a finished beauty. Now I do my partying sitting in front of my computer. I'm a little fluffier and a lot quieter, but with Fashion Doll Makeovers list I have the comradery and sense of belonging I've always enjoyed and I'm still having the time of my life. Email: les111@bellsouth.net

Deborah Fagan

I am an artist who now makes my home in Las Vegas, Nevada. Born in California to European parents, I have been exposed to a wide variety of art forms and cultures. Since early childhood, I have loved bright colors and light, which found myself with a paintbrush in hand early on. Influenced by the melting pot of culture and art in California, as well as my own European background, art became a natural expression of my surroundings. Art is a rich mosaic in my life. I paint anything that doesn't move...

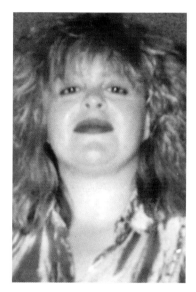

televisions, refrigerators, walls, doors, windows and now dolls!

I have studied art for many years. I have had formal training as well as assisting some of my artistic mentors. I have sculpted dolls at one point, but now I put most of my energies into fashion doll makeovers. Using the blank body as a canvas, I transform the piece with fine quality paints and layers of fine fabric.
Email: Skybloopnk@aol.com -
Website:
http://hometown.aol.com/skybloopnk/myhomepage/business.HTML

Karin Roberts

I started collecting Barbie® dolls in 1997. My personal collection and knowledge of the hobby grew by leaps and bounds. Along the way I discovered the Barbie® doll's cute little sister, the Kelly® doll. I became so enthralled by the Kelly® doll that I started a website dedicated entirely to her and an Internet group called the KellyKlub. About that same time, a talented friend, Tim Wooten, introduced me to fashion doll makeovers. His encouragement and support fueled my first fashion doll

makeover. I have found customizing to be highly addictive. I joined the fashion doll makeovers group in search of more tips and tricks, but instead found a great group of artists and friends. There is never enough time to bring all my ideas to fruition, so I have learned to enjoy the process as much as the finished project. I create and design almost exclusively for the Kelly® doll and her l'il friends.
Email: karin@lilfriends.net -
Website:
http://www.lilfriends.net/

Tracie Hutcherson

I am a housewife and mother of two beautiful children. My mother taught me to sew when I was ten years old. I began sewing again after I read Jim Faraone's book *Fashion Doll Makeovers, Learn from the Artists*. Most of my childhood dolls needed some repair work, so I put Jim's tips to the test. Later, I started looking on-line for other people who were also interested in fashion dolls. I've been doing

this for two years now, mostly for gifts or for my own enjoyment. I recently learned to design my own patterns in order to bring to life the dresses I see in my imagination. My favorite part of doing makeovers is creating something that will be enjoyed for years to come.
Email: secondlookdolls@yahoo.com - Website: www.geocities.com/secondlookdolls

Kert Hoogstraat

I began doing fashion doll makeovers over five years ago. As a collector, I wanted something more exclusive for my collection, something no one else could have. There were a few mavericks back then, the folks who started this whole marvelous, artistic trend, Mark Ouellette, MiKelman, Steve Skutka, James Bogue and Jim Faraone. I saw the work they were doing and got what I need to follow in their lead. I was off on the most rewarding, enriching and exciting artistic trip of my life. A trip that continues every day!

I have been fortunate to have my work featured in *Barbie Bazaar®*, *Miller$ Fashion Doll®* and *Second Fashion Doll Makeovers*. In 1999, the readers of *Barbie Bazaar®* magazine made my artistic dreams come true by voting my creation "Queen of the Silver Screen" as the Collector's Choice of the first domestic BMAA competition. Being given those two crystal awards by the people who love dolls as much as I do is a memory that I will cherish with a full heart the rest of my life.
Email: kertkraft@aol.com - Website: www.kertkraft.com

Harriett V. Weymon

I started creating fashion doll makeovers in 1990 as a hobby, shortly after I started collecting them. I credit my two sons with this fashion doll makeover and collecting

discovery, since it was the two of them, who persuaded my husband to get me a Barbie® doll for Christmas. I have been sewing since I was a girl, so when I found patterns for Barbie® doll clothes, my creative spark was ignited. I started with party dresses, and went on to ball gowns and bridal gowns. I like working with Mattel™ fashion dolls, but have plans to begin customizing larger fashion dolls such as the Elle® doll and the Gene® doll. Most of the dolls I've created have been gifts, and I just started creating for doll swaps. I haven't decided to market my dolls yet because I haven't yet learned how to reroot hair, and do facial repaints, but those skills will be obtained in time.
Email: allmydolls@houston.rr.com - Website: http://home.flash.net/~jwey/weyweb005.htm

Luci Lynette North

I guess you could say I've always loved dolls, although the way I work with them now is different than when I was a girl. The two ways I like to play with my dolls when I was little was to dress them with wet toilet paper, which could be molded into any shape I liked and I would also behead them. I loved to play French Revolution.

I attended Mission College and majored in Fine Arts and Design. I enjoyed it immensely, but I could still feel the draw to dolls. I decided that Design and Fashion Dolls could work together perfectly. Now I still dress them and put makeup on them, all that I ever wished my dolls could be but never were I can create. The sky is the limit. I just wish their heads still came off as easy as they use to for rerooting purposes!
Email: Lucilynette@aol.com

Rachel Backway

My passion for the Barbie® doll started when I was about 6. My grandmother was very indulgent and I enjoyed a childhood filled with the Barbie® doll and all her accessories. I first started to collect 2 years ago and very recently started to makeover my own dolls. Since then I have met many wonderful artists who have given me a lot of encouragement and support. I am constantly learning! I enjoy creating fantasy dolls including fairies, sorceresses and birds, but I am branching out to other areas

as I learn more techniques. My latest designs are based on beautiful Australian native birds. Galerita is the first in this series and she represents the Cockatoo in all her white and pale yellow glory. My ideas are endless and I very rarely find that one of my creations turn out as I would have initially expected it to. This is the fun of fashion doll makeovers!
Email: azhure@cnl.com.au -
Website:
http://www.cnl.com.au/users/azhure/index.HTML

Tess Barton

I live in Dallas, Texas. When I'm not working with dolls, I'm a doctor of Pediatric Infectious Diseases. I guess I was a "makeover artist" from early childhood when I used to make horrible outfits out of socks, and repaint my poor doll's face with paint markers. But serious doll customizing really started when I became disenchanted with the lack of variation in dolls and especially in the lack of realistic clothing for them. I prefer making daywear and casual outfits, both vintage and modern.

I'm a very slow worker, mostly because that doctoring side career takes up most of my time. For me, the most important thing is making the doll look like a real person, only tiny. Although I do sell dolls on occasion, my favorite thing to do is swap with my friends. What could be more special than something handcrafted just for you?
Email: tessb@texas.net -
Website:
http://home.beseen.com/hobbies/boogtb/DollHome.HTML
or www.a-la-carte.bigstep.com

Jean Birk

I am just beginning my adventure into the world of fashion doll makeovers. But it makes sense for me to pursue this adventure! I have been collecting dolls for several years and also have a long history of dabbling in the arts and crafts - painting, sewing, beading, photography, and most recently, website development! Now I can pull many of my artistic interests together in fashion doll makeovers and enjoy them all at once. It's quite a challenge, as some interests need further development and refinement! But what's life without challenge. It might as well be in something I enjoy!
Email:
heartinhandtreas@netscape.net

Zena Myall

I was born and raised in England and moved to the United States in 1984 when I was 13. I currently live in Williamsburg, VA. with my husband and parents. I have been designing my beautiful creations since the fall of 1996 when I decided to make some unique, one-of-a-kind Christmas gifts for fellow Barbie® doll collectors. I enjoyed sewing for the 11½in (29cm) dolls so much, that I have turned it into a full time hobby.

I've always had a love for sewing and crafts and I've learned to incorporate those skills into a specialty design area of making fashion doll brides that reflect the actual wedding dresses worn by their owners, which makes a very unique token of remembrance of that special day. My range of ideas always leads me to believe that each creation is different and unique, which makes both my formal dolls and fantasy creations uniquely mine.
Email: ZeGirl@aol.com -
Website: www.ZeGirlsDolls.com

Lynn Smith

My interest in fashion doll makeovers and writing has led to my working on a wide variety of doll customizing projects including magazine articles, workshops, books and patterns. Karen Cooper and I worked together to write and self-publish the book *Artist Makeover Dolls* in conjunction with our 2001 National Barbie© Doll Convention workshop. *Fashion Designs for 11½in (29cm) Fashion Dolls* and *Fashion Dolls for 15/16in (38cm/41cm) Fashion Dolls* are two more of my recent self-published projects. These two books are

collections of my own original fashion doll patterns. In addition to the pattern books I also offer individual patterns and subscriptions to my new release patterns. These books are available through mail order or from my website. For more information regarding the books, pattern subscription, synthetic hair, or my customized dolls, please visit my website. Look for more about me as a featured artist in Jim's 4th book.
Email:
lynnsmith@designsfordolls.com -
Website:
http://www.designsfordolls.com

Anke Scharfenberg

I am 29 years old and come from Germany where I am a banker at a local bank here. I collected Barbie® dolls for about 2 years before I started with customizing dolls after I realized that something was missing....the good feeling you get when you create something new. After a while I discovered how many wonderful things I can do with fashion dolls that I found at the flea markets about 6 months ago. As there are not many fashion doll makeover artists around here, I had to discover for myself how to start creating and I bought a couple of OOAK dolls on eBay™. This finally inspired me to try one of my own and when I got a hold of Jim Faraone's *Fashion Doll Makeovers* book I could finally start creating. My favorites are the fantasy and fairytale figures and I am very fond of the African-American dolls, but they are very hard to get in Germany. I want to thank all those people who were there for me when I started, especially Frank Janas, my boyfriend and his mother Brigitte, who has also got infected on fashion doll makeovers.
Email: ankecatwomen4@aol.com
Website: http://www.
Catwomens-magic.exhome.de

Marylou Belcher

I have always loved dolls. The first ones I remember were the homemade variety—faceless creatures with pipe cleaner armatures and extensive wardrobes. As mother to eight kids, my mother sewed. A lot! Money was tight, but my folks always managed to buy me dolls. The Barbie® doll and I were born the same year, but didn't meet until 7 years later. My sister got a TNT for her birthday. I loved her! I've been hooked ever since. I'm a mother of three now (and grandmother to two). I sew in an effort to maintain my sanity (with questionable results). I enjoy being able to combine my interests in history, sewing and dolls. I prefer to make historic costumes, drafting my own patterns rather than use commercial ones (I'm never satisfied with the fit). While Babs is still #1, I use the slightly larger fashion dolls these days, because the fabrics lie better.
Email:
gimik_1971@yahoo.com

Angel Mitchell

I started creating fashion doll makeovers during the summer of 1999 after researching vintage restoration on-line. I came across so many beautiful designs and shortly thereafter designed my first doll. I became instantly hooked. My first love is the Barbie® doll and most of my designs are made with her, but I also have a fondness for the Gene® doll. I try not to limit my designs to a certain style but I admit, most are eveningwear inspired by fantasy. I also work with my mom on certain designs. She and a very dear friend have been a wonderful source of support and inspiration. Fashion doll makeovers have opened up a whole new world and I've met so many wonderful people and have learned so much. I offer a vintage Barbie® doll restoration service, accept commissions and sell on my website. I love customizing—it's a passion.
Email:
angel@customdolldesigns.com -
Website: http://www.
customdolldesigns.com

Heather Diane

I was born July 3, 1981 and raised in Brooklyn, N.Y. Most say I am the youngest makeover artist they know. I have a lot of fun altering my own appearance in ways that are "unusual" to every day society. Making over fashion dolls and being a beautician is perfect for me to express my artistic ability on a daily basis.

My doll craze began with Jem® dolls in 1997. Like me, they also have an "outrageous" look. I soon tried creating characters that were in the cartoon but not in the doll line. I then discovered the Gene® doll who replaced the Jem® doll as my favorite fashion doll.

Dragon Lance and other fantasy novels have been a great inspiration to me. I enjoy creating my favorite characters from the books, using their descriptions and the way that I envision them to look. There are enough characters to keep me busy for quite a few years!
Email: heatherdiane@ realmofdreamz.com
Website: www.realmofdreamz.com

Susan Yslas

I'm Susan Yslas aka Swapmama from southern California. I live with my husband, Jess, two sons, Kevin and Eric, two male dogs and one male iguana. Thus, the reason the Barbie® doll popped back into my life. In 1959, the Barbie® doll became my favorite doll. In 1995, out came the reproduction Solo in the Spotlight® and I was hooked! 375 dolls later I am still collecting strong. I collect new Barbie® dolls, but have a small collection of vintage. My love for the Barbie® doll has moved towards customizing. I prefer to make dolls in fancy gowns, yet I have ventured out and made some centaurs. Dolls have taken me to many sewing and painting classes. Plus the Barbie® doll has pushed me to learn the computer and I joined and participated in numerous doll lists. This has brought me much happiness and pleasure. How can anything that has brought so much happiness be bad?
Email: res0486f@gte.net

Imelda Sanchez

So much has happened to me since being a featured artist in Jim's 3rd book. It has been such a fun and exciting adventure! I joined Jim's on-line list when it was first started, and have learned so much from all the artists there. One of the areas I really wanted to work on in my designs was facial painting. I didn't even have to ask because that subject was addressed on our list and all my questions were answered. After experimenting, I have found what works best for me. I don't set many limits on what to create, but detailed lingerie for my dolls is what I really enjoy designing. I usually don't get any further then the lingerie because I think it is too pretty to cover up with clothes. With Jim's books and the help from my Yahoogroups friends, I hope to continue living my fantasies through my dolls for many more years to come!
Email: mariza1@mindspring.com
Website:
http://www.azstarnet.com/ ~dfannin/marizacover.HTML

Barbara Harrison

As a child growing up in Columbus, Ohio, I made my own paper dolls and outfits for them. As the mother of two sons, I began making Barbie® doll clothes for my nieces. I took some to work to show my co-workers and they asked to buy some. That is how I began to sew and design my clothes. I even sold them at Christmas Bazaars in my neighborhood. I did it more for the fun and not so much as to make a profit. I bought every pattern I could. I bought a Barbie® doll just to fit my clothes and to get the placement for the snaps right. I was hooked! That is when I began collecting the Barbie® doll. In 1998, after relocating to South Carolina, I met my friend Doris in a fabric shop where I worked. We began to talk Barbie® doll and became friends. She has taught me how to re-do their hair and how to accessorize. I have, at last, found a friend who does not think that I am crazy to play with dolls!
Email: GRANDL@aol.com

Bunny L. Dedes

Since 1998, I have been the artist and creator of "BLD Michaud's Original Designs". Born and raised in Florida, I am the youngest of seven children and the mother of four sons. I started creating my "OOAK Designs" out of the fond memories and love for my favorite fashion doll.

I am married and live in Connecticut with my husband and four sons. After the birth of my last son, I decided to pursue a new career while at home with my family. I found myself back in school studying for a "Degree in the Arts". My greatest love is sculpture and recreating the expressions of children either with my hands and clay or canvas and watercolor.

I admit that while creating my designs, my biggest gratification is when a doll is complete and someone discovers splendor in my work. It give me enormous satisfaction to see my designs got to new homes around the world.
Email: RPDEDES@PRODIGY.NET -
Website: http://pages.prodigy.net/rpdedes/

Barbara Fowler

One of my favorite Christmases was the year Santa brought my Barbie® dolls. I spent the next summer making hats and purses, selling them so I could buy fashions. When my mother brought all of my dolls to me a few years ago, I was reminded of how much I loved dolls. With the "help" of a friend, I started collecting Barbie® dolls. From there it was a short journey to fixing the hair of garage sale finds, adding eyelashes and learning to repaint makeup. I pulled my husband into the doll world kicking and screaming but now he also derives great pleasure from it. We opened a small doll shop, took sculpture classes with Jack Johnston and became doll doctors. He calls himself the surgeon and I do "hair and makeup". Customizing and restoring dolls fills the need to be creative and allows me to meet great people and artists.
Email: dollaholic@hotmail.com -
Website: www.bgsdollhouse.com

Caryl DeHerrera

I am a native Californian. I've lived most of my life in New Almaden with my family and husband of 25 years. I am fortunate to live in such a picturesque area with a pleasant little creek across the street, surrounded by mountains, horseback and hiking trails. I am somewhat of an ecologist. I've ridden horses most of my life and absolutely love animals. As a young girl I was always

infatuated by dolls and was passionate for art. In the last year, I combined the both of them and started making OOAK fashion dolls. I like to create new images, and incorporate them into doll crafting. I love to make fantasy come to life in my art. My wish is for everybody's fantasy to come true and keep on pursuing your dreams.
Email: BCZion13@aol.com - Website: www.FantasyInArt.net

Laurie Samford

Hi! I'm the proud mom of two grown children, a "wild-child" dog and several lap-cats. My daughter, Leslie, works in the theater, and my son, Andy, is a musician. I'm currently employed full-time in a clerical-support position at a local regional theater and part-time by a national closeout store, perfect jobs for me since I love live theater and shopping for bargains. I have a happy life and want to thank my children and co-workers for their love and support.

I enjoy a variety of interests and like trying new crafts. Jim's first makeover book got me interested in boil-perming and designing fashions, but my projects took off when I joined this Yahoogroup™.

I'm grateful to Jim and everyone here for their generous sharing of knowledge and experience. It's just fun seeing all the new creations, and I love being part of the gang.
Email: lsamford@hotmail.com - Website: http://www.geocities.com/starrynightskater/

William Stewart Jones

I am a retired professor of Theatre Design. My daughter, Kimmerie introduced me to fashion doll makeovers when she loaned me Jim Faraone's first book. Although I'd made toys and dolls for my children when they were little, I hadn't tried changing a commercial doll. All my dolls tend to be labor intensive, whether it's fantasy, period costume dolls or historical figures. Altering the position, repainting entire body colours, rerooting in mixed colours or with beads and unusual

materials, dyeing, painting and altering fabrics, all add to the creative fun of fashion doll makeovers. Everyone has a different approach to the use of fabric and painting faces. After years of teaching costume design, makeup and theatre crafts, I find all those skills are necessary in the creation of my dolls. Fantasy figures give me an opportunity to design costumes, makeup and headresses that no human could wear, and to let my imagination soar.
Email: wsjones@basingstoke.org
Website: www.daddysdolls.com

J'Amy Pacheco

If it weren't for the Internet, I likely would not be a customizer. My first week on-line, I "met" Jim Faraone in a chat room and learned that one could curl the Barbie® doll's hair with boiling water. The concept fascinated me, and I was soon wrapping-and-dunking. My specialty is customized shoes. I got the idea from a museum's catalogue, which included reproductions of antique shoes. I copied a pair for the Barbie® doll, and my friends encouraged me to make more. My mother, LaRaine Weishar and I started working together in early 2000. She's an accomplished seamstress; I'm good with hair. It was a natural fit, and I can't imagine a better partner.

I'm a journalist and the mother of a pre-schooler. Fashion doll makeovers provides me with the creative outlet I need at the end of the day. Now, if I could only figure out how to put more hours in those days.
Email: jpwrite@earthlink.net

LaRaine Weishar

My father was an artist who made his living hand-painting silk neckties. I apparently inherited his artistic gene, because I've always been interested in painting, sewing and crafts. My interest in dolls took off when I retired and my daughter-in-law showed me a copy of *Dollcrafter®* magazine. My husband said, "You could do that!" and eventually drove me all over the country to take porcelain doll-making lessons. After four months of lessons, my teacher encouraged me to enter the

Bohler Show. I walked away with second place ribbons for each of my dolls. The next year, all my dolls received first place ribbons, and one received "Best of Group".

My daughter introduced me to fashion doll makeovers, and we teamed up on 2000 as "LaJa Designs." Fashion doll makeovers combines all of my "loves"—fabric, costume design, sewing, painting—into one medium.
Email:
larraine.weishar@verizon.net

Janet Cretsinger

I learned to sew on a treadle sewing machine when I was 5. My first "model" was a 1950's Nancy Ann, and circle skirts were about the extent of my talents. Later, I would use commercial patterns while my designing centered around drawing paper doll clothing. Real life has a way of intruding into dreams and I completed a career with the government while pursuing a multitude of different crafts. With the arrival of the Gene® doll (and a timely early retirement) I started sewing for current day fashion dolls. I like to specialize in outfits that might have been seen on the runway in the 40's and 50's. I develop a total ensemble starting from the inside with undergarments and working outward ending with complete accessories from head to toe. I spend many happy hours shopping for fabrics, designing and sewing.
Email: janetceles@aol.com -
Website:
http://members.nbci.com/
sunnybug

Gantipa Chawandee

I live in Bangkok (Thailand). I only started creating fashion doll makeovers one year ago. I like to design in Thai styles and other different styles that reflect my culture. The custom of Thai classical dancing is one of the most fancy styles decorated by gold jewelry, sparkle fabrics and Thai silk. I am learning new things each day and will continue to create for as long as I can. Email: zeesee9@yahoo.com - Website: http://zeeseethaidolls.homestead.com/index.HTML

Rebecca Satterberg

I love costuming my dolls, and entering them in competitions. This is an awesome adventure for creative expression and a great way to meet other doll enthusiasts. You may find that the item you are working on is competition worthy the first time through. Sometimes a part or parts will have to be redone many time until you are happy with the result. Either way the feeling of accomplishment after you have put the time and effort into this type of project will be worth it. Email: reba@lareba.com - Website: http://www.lareba.com/index.htm

Annie Muscatelli

For as long as I can remember I have loved dolls. As an only child, I spent hours with them in my imaginary world of make-believe. Around my grade school years I found an interest in "playing store". I begged my mother for sales receipt books, so I would be the shopkeeper and the customer adding up the purchases and the love of retail never stopped growing. I have owned several Gift Shoppes and am still involved in selling to the public.

I have had 8 wonderful children and they have all worked with my husband and I in these businesses. Hence it came as no surprise to me when two of my daughters, Jenny Sutherland and Chrissy Stewart of JaC Designs used their talents in creating OOAK and repaints and offering them to the public. We love it! Email: anushka5@earthlink.net Website: http://www.geocities.com/jac_designs/index.HTML

Kathleen Forsythe

I currently reside in the central part of Utah. I am 46 years old and the mother of 2 sons. I have been sewing for over 30 years and have been more active in fashion doll costume design for the last 20 years. I was introduced to makeovers 2 years ago and I love it!! I wanted to learn how to restore dolls that I had found at yard sales or thrift stores for charities. They are a challenge to me and what I am able to do. I began using the Mego™ Cher doll and am still

very active in re-creating her costumes and clothing. I use pictures to go by and change the look of the doll to match the picture. Now I have branched out into doing other vintage dolls. I have begun to do historical gowns and dolls to match them. Initially when I get a doll, it's a blank canvas, and I create whatever look I want. Email: dolls@hmdigital.net - Website: http://www.geocities.com/toposdesigns/

Amy Harmon

I happily reside with my husband and two daughters in the great state of Kentucky, where I was born and raised. I am a work at home mom, dabbling in Real Estate and Consumer Direct Marketing. A few years ago collecting dolls led to customizing and repainting, after I discovered Jim Faraone's first *Fashion Doll Makeovers* book. My favorite aspect of fashion doll makeovers is repainting the entire face. Styling the hair is usually time consuming but worth the effort. It's always fun to choose a costume style and fabric. I've learned that talents abound in this craft and you only compete with yourself. True enjoyment comes from developing your own style of customizing.

Thankfully, I am blessed with a husband and family who not only tolerate, but sometimes even delight in my creative endeavors. I thank God for the opportunity to share my creations with others.
Email: Amyh41503@aol.com
Website: amylouiseoriginals.com

Gary Mak

Bonjour les amis! I live in Montreal, Quebec, Canada. Montreal is a French speaking part of Canada. When I was young, I always loved to design and create outfits for my Barbie® doll and Jenny® (Japanese Barbie® doll). Finally I decided to go to Fashion Design School at LaSalle College in Montreal. I took a Ladies' Wear Design program. I have knowledge of designing, drafting, pattern making, sewing, draping, computer designs, fashion history, theatre custom design, textile printing, etc.

Recently, I discovered the Gene® doll. I really enjoy creating outfits for her. She is the perfect model. She is a legend of her own. I am honored to have an opportunity to be her designer. I still have so much to learn to create outfits for the Gene® doll. There are so many talented artists in the Gene® doll world that I can learn form.
Email: makgary@yahoo.com

Helen Skinner

What started out with local doll and craft shows grew into traveling farther and seeing new places. Then the Internet made the whole country accessible for our business. Selling on a website soon made the opportunity to attend doll conventions and events I had only dreamed of seeing for years. Creating a new look for fashion dolls is such a varied and wonderful field that opens up so much for the collector today. Trying to keep your work fresh and changing is always a challenge for today's artists. I have taken classes at local sewing centers to help refine my sewing ability. Many tips on finishing seams well, along with working with fine fabrics have really helped my finished product. Beading classes are another way to learn great tips to use in your creations. Keep the creative process fun and your dolls will be a delight.
Email: MSkinzo@aol.com -
Website:
http://members.aol.com/
MSkinzo/montys.htm

Nikki Avery

Okay, it's true...I never outgrew Barbie® dolls. I refused to "retire" my dolls and played with them right into my teen years. As a teenager, I made clothing for them using bits of lace and draping pieces of fabrics around them. When I was in college I had my first doll find at a thrift store. She was covered in a black sticky residue. All I could see were beautiful eyelashes and the words "Mattel™" on her

buttock. Her price tag read 75 cents and I took her home with me. 1 week later after intense cleaning and styling I discovered I had a very nice Twiggy® doll under all that filth! Little did I know that a few years later I would be cleaning and coifing dolls every day!!
Email: BabyroseJ@aol.com - Website:
www.vintagefashiondoll. homestead.com

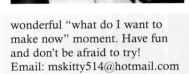

Jill "Kitty" Racop

I never would have dreamed after giving the Glamour Misty® doll her almost-flattering bob, that over 30 years later I would still be trying to change the Barbie® doll and her friends to suit personal taste. But the challenge is still there, every time one looks at a "well-loved" doll or an uninspiring NRFB and thinks, "What could he/she really look like?" My collection actually began in 1974, safe (for a while) from revision. But the bug would not die, eventually a halting attempt at repainting produced pleasing results, a fumbling reroot proved tedious but effective and a green marker plus metallic green paint plus a Beauty Secrets

Barbie® doll resulted in a crude, but to my eyes beautiful, aquatic Guardian Goddess. Now, there is always a bin of Goodwill® guys and girls just waiting for that next

wonderful "what do I want to make now" moment. Have fun and don't be afraid to try!
Email: mskitty514@hotmail.com

Stephanie Gazell

I started collecting dolls in 1989. The vintage Barbie® doll was my first doll interest, along with the Francie® doll, Midge® doll and the rest. I tried repainting in the early 90's and thought, "Well, that's fun!", but I didn't continue with it, due to other creative interests taking a front seat. I focused on pencil portraiture and illustration and widened my doll collection to other 60's fashion dolls. The Gene® doll came along and my doll collection changed overnight. Along with the Gene® doll came an exposure to a worldwide

community of collectors and artists. As the Gene® doll was quietly taking over the house, I considered repainting again. With a lot of help from Katharine Rayland, I repainted a Daughter of the Nile Gene® doll. A Bellmont Ball Doll Auction followed soon after. I am a Human Resource professional, in the biotech industry and live in the Boston area with my husband, Tom, a musician and woodworker. Dolls, and art, in many forms, will always be a part of my life.
Email:
STEPHTOMGAZELL@cs.com

Sandy Cunningham

I have been collecting fashion dolls for about 6 years. A couple of years back on vacation in Las Vegas I was inspired by the wonderful wild glitz, glitter, feathers and glamour of the showgirls. Upon returning home, I decided to try a showgirl design for fashion dolls, and the rest is history. Since that time I have created numerous showgirls and branched out into fairies and other fantasy creations, including makeovers on Kelly® size dolls. I have met and made friends with some great doll artists along the

way. Doll artists are the neatest people, that mostly all help and support each other, which makes it so much fun. I love wild color combinations, glitter, glitz, sparkle and shine, so my creations are easy to spot. My very favorite is giving my girlies "technicolor" hair. My designs have found homes nationwide and internationally.
Email: raysan@oknet1.net - Website:
http://sandesigns.tripod.com/tinyfantasy.HTML
or http://fantasydesigns.terrashare.com/

Natalie Tetzlaff

In college, my best friend Amanda bought me a Mermaid Midge® doll. That rekindled my love of the Barbie® doll and began my love of fashion doll makeovers. Originally from Wyoming, I moved to Cleveland three years ago with my husband, Roger. Besides fashion doll makeovers, I enjoy reading, writing fantasy stories and raising cockatiels. I work as a Nursing Assistant at a long time care facility.

Many of my Barbie® doll clothes were made by my

grandmother. She was a talented seamstress who also made most of my clothing. I love making all kinds of dolls, from high fashion to bridal, but fantasy is my favorite. I try incorporating unusual items into my designs. The Barbie® doll is my primary doll; she is versatile and affordable. Last year, I started repainting and now enjoy the challenge. My favorite are red-haired dolls!
Email: natalie@baddogink.com - Website:
http://www.geocities.com/justa_duck/barbie.HTML

Pat Feick

As an office manager for a national company for 20 years, I had very little time to design dresses for fashion dolls, however, I did make some outfits for my daughter's Barbie® dolls. After I left this company, I started an antique and collectible business. During these years, I continued to add to me daughter's Barbie® doll collection. Then two years ago, my daughter asked me to sell her vintage Barbie® doll collection on eBay™. While selling her dolls, I became

aware of all of the other fashion dolls on the market, and after viewing the OOAK auctions, I joined the Fashion Doll Makeover board, and found Jim Faraone's *Fashion Doll Makeover* series. The wonderful ideas in these books and the ideas on the Fashion Doll Makeover board inspired me to start designing for fashion dolls.
Email:
neversink1@earthlink.net - Website:
http://www.earthspirit.homestead.com

Jenny Sutherland

I have loved the art of drawing since I've been a child. I started oil painting when I was 19 and fell in love with the realism I could achieve with paints. A year or two into painting, I realized what I was trying to achieve was to bring my art to life. In early 2000, I noticed auctions on eBay™ of dolls that have been customized. Right then it hooked me! This encouraged me to start my painting again, but on the Gene® dolls. This

avenue of art has helped me bring my painting to life. The styling of the hair also comes from my natural ability of cutting and styling, which I have been doing since I have been 15 years old. I feel I am lucky to be able to live my dreams out and share what I love to do with others. It's a dream come true.
Email: jacdesigns@earthlink.net - Website: http://www.geocities.com/jac_designs/index.HTML

Trish Hurley

All artists share one thing—we all dip our pens in the same well source of creative imagination. Disney® opened a magic door for me. What followed became the costumes of 1001 dreams. Sewing and playing dolls from the age of six, I've learned from many people, books and films. After 2 degrees and hours of research, I can say, "I did it." I've watched my designs, ebb and flow in musically directed steps across a lighted and decorated stage. The challenge to be imaginative, yet work in a scale,

produces the same eclectic demands. "Dressed in a dream," my work makes time stand still and becomes immortal. Be it fashion, fantasy or historical, I enjoy creating it all. My favorite designer is Erté, and my love of Celtic knot work shows up in a few of my designs. My muse demands I create, my heart demands I share, and the results are of endless value.
Email: SewcuteT@centurytel.net
Website: http://members.spree.com/shopping/sewcute/

Chrissy Stewart

My name is Chrissy Stewart and I am the Seamstress of JaC Designs. When I first started sewing 5 years ago, I made clothing for adults and children, now I only sew for the Gene® dolls and the Tyler® dolls. Our goal is to make our dolls as realistic as possible, and have as much fun making them! I love sewing "old world" dresses—those are my favorite! I have just recently opened my new shoe store for the Gene® dolls and Tyler® dolls called "The

Cobbler's Corner". Here you will find all handmade shoes from throughout history, and even some movie prop shoes. I am also opening a hat shop for the Gene® dolls and Tyler® dolls, called "The Mad Hatter", that will be open sometime in 2001. This group is great, we all share wonderful tips and advice with each other, it's like one big family.
Email: sassyass7@earthlink.net - Website: http://www.geocities.com/jac_designs/index.HTML

Ken Bartram

Fashion dolls look like miniature mannequins! LOVE THAT! I have really enjoyed repainting and restyling hair on my dolls. I am a collector as well as a repainter/restyler. I'm having fun redoing larger dolls like the Alex® doll, the Tyler® doll, the Gene® doll, the Tonner® dolls and now the Madra® doll. I am partners with Patricia Cronin, who makes haute couture clothes for my dolls. We sell our joint efforts in dressed dolls through our websites.
Email: KenPaints@aol.com
Website:
http://hometown.aol.com/ kenpaints/myhom pagefreshfaces.HTML
or
http://hometown.aol.com/ kenpaints/myhomepage/ artgallery.HTML
or
http://hometown.aol.com/ kenpaints/myhomepage/ photo.HTML

Cliff Lovering

I taught myself to reroot on my '64 bubble. For some reason, as a child, I cut her hair off. I was very good at crochet, so my first thought was to use the crochet hook. This was long before any of the magazines or books came out with instructions, so I had to devise a method by myself. What I came up with creates a rooting that looks like the original machine rooting on the inside of the head, a very distinct braided look. The

hair will not pull out with the normal combing it goes through to be styled. The drawback is the amount of time the rerooting takes. When I do a dressed doll I start with a creative thought, then build the doll around the idea. I sew the clothing onto the doll. When I use beads they are sewn or even woven on a sewn on lining.
Email:
c.lovering@centurytel.net

Jennifer L. Brown

I have been doing fashion doll makeovers for only a year or so. I got interested in fashion doll makeovers through a friend who introduced me to Jim Faraone's books on doll makeovers. I was

soon hooked. I have only made a few dolls, primarily for private swaps with other artists. As the mother of three very young children, I do not have a lot of time to do many dolls, so it is primarily a hobby. I enjoy collecting Barbie® dolls, customized dolls and other fashion dolls. The Internet and FashionDollMakeovers@yahoogroups.com has been invaluable to me for learning new skills and getting support in this growing hobby. I hope to sell my work someday, but that is not the reason I love to create OOAK dolls. I create these dolls because I think they are beautiful and can bring joy to those who own them.
Email: Kotyonok@esva.net

Debbie Sherart

I started doing fashion doll makeovers after finding an ash blonde "swirl" ponytail in a thrift store for 25 cents. At the time I was making cloth dolls and turned to making clothing for the Barbie® dolls. I also re-did other "yard sale" dolls. About 15 years later, I found Jim's first book and was in awe and hooked. I make fantasy dolls thanks to seeing Bob Mackie's Neptune. I enjoy the entire process, turning a yard sale doll into a fabulous mermaid or fairy, even a glamorous gal ready for an evening out. I have always done crafting, and I have always loved dolls. Combining the two loves has been a wonderful experience. I feel that I have made some wonderful friends, both on-line and off-line. I hope to continue to learn and make new friends. Email: uplifted_feathers@yahoo.com - Website: http://arilinn.homestead.com

Svetla Vavova-Clifford

I was raised in Bulgaria but still fortunate enough to get a Barbie® doll at age 13. With my mom's help, I ended up sewing a few simple outfits for her. I did eventually grow out of playing with Barbie® dolls and it wasn't until years later that I found my way back to "playing" with fashion dolls. A year and a half ago, I accidentally came across a fashion doll makeover site. Not being able to afford those dolls, I decided to try making them. Originally, I thought that I would only create for myself, but this hobby turned into a passion. I truly enjoy putting painstaking detail into my dolls My dolls are mostly fantasy creatures or glamorous ladies. I repaint their faces, restyle and sometimes reroot their hair as well as create their costumes mostly without patterns.
Email: svavova@hotmail.com - Website: www.uydolls.com

Lori Velazquez

The first Barbie® doll I can remember owning was a "My First Barbie®" doll from Mexico that I received for my 4th birthday. As the years went on, I still kept my love for dolls and dressing them in neat outfits. It was around 1995 that I learned about an anine show called Sailor Moon®. This later served as my inspiration for collecting and later trying to customize my own dolls. I have looked long and hard to try and find these dolls. Much to my dismay I had discovered that certain of my favorite characters had not had dolls made of them. Even worse, their outfits from the series weren't available to purchase. So I decided to create my own. One of my goals is to create a pair of dolls that correspond to the main characters of a fantasy story I wrote a few years back.
Email: galexia@ix.netcom.com - Website: http://www.wraamyth.com

Doris A. Mixon

I was born in Los Angeles, CA. in 1951 and have lived in California all my life. Attending college gave me the self-esteem and determination I needed to start a doll design business of my own 5 years ago. I wrote for *Miller's Fashion Doll*® magazine for two years and now for *Doll Reader*® magazine as a free-lance writer. I also have a book called *Miniature Mannequins* by Hobby House Press. I also do freelance doll designs for Paradise Galleries in San Diego. I recently started a company called "Fashion Boulevard", a new and upcoming fashion doll company, that manufactures couture fashion for the 15-½in - 16in (39cm - 41cm) fashion dolls and will soon have a new 16in (41cm) fashion doll on the market. This has been a dream of mine from the time I started designing my own doll fashions.
Email: DMixon46@aol.com -
Website:
www.Fashion-Boulevard.com

Michelle James

I started out creating only Barbie® dolls and friends, but I'm currently creating for the Elle® dolls and the Gene® doll. Through Jim Faraone's books, I've come so far with my creations and doll designs. I've sold dolls to people as far as Japan, the Netherlands and Germany. I've been collecting dolls since 1997 and doing fashion doll makeovers since the summer of 1999. All my designs are OOAK creations. I rarely use commercial patterns, unless I want a certain tailored look. I do a total makeover of the face, hair, outfit and accessories, to create an entirely new OOAK design! Jim's books and the talented people on FashionDollMakeovers@yahoogroups.com have helped me develop and further my skills. I can only hope to further my talents in order to share my beautiful creations with others.
Email: MJames33@excite.com -
Website: www.jasmardolls.com

Brad Jensen

The fashion doll makeover community has been a wonderful environment in which to grow and learn as an artist and designer. Even though we all gather information from the same sources and talk to the same experts, the outcomes each artist produces are surprisingly different. This diversity makes for an exciting and growth inspiring relationship. I am fortunate to know 3 other designers on a personal level—Mary Beyer, Imelda Sanchez and Dorothy Fannin. All of us work hard to produce quality work that is beautiful and at the same time our work is as different and unique as our personalities.

Through Jim's FDM list we are able to share ideas and concerns with hundreds of designers and supporters. This sharing of ideas broadens our knowledge and helps us continually improve our craft. Along the way we are also able to make new friends in an environment where support and encouragement is primary and competition is secondary.
Email: brad@bradjensen.com -
Website: www.bradjensen.com

Sharon Smith

I am an empty nester with 3 grown children, 2 grandchildren and 2 pets. My wonderful husband, Gary, has been my greatest supporter in all my artistic efforts for our whole 30-year marriage. I collect several different dolls including the Barbie® doll, the Gene® doll and the Ginny® doll. I saw my first makeover dolls on eBay™ in late 2000 and was intrigued. I knew I had to try this. I have been an artist all of my life and couldn't resist.

At this time, I am only repainting faces and restyling hair, although I am going to begin to sew for my dolls in the near future. My goal is to improve my style as much as possible with the help from all of the talented people on this mailing list. I have a fantasy line planned using the little Strawberry Shortcake® dolls, but that is in the future.
Email:
ssmith@thegildedrose.com -
Website:
http://www.thegildedrose.com

Stefanie Baumler

I live in Central Ohio. I started doing fashion doll makeovers at the beginning of 2000 after joining a Barbie® doll club and seeing some of the member's makeovers. I knew it was something I would love to do, as I have always been a "crafty" person. After getting Jim's 3 books it was in no time that I dove in full force. I have worked only on Barbie® dolls thus far and don't have any immediate plans to cross over to other fashion dolls at this time. I enjoy all aspects of the makeover process, but I especially enjoy beading my costumes and making the matching jewelry and accessories. I do mostly evening wear, but have dabbled with fairies and other looks as well. I also have an ever-growing collection of modern Barbie® dolls, which are always inspirational when I'm working on a doll.
Email:
stefanie@baumshelter.com -
Website:
http://www.baumshelter.com/ourpage/DreamWeaverDesigns.htm

**Mario Paglino/
Gianni Grossi**

Fashion and Art are always in our country's culture. We are 2 Italian boys, Mario (27) and Gianni (30), from Turin. We have loved the Barbie® doll since childhood. Only 3 years ago we started collecting and 2 years ago we began creating fashion doll makeovers. I, Mario, am an employee and Gianni is a graphic designer; we both love fashion, the Internet and graphics. I have drawn costumes since I was a child and it's from my sketches that our creations get life. We search for glamour in our dolls and search for high quality fabrics for the dolls' look. We try to share our ideas and create unique dolls. We took part in the Italian Convention in Bologna and our "Audrey Chic" won 3rd place in the contest. We were in the Napoli Convention, and in Calenzano (Florence) and 2 months later, we opened our website showing our creations.
Email:
magia-2000@libero.it -
Website:
www.magia2000.com

About the Author

The author of the successful series of books "Fashion Doll Makeovers, Learn from the Artists, Jim Faraone, is an avid doll collector with a collection of over 3,500 dolls of all kinds. He is not just a doll collector but also collects paper dolls, paper toys, 40's, 50's and 60's plastic dollhouse furniture, children's aluminum cookware and accessories, celebrity autographed photos and more as time goes on.

A respected artist, Jim has had his artwork featured twice in the UFDC (United Federation of Doll Clubs) publication *Doll News*. His award winning artwork has also been featured souvenirs at many conventions and has been on display at the Metropolitan Museum of Art in New York City.

His articles on the BARBIE® doll, advertising dolls, celebrity dolls, fashion doll makeovers and paper dolls have appeared numerous times in several magazines including *Miller's, Contemporary Doll Collector, Dolls in Print* and *Doll Reader*. He has also covered many of the various doll and paper doll conventions in magazines and on the Internet.

Jim has also won 2 Crystal Awards for his creations in the *Barbie Bazaar*, 2000 BMAA Contest and 2 Second Place Ribbons in their 2001 FDMAA contest, as well as other awards for his creations and services in the fashion doll makeover world.

Jim is internationally known in the collecting field and is actively involved with many of the conventions. He organizes and runs many of the Artist's Galleries which feature the new work of professional and non-professional artists. Jim is an avid believer in supporting the well-deserved artists and giving those the recognition that they deserve. Jim has been commend-

ed several times for his strong determination in giving the artists a place in the spotlight. He has run several workshops and seminars on painting techniques, paper doll artwork, getting published, jewelry making, and the recreation of the fashion doll, taking each budding artist step-by-step through the trials and tribulations of creating. He has also co-chaired a Fashion Doll Convention in California and the competition for the 2001 BARBIE® doll convention in Dearborn, MI., as well as

co-chairing the 2002 International Paper Doll Convention in Williamsburg, VA.

Jim and his collectibles have appeared in several magazines and newspapers around the world, including the front cover of *USA Today*. His recreated fashion dolls have also appeared on several television news segments.

He likes variety, so he creates everything from Haute Couture ensembles, caricature dolls, vintage suits, to hand beaded and

sequinned evening gowns. His newest line consists of Erté inspired Art Deco creations and his "Insect" line, transforming the fashion doll into various types of insects has been a big hit as everyone is now starting their own "bug" collection of Faraone Originals. His intricate beadwork has astounded many a collector who own one of his detailed creations in their collection. All of his full-skirted creations have beneath the flowing skirts, tiny lace trimmed panties, garter belt with rhinestone "clasp" and stockings. He enjoys adding the small detail work on his creations. Even a few fashion doll manufacturers have praised his work and creations.

Jim has now added a new line of Faraone Originals *Simply Classique* jewelry for the Gene® doll, Kitty Collier® doll, Tyler Wentworth® doll and other dolls of their proportions. A jewelry designer back in the 70's, Jim has even designed for Anne Klein and his adult jewelry creations have been featured in Vogue® magazine and other magazines.

Jim Faraone has made his hobby a lifetime infatuation and the joy, comfort and friendships he's made over the years are always treasured. He truly enjoys hearing from collectors and artists around the world. Feel free to contact him with any comments or feedback on his books or become a member of his free internet list at FashionDollMakeovers-subscribe@yahoogroups.com.

Jim Faraone
19109 Silcott Springs Rd.
Purcellville, VA. 20132
(540) 338-3621

Email: jimfaraone@erols.com
Website: http://www.erols.com/jimfaraone/